'John C. Lennox is not only one of the be[st]
and defending the Christian worldview
teacher. Whether he's preaching on the L
about the lives of Daniel, Joseph, and no
and application for believers of all ages and backgrou[nds]
In a day when the deep study of Scripture is often neglected, I'm thankful
that Dr Lennox has given us this new volume on Abraham, the Father of
all who have faith, and the friend of God.'
**Brian Brodersen**, Pastor, Calvary Chapel, Costa Mesa, CA, USA

'John Lennox – both an accomplished mathematician and a serious
Christian – has blessed the world with many works showing why science
and faith make good companions. Now he has blessed us with another,
this time an exposition of the Abraham story in Genesis, which displays
many virtues. He wants you to be sure that the stories are true, but also
that they have a bearing on us today. In this well-written and thoughtful
book, he keeps his eyes on the ancient settings of these tales, but also
on the New Testament, traditional Jewish reflections, and modern
application. In all of this he reminds me of another Oxford–Cambridge
academic, who likewise came from Northern Ireland, C.S. Lewis: an
"amateur" in Biblical Studies, who has something to say, not only to
us "professionals," but especially to the general public. I am pleased to
commend this book to you.'
**C. John Collins**, Professor of Old Testament, Covenant Theological
Seminary, St Louis, MO, USA

'I was not prepared for how much I would enjoy Professor John Lennox's
*Friend of God*, probably the greatest book ever written on the life of
Abraham. A book with massive scholarship but with personal anecdotes,
this will encourage the ordinary Christian. *Friend of God* is both an
apologetic achievement and one that will increase the reader's own faith
– and make him or her desire to be a friend of God like Abraham.'
**R. T. Kendall**

*Friend of God* is an insightful, profound and deeply relevant exploration of the person of Abraham. We learn what it means to be human and to have a relationship to God. Author, John Lennox, also carries these essential truths into the heart of our contemporary distress: like connecting the ancient story of the Tower of Babel to contemporary author Yuval Harari, who insists we are on the brink of creating a new kind of species who will become human gods who will live forever. I finished reading with tears of gratitude to God for how he pursues us in order to offer his indescribable gift.
**Rebecca Manley Pippert**, author, speaker, evangelist: founder of Becky Pippert Ministries

'Reformed faith has three components – evidence, meaning and action. To take each in turn, I had no idea there was so much evidence for Abraham. I think I just thought it was so long ago, one just had the precious chapters of Genesis, which were uncorroborated, but you will be staggered by the evidence for this patriarch. Again when it came to the meaning of Abraham's life, though I was familiar with the narrative and most of the 60 New Testament references, I discovered my understanding was so shallow as my eyes were opened to text after text. Lastly, of course, once the evidence and meaning have been grasped, then the difference it makes to one's living faith is quite thrilling. I shall never read Hebrews 11 verses 8 to 10 with the same mindset. We need to thank Professor Lennox for waking a sleeping giant of Scripture for us.'
**Rico Tice**, All Souls & Christianity Explored

# Dedication

This book is dedicated to our friends Alex and Iris McIlhinney. It was Alex who first suggested that I should give a course of lectures on the life of Abraham. My wife Sally and I wish to thank them for years of valued friendship, encouragement, sparkling conversation and wise counsel.

# About the author

**John C. Lennox** MA MMath, MA (Bioethics) PhD DPhil DSc is Emeritus Professor of Mathematics at the University of Oxford and Emeritus Fellow in Mathematics and Philosophy of Science at Green Templeton College, Oxford. He has lectured on religion and science at many prestigious institutions around the world, and has publicly debated Richard Dawkins and Christopher Hitchens, among others. He is also the author of many books including, *Joseph: A story of love, hate, slavery, power and forgiveness; Against the Flow: The inspiration of Daniel in an age of relativism; Gunning for God: Why the new atheists are missing the target; God and Stephen Hawking: Whose design is it anyway?; Can Science Explain Everything?; Cosmic Chemistry: Do God and science mix?; 2084: Artificial intelligence and the future of humanity.* John is married to Sally and they have three children and ten grandchildren.

# FRIEND OF GOD

The inspiration of Abraham in an age of doubt

John C. Lennox

First published in Great Britain in 2024

SPCK
SPCK Group
Studio 101
The Record Hall
16–16A Baldwin's Gardens
London EC1N 7RJ
www.spck.org.uk

*British Library Cataloguing-in-Publication Data*
A catalogue record for this book is available from the British Library

ISBN 978–0–281–08911–6
eBook ISBN 978–0–281–08913–0

1 3 5 7 9 10 8 6 4 2

Typeset by Fakenham Prepress Solutions, Fakenham, Norfolk NR21 8NL
First printed in Great Britain by Clays Limited
eBook by Fakenham Prepress Solutions, Fakenham, Norfolk NR21 8NL
Produced on paper from sustainable sources

# Contents

# Contents

## Part 4
## GENESIS 20.1—22.19

## Part 5
## GENESIS 22.20—25.11

# Preface

I am indebted to the late David Gooding, MRIA, Professor of Greek at Queen's University Belfast, who was my mentor, friend and colleague for many years. Above all, I treasure his unique insights into Scripture and it was through him that I came to love the book of Genesis.

I am also grateful to many others who have written about Abraham from the perspective of those who trace their spiritual descent from him, as well as to many Jewish commentators who regard Abraham as their physical, cultural and, in many cases, spiritual ancestor.

# Introduction

This book is an attempt to understand the life and work of a towering historical figure from whom billions of people trace their spiritual descent. The biblical account of Abraham's life and significance could well be framed as a tale of two cities. The account starts in the Old Testament with the Genesis record of the building of the great cities of the ancient Near East – in particular, Babel or Babylon – while in the New Testament Abraham is described as a man who was 'looking forward to the city that has foundations, whose designer and builder is God' (Heb. 11.10). That city appears in the book of Revelation as the New Jerusalem, where it is described as the faithful bride of Christ and contrasted with another city, 'Mystery Babylon the Great', an unfaithful prostitute. Not only Abraham's life, then, but the entire Bible can be thought of as a tale of two cities.

Abraham is unquestionably one of the most outstanding and influential figures in world history. In two earlier books I wrote about the lives of two other famous biblical characters, Joseph and Daniel, who rose to become the leaders of great empires in the ancient Near East: Joseph ran the economy of Egypt, and Daniel led the administration, first of the Babylonian empire and then of the Medo-Persian empire that succeeded it. They were supremely competent as leaders, their lives energised and shaped by their faith in the enduring reality and presence of the living God.

However, in terms of influence, neither of them is in the same league as their common ancestor Abraham. The late Lord Jonathan Sacks, former Chief Rabbi of the United Kingdom and Commonwealth, wrote:

Abraham performed no miracles, commanded no armies, ruled no kingdom, gathered no mass of disciples and made no spectacular prophecies. Yet there can be no serious doubt that he is the most influential person who ever lived, counted today as the spiritual grandfather of more than half of the six billion people on the face of the earth.[1]

In particular, around 13 million Jews, 2.4 billion Christians and 1.6 billion Muslims claim him as such, and for Jews, who call him Avraham, and Muslims, who call him Ibrahim, he is their physical progenitor as well.

Joseph is only mentioned six times in the New Testament, and Daniel once, whereas Abraham's name occurs more than sixty times. Even a cursory reading shows that he plays a fundamental role, particularly in the letters to the Romans, Galatians and Hebrews, where he is held out to us as the great exemplar of what it means to trust God. In those letters there are lessons taken from Abraham's faith in God, particularly in connection with his migration from Babylon to Canaan, his offspring and their inheritance of the land.

Abraham's experience was, in a sense, the mirror opposite of that of both Daniel and Joseph. Abraham was called to leave the region of Mesopotamia to which Daniel was later forcibly deported and yet eventually administered. Also, Abraham was forcibly ejected from Egypt, the land to which Joseph would later be taken as a captive and yet would eventually rule.

Unlike Joseph and Daniel, Abraham never became a leader wielding administrative power. He never ruled a nation, let alone an empire, although he prospered materially. He lived first with his relatives as a city dweller in Ur, moving later to Haran in northern Mesopotamia for a time. He then migrated further west to live an essentially nomadic life as head of a small clan in and around the land of Canaan. His journeys were never merely geographical, but had a spiritual dimension in that they were journeys of faith in God.

God called Abraham to a unique role as the genetic ancestor of a physical nation through which God promised to bless the entire world and to be the spiritual ancestor of all those who trusted God. Joseph and Daniel were prime examples of the partial fulfilment of that promise. The fact that God chose one particular man to be the vehicle of universal blessing is a striking example of what is often called 'the scandal of the particular'. The supreme example of this is, of course, the claim that Jesus Christ, Abraham's most important descendant, is the only way to God: 'And there is salvation in no one else, for there is no other name under heaven given among men by which we must be saved' (Acts 4.12). There is a lengthy classical philosophical tradition, starting with Plato and

Aristotle, about the nature of and relation between the particular and the universal that we cannot develop here. Sufficient to say that in this biblical narrative one particular man is chosen as the vehicle of blessing to many particular men and women. I, in particular, have come into that blessing. The 'universal' here is, therefore, far from an abstract concept.

The particular man Abraham was no superhuman superhero in the classical mould. He is presented to us as a flawed man, a man who worried about his own safety and twisted the truth to try to ensure it, and a man who struggled in his marriage to Sarah with the physical process of being fruitful and multiplying. Christopher Watkin's comment is apt:

> Abraham is not always a good or wise man . . . Clearly, Abraham is not right with God because he always trusts God but because the foundation of Abraham's story (though not every note in its melody) is that he acts on the belief that God fulfils promises.[2]

We shall investigate the much-misunderstood nature of 'faith' and 'belief' in Chapter 11.

The trials of Abraham and Sarah in these different areas inject a great deal of fascinating human interest into the account as they wrestled with each other (and with God!) about these matters.

Sarah's childlessness led to what turned out to be a presumptuous attempt on her part to help Abraham fulfil God's promise of a son and heir by taking their Egyptian servant, Hagar, as a surrogate wife. This stratagem backfired and generated a great deal of tension between the two women that resulted in Hagar and her son Ishmael being expelled when their own son Isaac was eventually born.

In fact, Abraham's marriage was far from tension free in general, yet God used the pair of them to play a major role in his self-revelation in history. That should encourage us to realise that relationships, even marriages, do not have to be perfect in order for God to use them for his kingdom purposes.

Trust in God is the key to understanding the narrative. Again and again our attention is drawn to Abraham's and Sarah's faith in God – and its defects. For faith is a central theme in the Bible as a whole. We shall find that, contrary to widespread opinion, faith is to be understood as evidence-based trust and not the superficial credulity that so many atheists and sceptics erroneously imagine it to be. It is a trust that God himself will put to the test, sometimes in extreme fashion, as Abraham eventually discovered when God told him to offer up his son Isaac as a sacrifice on Mount Moriah. The narrative of the so-called Akedah, or Binding of Isaac, is nail-bitingly tense, yet it led to a complete vindication of the trust that Abraham had in God.

Nor was that the end of the story. In order for Abraham's descendants to be a blessing to the world, Isaac had to have his own descendants, so needed to marry and have children. The romantic account of how Abraham sent his trusted servant to find a wife for Isaac is one of the most delightful in all of literature.

The Bible subsequently relates how, over the centuries after Abraham's death, many of his spiritual descendants – men and women who trusted God as Abraham did – were called by God to live and witness around the world as conduits through which God's blessing would flow to the whole earth.

Way beyond this, one very special, indeed unique, descendant of Abraham played the central role in God's great plan of world redemption – Jesus the Messiah. The New Testament record begins with the words: 'The book of the genealogy of Jesus Christ, the son of David, the son of Abraham. Abraham was the father of Isaac and Isaac the father of Jacob...' (Matt. 1.1–2). Jesus Christ, the Son of God, Messiah and Saviour, of the seed of Abraham, was God's supreme blessing to the world.

This fact demonstrates that Christianity is not simply a philosophy, although it has a very important philosophical dimension and offers us credible and profound answers to the great world view questions of humanity. It goes beyond philosophy by having an essential historical dimension in the sense that the biblical narrative, particularly that part of it relating to Abraham and his descendants, is an integral and important part of world history. As we mentioned earlier, adherents of the three major monotheistic traditions – Judaism, Christianity and Islam – all claim Abraham as historical patriarch.

Yet in the case of Christianity there is another aspect altogether to the relationship of Jesus to Abraham. In a famous discussion recorded in John 8 Jesus made the following remarkable claim to some Jews:

'Your father Abraham rejoiced that he would see my day. He saw it
and was glad.' So the Jews said to him, 'You are not yet fifty years old,
and have you seen Abraham?' Jesus said to them, 'Truly, truly, I say
to you, before Abraham was, I am.'
(John 8.56–58)

Abraham was an ancestor of Jesus as far as his humanity was concerned,
but Jesus was never merely human, as he clearly indicated by saying that
he had existed eternally before Abraham had come to be.

However, physical descent from Abraham, though essential for
establishing the human lineage and identity of Jesus, was never the whole
story, as Jesus himself pointed out earlier in that same passage in John 8.
The group of Jews said to him:

'We are offspring of Abraham and have never been enslaved to
anyone . . .' Jesus answered them: '. . . I know that you are offspring
of Abraham; yet you seek to kill me because my word finds no place
in you . . . If you were Abraham's children you would be doing the
works Abraham did, but now you seek to kill me, a man who has
told you the truth that I heard from God. This is not what Abraham
did. You are doing the works your father did . . . you are of your
father the devil.'
(John 8.33–44)

They were physically descended from Abraham, but the Lord did not
count them as Abraham's children because they did not share Abraham's
attitude to God. There is, therefore, more to being one of Abraham's true
children in the biblical sense than having him as one's genetic forebear.
Indeed, we shall see that, in the spiritual sense, a person can be counted
as a child of Abraham without being physically descended from him. The
essential criterion is that one shares Abraham's faith in God.

That was difficult for many people who thought that it was physical
connection with Abraham that was the all-important factor, quite
irrespective of their attitudes and behaviour.

John the Baptist had earlier countered this misunderstanding with a
slightly different emphasis. Matthew records:

Then Jerusalem and all Judea and all the region about the Jordan were going out to him, and they were baptized by him in the river Jordan, confessing their sins. But when he saw many of the Pharisees and Sadducees coming to his baptism, he said to them, 'You brood of vipers! Who warned you to flee from the wrath to come? Bear fruit in keeping with repentance. And do not presume to say to yourselves, "We have Abraham as our father", for I tell you, God is able from these stones to raise up children for Abraham. Even now the axe is laid to the root of the trees. Every tree therefore that does not bear good fruit is cut down and thrown into the fire.'
(Matt. 3.5–10)

John warned them that being a child of Abraham was not as big a deal as they thought – indeed God could raise up children for Abraham from the very stones that were lying in the river beside them. Alfred Edersheim cites Bishop Lightfoot as pointing out that in the original language John spoke, there is a play on words here – *banim* for 'children' and *abhanim* for 'stones'. Lightfoot writes: 'Both words are derived from bana, to build, which is also used by the Rabbis in a moral sense like our own "upbuilding" and in that of the gift or adoption of children.'[3]

Paul explains this spiritual and moral dimension as he expounds the key Christian doctrine of justification by faith in his letter to the Romans:

We say that faith was counted to Abraham as righteousness. How then was it counted to him? Was it before or after he had been circumcised? It was not after, but before he was circumcised. He received the sign of circumcision as a seal of the righteousness that he had by faith while he was still uncircumcised. The purpose was to make him *the father of all who believe* without being circumcised, so that righteousness would be counted to them as well, and to make him the father of the circumcised who are not merely circumcised but who also walk in the footsteps of the faith that our father Abraham had before he was circumcised.
(Rom. 4.9–12, emphasis mine)

Similarly, in Galatians Paul writes: 'for in Christ Jesus you are all sons of God, through faith . . . And if you are Christ's then you are Abraham's offspring, heirs according to promise' (Gal. 3.26, 29). We shall explore this matter in much more detail later.

Many of my readers, like myself, are children of God through faith in Christ. According to this text we are also, therefore, Abraham's spiritual offspring through faith. Not only that, we are heirs of God's promises to Abraham.

We are perhaps so familiar with the idea of promise that we fail to realise what a marvellous thing it is that the God of the Bible is a God who makes and keeps promises. After all, promises play a key role in our lives from the very beginning. The essential characteristic of a promise is that it is anticipatory: its fulfilment is in the future. Most of us will recall promises made to us by our parents whose fulfilment brought great joy. Sadly, many others will recall the disappointment of unkept promises that were sometimes only made to get them to behave in a certain way. Promises kept promote trust. Promises broken generate distrust, to which the tragic litany of broken relationships – especially marriages – testifies.

Being an heir is a legal status that has to do with the promise of an inheritance.

We have all come across 'rags to riches' stories, one of the most famous being that of the brothers Zsolt and Geza Peladi who, in 2009, were homeless. They lived in a cave outside Budapest, Hungary, and scavenged scrap to survive. The siblings were eventually located by charity workers, who told them that they had inherited a fortune worth 4 billion pounds from a grandmother in Germany.

Such stories are rare and most of us can only dream. The reading of a will with its convoluted legal language can be very boring – unless, of course, our name happens to come up! And if it does, how rapt our attention to the precise provisions of the will instantly becomes!

What transformed the lives of the Peladi brothers was the fact that their names appeared in a legal document drawn up years earlier by a lawyer and executed by their grandmother. The chance of that happening to any of us is statistically vanishingly small.

And yet – what, then, if we now discover that those of us who belong to Christ are covered by an equally valid legal commitment made, not by a wealthy, ailing grandmother, but by God the almighty Creator and owner of heaven and earth? That legal commitment was made around 4,000 years ago to Abraham and, most importantly, it is still valid today.

I am staggered at how few Christians show real interest in it, even though they may pay lip service to the fact that they are Abraham's spiritual children in some vague and indeterminate sense. Admittedly, such a relationship with an ancient nomad in the Middle East is not the easiest notion to grasp, as the following personal experience illustrates.

Some years ago, while on a research visit to a university in Israel, I was invited to a meal in Tel Aviv by two Israeli engineers. They were a married couple I had met some years earlier when they were on holiday in Austria. Conversation flowed, during which I explained the importance of the history of Israel to my Christian world view.

Suddenly, the wife asked me: 'Why aren't you a Jew?'

Her husband was very embarrassed and burst out: 'You shouldn't ask that!'

I replied that it was a very good question and I was happy to respond to it. I quietly told them that I happened to be a son of Abraham! Talk about startled.

'Impossible!' they chorused. 'You are not a Jew, so how can you be a son of Abraham?'

I then asked them to define a Jew, putting it to them this way: 'Abraham had two sons Ishmael and Yitzak.[4] Was Ishmael a Jew?'

'No,' they said.

'Why not?'

'Because he didn't have a Jewish mother.'

'Really?' I responded. 'What about Yitzak [Isaac]? He had two sons: Esav [Esau] and Yakov [Jacob]. Was Esav a Jew?'

'No,' came the answer.

'But wasn't his mother Rivka [Rebecca] the mother of Yakov as well, and therefore herself a Jew?'

That was clearly a problem. After a slightly embarrassed silence on their part, I ventured: 'Could it be that it was not just a matter of purely physical descent but that God was choosing a particular line of inheritance?'

They grasped at it. 'That's it,' they said.

I pressed on: 'Well then, on that very same principle, a famous rabbi Saul [aka Paul the apostle] said that God has chosen that those who believe in Yeshua Ha Mashiach [Jesus the Messiah] are to be counted as children of Abraham in both a spiritual and a legal sense. In a spiritual sense because they trust God as Abraham did, and in a legal sense because those who share the faith of Abraham are counted as legal heirs of the promises that God made to Abraham.'

It was very surprising and unexpected news for them. They found it extremely difficult to comprehend, commenting wryly that I seemed to have more hope than they did.

Unpacking this matter of inheritance in some detail will be one of our main objectives in this book. However, in order to avoid confusion we shall have to be patient and deal with the issues as they arise in the narrative – otherwise we risk losing the impact of the story.

We now need to fill in some background historical information that can be skipped by readers already familiar with it.

# Abraham – a historical figure?

Of course, saying as we did above that Abraham is an influential historical figure assumes that he really did exist as an actual person living at a particular time in a particular place. Over the years it has been fashionable at times to question the historicity of many events and persons in both Old and New Testaments, including Abraham. However, the Bible has proved impressively resilient to such attacks, particularly the New Testament. Time and again manuscript and archaeological evidence has turned up to vindicate specific claims. Colin Hemer's magisterial work, *The Book of Acts in the Setting of Hellenistic History*, is a prime example of the kind of research that has done much to revive confidence in the historical accuracy of the New Testament.[5] A more recent book is that by Peter J. Williams of Tyndale House, Cambridge: *Can We Trust the Gospels?*[6]

What about the Old Testament – Abraham in particular? That this is a much more complicated matter we can illustrate as follows. Genesis describes a treaty that Abraham made with the king of Gerar. Such treaties were of great importance in the ancient world and questions have often been asked, such as: does the fact that we have no extra-biblical trace of this treaty not weaken confidence in the historicity of Abraham? Referring to this treaty, ancient Near Eastern expert Alan Millard, Rankin Professor Emeritus of Hebrew and Semitic languages at Liverpool, writes:

> This agreement exemplifies the problem of corroboration. If an archaeologist were to find that treaty, the Genesis account would gain in credibility among all historians. However, to find that treaty the archaeologist would have to dig to the appropriate level, unearth the royal palace and locate its archive room. Now ancient towns usually lasted for many centuries, so there is a great accumulation of debris, 70 or 100 feet high (20–30 m). The ruins of buildings, perhaps monumental buildings, of later times may cover those of the Middle Bronze Age, which could contain the treaty. All of those remains have to be carefully explored and recorded before the appropriate level is reached. If that level is reached, how does the archaeologist locate the palace? There may be some indications, but there can never be certainty until the spade strikes it. But what if the palace is found, will there be an archive room and, if there is, will the archives still lie there? Ancient archivists jettisoned out of date documents, just as we do, so if occupation continued in the palace for several generations after the date of the treaty, it may no longer be there. Another danger is that later building work may have dug into the ruins of the older palace, to lay foundations or to collect building material, and have disturbed or destroyed the archive. Cuneiform tablets are fairly durable, but they can be broken quite easily, by falling from shelves or by masonry collapsing on them.
>
> Moreover, although clay tablets were in use in the Levant during the Middle Bronze Age, Egyptian scribal customs were also current, so if it was written down, Abraham's treaty may have been written on papyrus or leather and such documents do not survive in the moist soil of the Holy Land. There are many obstacles, therefore, in the path of survival for that treaty. Also, many agreements were made orally, before witnesses, perhaps with an oath by the gods, and

so cannot be recovered. There is one more reason why no-one has found a copy of a treaty between Abraham and Abimelech: the site of Gerar has not yet been identified! A good candidate is Tell Abu Hureira, Tel Haror, but no document from there or anywhere else gives its name.[7]

On all of these grounds, Millard concludes:

It is most unlikely any record will be found about Abraham or Joseph in Egypt . . . Even though it provides no direct references to the patriarchs, archaeology may still offer help in studying the background to their lives. Are the stories in keeping with what we know about the period 2000–1500 BC in which the Bible seems to place them, or do they show signs of another era?[8]

On the basis of this principle of corroboration of primary evidence, Millard is convinced that they are very much in keeping with the era in question.

Kenneth Kitchen, Emeritus Professor of Egyptology at Liverpool, agrees with this measured verdict. He points out in his comprehensive work, *On the Reliability of the Old Testament*,[9] that there are essentially five kinds of biblical narrative texts: (a) Royal Historical texts; (b) Autobiographical and Biographical texts, Officials and Private People; (c) Historical Legends; (d) Purely Fictional Tales, excluding Historical People; (e) Tales of Mythology. Kitchen is an expert on each of these categories from both biblical and extra-biblical sources and I would encourage readers to consult his work if they want to know more than can be accommodated in this book.

I shall content myself with observing that he places the Abraham narrative in category (b). He writes:

Thus the fairest judgment – based on the overall evidence itself . . . would appear to be that a real historical family of a man Terah existed in and around Ur this side of circa 2000 B.C.; he and they moved on northwestward and his son Abraham and family moved southward into Canaan; after three generations the latter's great-grandson (Joseph) could care for the group in Thirteenth/ Fifteenth Dynasty Egypt in the East Delta. Abraham passed on family lore to his son Isaac . . .[10]

This view is also supported by Professor of Old Testament R. K. Harrison: 'From this brief survey of archaeological material from the second millennium B.C. of Assyrian culture, it will be clear that the patriarchal narratives are set firmly against a contemporary social and cultural background.'[11] More detailed material may be found in the book *Essays on the Patriarchal Narratives* edited by A. R. Millard and D. J. Wiseman.[12]

The New Testament gives its support to the historicity of Abraham in various ways. First, Abraham is included in the genealogies of Christ recorded in Matthew 1 and Luke 3. Jesus himself clearly regarded Abraham as a historical figure as evidenced by his famous statement: 'Truly, truly, I say to you, before Abraham was, I am' (John 8.56–58). Abraham's existence is as firm in Jesus' mind as the fact of his own eternal existence pre-dating Abraham. Similarly, Stephen in his defence before the Sanhedrin regards Abraham as the undisputed father of the nation to whom God appeared, and Paul does the same.

The fact that the biblical account of Abraham's life raises many unanswered questions is partly due to the minimalist character of Hebrew narrative that makes it very different from other literary genres. Jewish writer Robert Alter says that the

biblical narrative characteristically captures its protagonists only at the critical and revealing points in their lives, the biblical type-scene occurs not in the rituals of daily existence but at the crucial junctures in the lives of the heroes, from conception and birth to betrothal to deathbed.[13]

Alter goes on to list examples:

the annunciation . . . of the birth of the hero to his barren mother; the encounter of the future betrothed at a well; the epiphany in the field; the initiatory trial; danger in the desert and the discovery of a well or other source of sustenance; the testament of the dying hero.

Furthermore, Hebrew narrative in general does not suffer from the contemporary preoccupation with moods, emotions and thoughts. It is more concerned with actions motivated by the conviction that who and what people are is best seen in what they do. God often introduces himself in this way. Leon Kass points out that in Yahweh's encounter with Moses at the burning bush his speech is 'emphatically about his purposes and plans'.[14] We need to recognise that this biblical style is not inferior to other styles but is simply different and should be treated on its own merits.

The importance of Abraham's story to Genesis is shown by the fact that it occupies nearly one third of the book. We now briefly survey the structure of Genesis as a whole in order to place the Abraham narrative in its wider context.

## Structure and thought flow in the book of Genesis

These days most books are conveniently divided by the author into chapters arranged according to some scheme – thematic, historical and so on – that is set out in the table of contents at the beginning of the book. The biblical books are not like that. The familiar chapter and verse divisions were added long after the books were written. However, ancient writers had their own ways of dividing up their works. One of them is to use a repeated phrase, or a summary statement, or a statement that makes it clear the subject matter is entering a new phase or changing completely.

By common scholarly consent, Genesis contains such a phrase: 'This is the account of . . .' or 'These are the generations of . . .'. It is often referred to by its Hebrew name: *toledoth*.

Taking into account the way in which these *toledoths* are distributed, the book would then seem to be organised as follows:

### The beginning
1. *The creation of the universe and human beings 1.1—2.3*
2. *What it is to be human and the beginning of sin 2.4—4.26*
   The generations of the heavens and the earth 2.4

3. *From Adam to the judgement of the world 5.1—9.29*
   The generations of Adam 5.1—6.8, Noah 6.9—9.29

## The new beginning

4. *Abraham and his sons 10.1—25.11*
   The generations of Noah, Shem, Terah
   The death of Abraham
5. *Isaac and his sons 25.12—35.29*
   The generations of Ishmael 25.12, Isaac 25.19
   The death of Isaac
6. *Jacob and his sons 36.1—50.26*
   The generations of Esau 36.1, Jacob 37.2
   The deaths of Jacob and Joseph

We observe that in some of the sections the *toledoth* appears more than once, as indicated in the subheadings above. For example, in section 5 we first find the generations or account of Ishmael, which occupies a few verses, and then the generations of Isaac. Similarly in section 6 we first have the generations of Esau, which occupy a chapter, and then the generations of Jacob, which occupy the remainder of the book. A similar pattern can be detected through the entire book.

On this basis it seems reasonable to argue, as I did with my Israeli friends in Tel Aviv, that God was indicating his choice of the line of inheritance and marking it by means of the literary device that in each section the main line of descent appears second, after a brief description of the lesser lines.

# A summary of the contents of the major sections of Genesis

*Section 1* teaches us about the nature of God, the status of the universe and the status of human beings: God is the Creator of the universe by his word and human beings are unique in that they alone are made in God's image. God can speak 'to them'. The introduction to Genesis constitutes a powerful assault on the naturalism of both the ancient and modern worlds.

*Section 2* deals with the basic parameters of human existence (humans made from the dust of the ground, with aesthetic sense, need for food, curiosity, work, relationship with spouse and family) with life at its highest consisting in a (moral) relationship with God defined by his word – the essence of morality in freedom and responsibility. Human sin breaks the relationship and infects the world. Yet God makes provision and promises that one day 'the offspring of the woman shall bruise the serpent's heel' – that is, humanity will triumph.

This section traces morality back to its defining source in God and it constitutes an assault on the dominant moral philosophy of the contemporary Western world – utilitarianism. This is a consequentialist view of morality. In other words an action is to be judged solely in terms of its consequences on the principle of the maximum benefit for the maximum number of people, rather than being judged by whether or not it conforms to a divine commandment. The problem lies with the word 'solely'. It makes good sense in any decision to take account of the consequences, but that needs to be subjugated to a higher sense of right and wrong. Otherwise you can get the situation where a decision is made that the maximum benefit for the maximum number of people is to commit genocide on an 'undesirable' ethnic minority – as has too often tragically happened in world history.

*Section 3* tells of the development of the human race from Adam and its increasingly violent and corrupt behaviour, which leads to the chilling announcement by God: 'I will blot out man whom I have created from the face of the earth . . .' In section 1 God's word separates earth from sea – dry land from water – and in section 3 God intervenes in nature and by his word reverses that division and so brings lethal judgement on the world.

The New Testament uses the Flood narrative as a thought model to help us understand that what happened in the past foreshadows what will happen in the future. Jesus himself used it in this way to prepare people for a future cataclysmic intervention when he comes again: 'For as were the days of Noah, so will be the coming of the Son of Man' (Matt. 24.37). We read in 2 Peter 3 that God will one day destroy the earth by using one of its constituent elements – not water this time, but fire.

In this way the first three sections of Genesis can be seen to lay the foundations for three major biblical doctrines: (1) Creation; (2) Sin and (the promise of) Redemption; (3) Judgement and Salvation. We should also notice that each of the first three sections includes a reference to the creation of human beings (1.26; 2.7; 5.1) so that each of them can be seen to unpack a different aspect of the uniqueness of humans as God's image bearers.

The second half of Genesis represents a new beginning for humanity after the Flood. This half of the book also falls into three parts. In section 4 the narrative rapidly narrows to concentrate on a particular person, Abraham, and his sons. It ends with the death of Abraham; in 5 the narrative of Isaac and his sons ends with the death of Isaac, and in 6 the narrative of Jacob and his sons, particularly Joseph, ends with the deaths of Jacob and Joseph. We might therefore summarise the second half of the book using the phrase 'I am the God of Abraham, Isaac and Jacob'.

After opening with an account of the temporal beginnings of the universe, the earth and life on it, the book of Genesis concentrates mainly on providing a biblical anthropology in the original sense of that word – a *logos* (account) of *anthropos* (man, human being). Jewish polymath Leon Kass, in his brilliant book *The Beginning of Wisdom – Reading Genesis*,[15] suggests that the biblical narratives are powerful precisely because they present human life in all its moral ambiguity. They not only present to us what once happened in a particular time and place, but, in a very real sense, they throw light on what always happens and hence they act as a mirror in which the complexity of our own lives is reflected. That is, Genesis shows us not only what is first in time, but also what is first in importance when it comes to understanding fundamental things – God, the universe, life, language, morality, relationships, sin, death, salvation and much else.

The order in which these things are communicated to us should teach us something of how we in our turn should pass the message on. In particular, the Genesis narrative does not start with the moral failure of humans but with their value as made in the image of God. Today, with moral failure evident all around us, it is easy to start there. Yet that leaves our hearers without a positive context in which to face their moral turpitude. The Fall stands in the shadow of creation, so we need first to remind our hearers of the unique dignity and value that is conferred on us as God's image bearers. Then we can tell them about sin and salvation.

Thus, the first three sections of the book reveal to us what the world once was in all its glory, with human beings made in the image of God as the pinnacle of God's creation with all their wonderful capacities. It then relates the devastation wrought by the misuse of those capacities to disobey God, thereby introducing sin and alienation into the world: the banishing from Eden, the trials of life and the increasing violence of human behaviour that leads to the capital judgement of the Flood, with only the family of Noah saved through that judgement in the ark to repopulate the planet.

God begins afresh after the Flood. This time he calls a particular person, Abram, to leave his own country and set out on a journey to a new land in order to form a new nation that will live God's way. One of the major lessons is that, since sin entered into the world through human failure to trust God and consequent grasping at independence from him, the way back will necessitate learning to trust him and his word.

We learn about the complexities of this path back to God through the experience of it on the part of flawed men and women, in particular the patriarchs, their wives and families. They were each involved in a series of steep learning curves full of ups and downs geared to training them to trust God. Their stories can inspire us and give us real hope of doing the same.

We end this introduction by summarizing the stages of the life of Abraham.

## The stages of Abraham's life

*Background: 10.1—11.32*
The Gentile nations descended from Noah: Nimrod
The city and Tower of Babel: making a name
Death of Terah

*Stage 1: 12.1—15.21*
God's call to Abram
Denial of wife among Egyptians
The promise of name, seed and inheritance
Justification by faith

*Stage 2: 16.1—19.38*
Trust in God's promise or the works of the flesh?
A substitute wife: Ishmael born to Hagar
Lot: his daughters and his seed

*Stage 3: 20.1—22.24*
Security: in God or in his gift?
Denial of wife among Philistines
Isaac born and Ishmael cast out
The offering of Isaac
Justification by works

*Stage 4: 23.1—25.11*
Sarah's death and burial
A wife for Isaac from the Gentiles
Abraham's death and burial

# Part 1

# GENESIS 10.1—11.32

**SUMMARY**

A.  The sons of Noah (10.1–7)
B.  Nimrod and the cities of the ancient Near East (10.8–12)
C.  The city, tower and ideology of Babel (11.1–9)
D.  The other Semitic nations and Abraham's ancestry (11.10–32)

# 1

# The city that reached for the sky

Genesis 10 gives us important background to the Mesopotamian culture from which Abraham came. It starts with what is often called the Table of the Nations, which describes the repopulation of the earth by the descendants of Noah following the Flood. Robert Alter says:

> The Table of Nations is a serious attempt, unprecedented in the ancient Near East, to sketch a panorama of all known human cultures – from Greece and Crete in the west through Asia Minor and Iran and down through Mesopotamia and the Arabian Peninsula to northwestern Africa.[1]

It also lists many of the tribes and nations that are encountered in the biblical narrative and shows how they relate to each other.

Egyptologist Kenneth Kitchen points out several strands of evidence that converge on an early date:

1 The topic of the division of languages mentioned in Genesis 11 is very old – it is also recorded in a nineteenth-/eighteenth-century Sumerian composition in relation to a king who lived around 2600 BC.
2 The kind of structure exhibited by Genesis 1–11 is not known in the ancient Near East after 1600 BC and is characteristic of documents before that time.
3 The scribal use of cuneiform script spread from Mesopotamia as far as Canaan, Hazor and even Hebron by the seventeenth century BC, so that the account could have been written as early as that time.

Kitchen sums up the evidence as follows:

So no objection can be taken to the essence of Genesis 1–11 going westward at this epoch; its written formulation in early Hebrew may then have followed later and independently. The patriarchal tradition would then have been passed down in Egypt (as family tradition) to the fourteenth/thirteenth century, possibly then first put into writing . . . It is part of the oldest levels of Hebrew tradition, as were the Mesopotamian accounts in their culture.[2]

It is therefore an important *historical* document. It lists the sons of Noah, Shem, Ham and Japheth and their descendants as follows:

*The sons of Japheth (10.2–5)* A very brief account of the progenitor of the 'coastland peoples' is given, probably because they are of the least relevance to the development of the biblical storyline. Precise identifications have proved difficult. Gomer may indicate the Cimmerians, an Indo-European group from southern Russia that posed a threat to Assyria in the seventh and eighth centuries; Madai refers to the Medes, Yavan the Greeks – first Ionian Greeks then all Greeks, and Kittim is Cyprus.

*The sons of Ham (10.6–20)* Here more detail is given, including identifiable names. Many of Ham's descendants occupied the Arabian area, Cush (Ethiopia), Egypt, Put (Libya?) and Canaan. A prominent thing about this list is that it singles out for special mention one of Noah's great-grandsons, Nimrod, the founder of Babel (Gen. 10.8–10). He is said to be the first mighty man on the earth, a hunter whose prowess became legendary – 'a mighty hunter before the LORD'. The phrase is probably a superlative, but some think that it means 'against the Lord', since one meaning assigned to the name Nimrod is 'we shall rebel'. If so, that would neatly encapsulate the attitude of Babel, as we shall see below. Nimrod is an example of two things that have been of conspicuous importance to leaders and others throughout history – personal prowess and power. The ambiguity here introduced by the mention of 'the LORD' raises a question as to what Nimrod knew about God's dealings with Noah, whom he may possibly have known personally.

The list of descendants of Ham now concentrates on the line of Canaan and seems to consist more of tribes than individuals. It gives the origin of some that feature in the later biblical narrative under the collective name of Canaanites, including Jebusites, Amorites, Girashites, Hivites and Phoenicians (Sidon – the firstborn). In addition their land boundaries are given, and this information will become important in connection with the territory promised to Abraham.

*The sons of Shem (10.21–31)* In this list the name of Peleg stands out, as the narrator says that in his days the earth was divided – a possible reference to the consequences of the scattering of languages post-Babel. The list then continues to give several generations of the descendants of Peleg's brother Joktan.

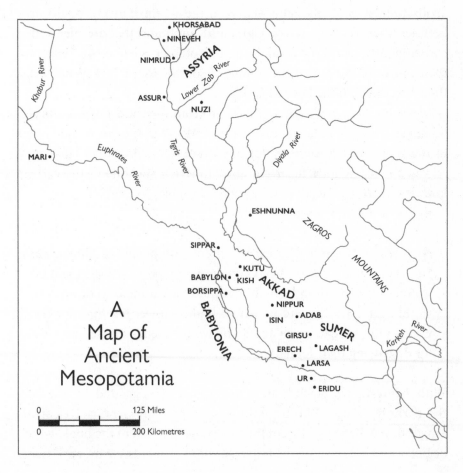

Taking the three genealogies together we see that most attention is paid to Nimrod, a descendant of Ham. He was a prolific builder of ancient cities: 'The beginning of his kingdom was Babel, Erech, Accad, and Calneh, in the land of Shinar. From that land he went into Assyria and built Nineveh, Rehoboth-Ir, Calah, and Resen between Nineveh and Calah; that is the great city' (Gen. 10.10–12). Eight cities are named here, including, notably, Babel (Babylon on the Euphrates), Erech (Uruk), Akkad (not identified geographically, but it gives its name to the Semitic Akkadian language) and Nineveh (on the Tigris on the outskirts of modern Mosul). Nineveh was the largest city in the Neo-Assyrian empire and, indeed, the largest city in the world for several decades. It figures prominently in the book of Jonah. Shinar is known to us as Sumer.

The setting is therefore ancient Mesopotamia,[3] one of the cradles of civilisation. It is, as its name suggests, the (comparatively small) area between the two great rivers Tigris and Euphrates that are mentioned earlier in Genesis as flowing in the garden of Eden (Gen. 2.14). They have their source in the Taurus mountains of south-eastern Turkey and wend their way down to the Persian Gulf.

Mesopotamian civilisation flourished from the third millennium BC. Southern Mesopotamia was divided into Akkad in the north and Sumer in the south, which were similar in culture but had distinct languages: Akkadian was Semitic in origin and Sumerian was one of the earliest known written languages of very ancient origin.

In his *Antiquities*, Josephus writes:

Now it was Nimrod who excited them [the people of Shinar, i.e. Sumer] to such an affront and contempt of God . . . He also said he would be revenged on God, if he should have a mind to drown the world again. To that end he would build a tower too high for the waters to be able to reach and so he would avenge himself on God for destroying their forefather.[4]

With Nimrod, we reach a new beginning, as suggested by the way the narrative starts: 'The beginning [*reshith*, as in Genesis 1.1] of his kingdom was Babel . . .' By contrast with the first half of the book, which begins with God creating the universe with key words 'create' and 'make', now the second half of Genesis begins with the building of some of the great cities of the ancient world with key words 'build' and 'make'.[5]

Earlier in Genesis there are hints about the beginnings of city civilisation. Cain, we are told, was the first to build a city that he called Enoch after his son (4.17), and one of his descendants, the violent Lamech, is said to have had a particularly talented family that developed agriculture, industry, music and the arts (4.19–22).

Genesis 11 now concentrates on the construction of one particular city, Babel (Babylon). H. W. F. Saggs, Emeritus Professor of Semitic Languages in the University of Wales and author of *The Greatness That Was Babylon*, writes:

> Though traces of prehistoric settlement exist, Babylon's development as a major city was late by Mesopotamian standards; no mention of it existed before the 23rd century BCE. After the fall of the 3rd Dynasty of Ur, under which Babylon had been a provincial centre, it became the nucleus of a small kingdom established in 1894 BCE by the Amorite king Sumuabum, whose successors consolidated its status.
>
> The sixth and best-known of the Amorite dynasts, Hammurabi (1792–50 BCE), conquered the surrounding city-states and raised Babylon to the capital of a kingdom comprising all of southern Mesopotamia and part of Assyria (Northern Iraq). Its political importance, together with its favourable location, made it henceforth the main commercial and administrative centre of Babylonia, while its wealth and prestige made it a target for foreign conquerors.[6]

By the sixth century BC it was the largest city in the world. Here is how Genesis describes the foundation of ancient Babel:

> Now the whole earth had one language and the same words. And as people migrated from the east, they found a plain in the land of Shinar[7] and settled there. And they said to one another, 'Come, let us make bricks, and burn them thoroughly.' And they had brick for stone, and bitumen for mortar. Then they said, 'Come, let us build ourselves a city and a tower with its top in the heavens, and let us

7

make a name for ourselves, lest we be dispersed over the face of the whole earth.'

(Gen. 11.1–4)

We note, first, that the description of Babel is placed between two overlapping lists of descendants of Shem. Second, the lists of the descendants of the sons of Noah end by indicating that there were several linguistic groups in each – verses 5, 20 and 31, respectively. Yet nothing is said in chapter 10 to account for the spread of those languages. Chapter 11.1–9 could be thought of as filling in the missing information by relating the confusion of languages after Babel. That would mean that the textual order may not necessarily be chronological, but rather explanation after the event, so that logical order takes priority. Placing the account of Babel directly before the genealogy of Abraham suggests that it is to be thought of as essential background for the account of his life.

Language and speech play a central role in Genesis, beginning with the formation of the physical cosmos by the creative word of God. The repetition of the phrase 'And God said . . .' in Genesis 1 tells us that the universe came to exist through a series of divine speech acts, each of which not only conveyed information but also had the effective power to create the reality described by that information.

The last occurrence in that sequence of speech acts is different from the others: 'God said *to them* . . .' (my emphasis). It gives us profound insight into what it means to be made in the image of God; namely, that we humans can hear and understand what God says and can respond to it. And it is that wonderful created capacity of speech communication that lies at the heart of the moral relationship between us and God.

The philosopher Ludwig Wittgenstein once wrote: 'The limits of my language means the limits of my world.'[8] Language is the foundation of civilised order. A common language facilitates communication and co-operation. This is to be seen particularly in the languages of mathematics and science, which transcend all international boundaries.

The first half of Genesis begins with a divine construction project. God creates the universe by speaking his word. The high point and goal of that creation was the making of human beings in God's image from the clay of the earth (making Adam from *adamah*). The second half of Genesis begins with a construction project initiated by humans speaking their words to each other and making bricks of the clay of the earth to make a city. God's image was alive; theirs was lifeless. Note the words that these two texts have in common: make, speak, man (human), earth, heavens.

What a vast category difference there is between the way those words are used in the two 'beginnings'. Think particularly of God's unparalleled words: 'Let us make man . . .' and the words of the inhabitants of Babel, men and women whom God had made: 'Let us make a name for ourselves . . .' God made a world for the habitation of humans who could enjoy fellowship with him – a world filled with meaning. Indeed, a world where, we are told, the Creator himself supplied some of the initial names: it was God who called the light 'day', the darkness 'night', the dry land 'earth', the expanse 'heaven'. God then instructed humankind to name the animals – the beginning of the fundamental academic discipline of taxonomy, necessary to every field of research. Also, the man called his created companion 'woman'. Central to that fundamental relationship is the faculty of speech.

It would seem that Babel did not involve giving a name to something God had made, but was rather a dispensing with God altogether and using the latest technology to pile up bricks in the hope of scraping their self-made name in the sky in a futile search for enduring reputation and significance. After all, they could not even have started to make their city if they had not possessed the God-given faculty of speech to communicate with one another.

This is a point made much later by Aristotle, the ancient Greek founder of political science, in his famous description of human beings as 'political animals' (*politikon zoon*), where the word *politikon* is related to the Greek term *polis* that means 'city', or 'city state'. Mesopotamia had city states long before the time of Aristotle, and the people of Babel were *city animals* in the sense, as he put it,

which a bee is not, or any other gregarious animal . . . Nature . . . has endowed man alone among the animals with the power of speech . . . Speech . . . serves to indicate what is useful and what is harmful, and so also what is just and what is unjust. It is the sharing of a common view on these matters that makes a household and a state.[9]

For Aristotle, commonality, for which he uses the Greek term *koinonia*, meaning partnership or fellowship, is central:

Since we see that every city is some sort of partnership, and that every partnership is constituted for the sake of some good (for everyone does everything for the sake of what is held to be good), it is clear that all partnerships aim at some good, and that the partnership that is most authoritative of all and embraces all the others does so particularly, and aims at the most authoritative good of all. This is what is called the city or the political partnership.

The household is the partnership constituted by nature for [the needs of] daily life . . . The first partnership arising from [the union of] several households and for the sake of non-daily needs is the village.

The partnership arising from [the union of] several villages that is complete is the city. It reaches a level of full self-sufficiency, so to speak; and while coming into being for the sake of living, it exists for the sake of living well.[10]

One reason for building Babel seems to have been fear of losing that sense of community. They felt threatened by dispersal, rather than pleased to fulfil God's command to be fruitful and multiply and fill the earth or, as Abraham's seed was called to do, be scattered around the world to bring God's ultimate blessing in the message of the gospel.

In order to ward off what they saw as the threat, Nimrod's contemporaries decided on a grandiose project that they announced by saying (literally): 'Come let us brick bricks and burn them to a burning . . . let us build for ourselves a city with a tower with its head in the heavens . . . let us make a name *[shem]* for ourselves lest we be scattered abroad on the face of the earth.'

At first sight it looks like a voluntary community project, but is that really likely in view of what we know of the autocratic structure of ancient Near Eastern civilisations? Is it not much more probable that the fear of dispersion was on the part of the ruling class led by Nimrod and that the making of bricks and the building of the city were achieved by the common practice of forced labour – somewhat similar to the way in which Pharaoh later used Hebrew slave labour to build his cities?

In themselves, burnt clay bricks were a brilliant technological innovation dating back to the dawn of history. We still use billions of them to construct buildings of all kinds, especially in mega-cities all over the world.

A fundamental question that has persisted through the centuries and led to a great deal of knowledge and understanding is: what is something made *of* (Aristotle's material cause)? The foundations of the city of Babel were made of clay bricks.

But there was another kind of foundation that answers a second question in which the Greeks, in particular, were subsequently interested: what is something made *for* (Aristotle's final cause)?

The answer to that question in the case of Babel is important. 'Making a name' by building a city and tower in order to avoid dispersion was a direct affront to God, who had made humans and commanded them to multiply and fill the earth – first Adam and second Noah after the Flood. The motivation behind building Babel is poles apart from God's later promise to Abram in Genesis 12.2: 'I will . . . make your name great.' They thought big things about themselves in their desire for a unique reputation and legacy, whereas God thought big things about the reputation he would give to Abram, and it would be in his name, not Babel's name, that all the nations of the earth would be blessed – by a scattering of Abram's spiritual seed in the diaspora.[11]

Babel was built in defiance of God's command that humans should disperse around the world. These people didn't wish to be scattered and thought that, by uniting in a metropolis, they could make a name for themselves without God.

Leon Kass says:

To make a name for oneself is to remake the meaning of one's life so that it deserves a new name. To change the meaning of a human being is to remake the content and character of human life. The city, fully understood, achieves precisely that.[12]

11

Harvey Cox emphasised this motif in his landmark book *The Secular City*, written in 1965:

> In our day the secular metropolis stands as both the pattern of our life together and the symbol of our view of the world. If the Greeks perceived the cosmos as an immensely expanded polis and medieval man saw it as the feudal manor enlarged to infinity, we experience the universe as the city of man . . . Contemporary man has become the cosmopolitan. The world has become his city and his city has reached out to include the world. The name for the process by which this has come about is secularization . . . Secularization occurs when man turns his attention away from worlds beyond and towards this world and this time (*saeculum = this present age*).

Former Chief Rabbi of the UK, the late Lord Jonathan Sacks, wrote:

> cultures that lose their religious faith eventually become individualistic and relativistic – people become self-seeking. The Enlightenment led to people placing faith in science and sacrificing Europe to the twin gods of race and nation. Soviet communism, the greatest ever attempt to build a society on scientific principles and social engineering, crushed human freedom until the empire collapsed under its own dead weight.[13]

In his famous book *The Meaning of the City*, Jacques Ellul develops the thesis that the city represents humanity's attempt to replace God. For Ellul, it is Cain who built the first city, Enoch, that sets the agenda for the city as opposed to God. Ellul writes perceptively of the city that:

> It is the desire to exclude God from his creation. And it is this solidarity in a name, this unity in separation from God, which was to keep men ever again being separated on earth. And the sign and symbol of this, man's environment, built by man for man, with any other intervention or power excluded, that man could make a name for himself. It was there that this pretension of becoming a subject, never again to be an object, could be realised. The cities of our time

are most certainly that place where man can with impunity declare himself master of nature. It is only in an urban civilisation that man has the metaphysical possibility of saying 'I killed God'.[14]

Consistent with that perspective, in the secular city the tower is a symbol for man himself as the creator of his own meaning. He builds because he is afraid of having no identity or meaning in the world, because he wishes to belong to something greater than himself.[15]

The Tower of Babel was the world's first skyscraper and it is no accident that the city's main temple was called *Esagil* – the house with the raised head. From then on people have constructed high buildings as symbols of human pride in achievement. Philip Nobel, writing for the American Enterprise Institute says:

The most primal motivation for skyscraper construction is to stake a claim, to mark the land, to show how your power can change the world, both physically and psychologically. Nothing says 'I am master of the universe' more clearly than the erection of a tall building. And if it can be taller than all the rest, so much the better . . . Before the Petronas Towers, no one knew where Kuala Lumpur was . . .

Skyscrapers are built to make space, they are built to make money, but they are also built to make a point: they are built to awe. And when we do get our true mile-high tower – in 2030, or sooner, or later – one thing is certain: behind the financing, the army of workers, the engineers' numbers, and the architects' specs, there will stand . . . a giant ego – personal, corporate, or national, but still requiring its likeness to be etched in the clouds.[16]

The ideology of the modern skyscraper is essentially that of ancient Babel: Nimrod's driving ego pushing out the boundaries, exceeding the limits, flaunting wealth and power, reaching for the sky and grasping at immortality. Babel was an attempt to capture the imagination and create enduring identity by technological achievement and prowess that represented the power and triumph of human rationality.

Building was also an integral part of ancient worship of the gods. One interpretation of the name Babel is 'gateway to the gods'. In later history the tower or ziggurat[17] in Babylon was called *Etemenanki*, 'the house of the foundation of heaven and earth'. It had a square base and an external stairway winding around the tower until it reached a temple at the top, where the gods were thought to come down to human beings. It was, therefore, thought of as a 'gateway to the gods' and sought to link the city with the cosmos by trying to harness and control its powers and use their knowledge to predict the political fortunes of their rulers. And we can imagine that they imagined the bigger the tower the more powerful the gods they might attract to inhabit its temple.

In spite of its permeation with idolatry, there were many positive sides to Babylonian culture. For instance, its medicine, engineering, literature, art and mathematics were astonishingly advanced. Their astronomers/ astrologers were the first to plot the courses of the stars and use the information to try to predict the seasons and the coming of rain. In that respect, they were the forerunners of contemporary astronomers and meteorologists to whom we are all indebted.

However, heaven soon proved to be beyond their reach. Indeed, Isaiah later gives a vivid description of the soaring arrogance of Babylon and tells us that the only thing in it that reached heaven was its sins

You said in your heart,
'I will ascend to heaven;
above the stars of God
I will set my throne on high;
I will sit on the mount of assembly
in the far reaches of the north;
I will ascend above the heights of the clouds;
I will make myself like the Most High.'
(Isa. 14.13–14)

In other words, the building of Babel had the very same motivation that led humans to rebel against God in the first place by giving in to the temptation to 'be as gods'. It was, to use the title of the book by Yuval Noah Harari, a *Homo Deus*[18] project and the progenitor of many others, including the desire to create a super-intelligence, as Harari's book shows.[19]

Commentator Gordon Wenham points out[20] that in the account of the building of Babel there is subtle Hebrew wordplay to emphasise the foolishness of this human-centred city-tower project. 'Come, let us make bricks (*nilbenah*).' God's reply is: 'Come . . . let us mix up (*nabelah*)', both of which evoke the word *nebelah* (folly).[21] The three stem consonants *n b l* are prominent by their repetition and flow rhythmically into *b b l*, the city. Note: *babel* is etymologically equal to 'gate of god' from the Babylonian perspective, whereas in Hebrew it is linked by word association with *balal* – to 'confuse' or 'mix up'.

Wenham adds that the Hebrew word for flood is *mabul* (with stem consonants *m b l*) so that the whole section could be entitled: From *m b l* to *b b l* – From the Flood to Babel.[22] One might even say: From *m b l* via *n b l* to *b b l*.

This ancient tower, dominated by the powerful ego of Nimrod, stretched up towards the heavens, yet didn't quite make the distance since, as Genesis 11 puts it with delightful irony, God had to 'come down' to see what they were building.

> And the LORD came down to see the city and the tower, which the children of man had built. And the LORD said, 'Behold, they are one people, and they have all one language, and this is only the beginning of what they will do. And nothing that they propose to do will now be impossible for them.'
> (Gen. 11.5–6)

Note carefully the expression 'children of man' – that is, human beings. Not surprisingly, there remained an unbridgeable gap between what humans could do and heaven in more senses than one. Contrasting starkly with Genesis 1, where God saw 'that it was good', here he saw that it was anything but good.

God makes a chilling remark about the builders of Babel: 'this is only the beginning of what they will do. And nothing that they propose to do will now be impossible for them.' This beginning was nothing like the magnificent beginning announced in Genesis 1.1. The Hebrew word *zamam* translated 'propose' is often used with the negative connotation 'plot', so the text may be indicating that the construction of Babel was a defiant anti-God plot.

Is the statement that nothing would be impossible for them a hint that human beings, created in God's image, had immense creative capacities and that there were projects they might well complete that went far beyond what anyone might have expected them to be able, or even allowed, to achieve, and that some of them would prove disastrous?

In many legends about Babel God is said to have destroyed the city. Genesis does not say so. We are told that God intervened and brought the project to a stop by frustrating their communication through mixing up their languages – an action that resulted in their unwilling dispersion. Genesis simply states that 'they left off building'.

However, that does not necessarily mean that God will always intervene to stop human projects at a point where we might expect.

For instance, the book of Revelation speaks of a future, anti-God, tyrannically evil world power, whose rule is enforced by a constructed image that is somehow given at least some of the properties of (artificial?) life. The imagery used is of two wild beasts[23] that come to power consecutively:

And it [the second beast] was allowed to give breath to the image of the [first] beast, so that the image of the beast might even speak and might cause those who would not worship the image of the beast to be slain. Also it causes all, both small and great, both rich and poor, both free and slave, to be marked on the right hand or the forehead, so that no one can buy or sell unless he has the mark, that is, the name of the beast or the number of its name. This calls for wisdom: let the one who has understanding calculate the number of the beast, for it is the number of a man, and his number is 666.
(Rev. 13.15–18)

Sufficient for our purpose here, the text tells us that the mysterious number of the beast, 666, denotes a human being that has Nimrod-like totalitarian power and to whom nothing seems impossible.[24]

God clearly regarded the Babel project as directed against him. It was a massive glorification of human ego and prowess in rebellion against God that started with the Fall and runs throughout the whole biblical narrative until its final hideous incarnation is destroyed by the return of Christ in power and glory.

Speaking of hideous, the Scottish herald and distinguished poet Sir David Lindsay (1495–1555) wrote *Ane Dialog betwix Experience and ane Courteour of the Miserabyll Estait of the World*, in which he described the shadow of the Tower of Babel in the following dramatic terms: 'The shadow of that hyddeous strength sax myle[25] and more it is of length.'[26] This is the source of the title of C. S. Lewis's dystopian science fiction novel, *That Hideous Strength,* that presciently shows the dangers in using morally unbridled science and technology to try to alter and control humankind.[27]

Thus, God did not destroy the hideous strength that was Babel. He caused a breakdown in its inhabitants' ability to speak to one another. He removed their common language and separated them into a multiplicity of language groups so that co-operation was impeded and their Babel project collapsed. Robert Alter captures this beautifully in his translation of 11.9: 'Therefore it is called Babel, for there the Lord made all the language of the earth babble.'

Scholars are divided as to whether the diversification of languages was the cause or the consequence of the scattering of the people. The latter view could be seen as fitting in with the idea that Babel represented a rebellion against God's command to fill the earth. In any case, what they feared most was what in fact happened – they were scattered abroad in the earth.

However, much later in world history another event occurred that marked a reversal of what happened at Babel – the creation of the Church on the Day of Pentecost (Acts 2). On that day people from diverse language groups who had gathered in Jerusalem for the Jewish festival were suddenly empowered to understand in their own languages what the apostles were saying about the mighty works of God. It was a manifestly supernatural event that was itself a mighty work of God, and it connected linguistic commonality with the Holy Spirit. Holiness was the exact opposite of all that Babel and later Babylon stood for: Pentecost involved God coming down to dwell on earth, not men and women building up to dwell in the heavens.

Pentecost inaugurated the Christian Church, or 'body of Christ', whose message was fruitful and multiplied throughout the world in the coming into being of myriads of churches. It is apposite that Jesus and his apostles used the metaphor of building in connection with the Church – with Jesus the chief cornerstone and his people living stones that formed the building – the ideological polar opposite of Babel and its tower (1 Pet. 2.4–5).

And what of our world today? The shadow of the Tower of Babel in terms of time is much more than 'sax myle' – it reaches to the present time. Leon Kass makes a perceptive comment about the ancient culture into which Abraham was born: 'There are the Mesopotamians, who first begin to measure the stars, who build the Tower of Babel, where all humankind comes together to build a technological refuge for humanity where man might be a god to man.'[28]

We are there again today. The universal language of the Christian Church has become submerged by a revival of the ideology of Babel. With the unifying power of the language of science, humans are now engaged in building their techno-world with dizzying speed – even attempting to re-engineer themselves into super-intelligences with unlimited understanding.

Advanced technology has already given us undreamed of means of communication and connected the world by the internet of things. In the words of Mark Zuckerberg, Facebook would 'rewire the way people spread and consume information'.

Writing in 2022 in *The Atlantic*, social psychologist Jonathan Haidt said:

> The story of Babel is the best metaphor I have found for what happened to America in the 2010s, and for the fractured country we now inhabit. Something went terribly wrong, very suddenly. We are disoriented, unable to speak the same language or recognize the same truth. We are cut off from one another and from the past.[29]

In his perceptive analysis he points out that social media has weakened all three of the principal factors that consolidate thriving democracies: social capital (extensive social networks with high levels of trust), strong institutions and shared stories. The tragedy is that social media has, in particular, undermined trust by undermining relationships through spreading dislike, distrust, outrage and hate. As a result we have become in many ways further apart than ever. International tension has increased and multitudes of people are scattered throughout the vastness of cyberspace, their lonely silence broken, not by human speech, but by the tapping of countless impersonal keyboards and blind touchscreens.

Haidt says: 'Facebook, Twitter, YouTube, and a few other large platforms unwittingly dissolved the mortar of trust, belief in institutions, and shared stories that had held a large and diverse secular democracy together.' I would add that what Zuckerberg's metaverse will do to aggravate that situation is nothing less than horrific.

Haidt also points out that the 'dart guns' of social media empower trolls and provocateurs and silence decent citizens. They also amplify political extremes while attenuating the voice of the moderate majority. Perhaps most importantly, by supplying its dart guns indiscriminately, social media deputises everyone to mete out 'justice' without any due process so that innocent people are punished on Twitter, for example, for what are often banal or imagined offences. The problem is that there may be very real consequences, including job loss and even suicide. Haidt says: 'When our public square is governed by mob dynamics unrestrained by due process, we don't get justice and inclusion; we get a society that ignores context, proportionality, mercy, and truth.'

Haidt is fearful for American democracy:

If we do not make major changes soon, then our institutions, our political system, and our society may collapse during the next major war, pandemic, financial meltdown, or constitutional crisis . . . We must harden democratic institutions so that they can withstand chronic anger and mistrust, reform social media so that it becomes less socially corrosive, and better prepare the next generation for democratic citizenship in this new age.

In his 2014 book *The Revolt of the Public*,[30] former CIA analyst Martin Gurri predicted the fragmentation of society by social media. He maintains that the information explosion that began with the internet has subverted authority. Consequently 'the public isn't one thing; it's highly fragmented, and it's basically mutually hostile. It's mostly people yelling at each other and living in bubbles of one sort or another.'

Using the full power of our technology, in those bubbles we are babbling today like never before on social media that devours our time and concentration and, so the psychologists tell us, are not only in danger of reprogramming our minds, but actually doing so – particularly the minds of the young.

There are many kinds of 'language' that fragment our culture. The old don't understand the young and vice versa. There are the languages of political correctness, of postmodern relativism, of technospeak, of cancel culture, confusion about gender and sexuality, racism and woke. Even a single word that is spoken without any malicious intent by a lecturer, journalist or teacher can lead to a firestorm of social media protest and hate, often resulting in utterly unjustifiable investigative processes, muzzling or dismissal.

Old-style healthy and true tolerance – where 'I tolerate you' meant 'I disagree with you but will defend your right to say what you wish' – has been replaced by a relativistic paralysis on criticism where we dare not offend, or the thought police will act. We have to accept all views as 'true' and make sure that everyone has a 'safe space' where they are dangerously immune from learning anything new or helpful.[31]

As Dorothy Sayers trenchantly says of this perspective:

In the world it calls itself Tolerance; but in hell it is called Despair. It is the accomplice of the other sins and their worst punishment. It is the sin which believes nothing, cares for nothing, seeks to know nothing, interferes with nothing, enjoys nothing, loves nothing, hates nothing, finds purpose in nothing, lives for nothing, and only remains alive because there is nothing it would die for.[32]

Jesus refused to get involved in many of the controversies of his day and Paul warned us to avoid 'foolish controversies, genealogies, dissensions, and quarrels' (Titus 3.9). They did not go around unnecessarily looking for trouble. But nor did they espouse the sort of risk aversion mentality that shies away from upsetting the power brokers and refuses to do anything to provoke them.

This 'dictatorship of relativism', as Pope John Paul II called it, is a recipe for disaster. Real communication becomes impossible as intellectual life becomes pathological, illiberal and aggressive. Psychobabble (psycho-Babel?) dominates the omnipresent social media, most of it achieved at fearful cost, making man a god to man, while paradoxically, particularly in the academy, atheistic naturalism reduces man to meaninglessness by homogenizing all distinctives and smoothing out all tensions.

Russell Moore, Director of the Public Theology Project at *Christianity Today*, in a response to Haidt's article cited above, makes a very important point:

> We need a shared story, but a story without tension is no story at all. Our story is of a God who brought us out of the land and slavery of Egypt (Ex. 20:2), of a God who 'raised Jesus from the dead' (Rom. 8:11, emphasis mine). Our story is so repugnant that the apostle Paul had to keep reiterating that he was not ashamed of it (Rom. 1:16).
>
> Pentecost brought about unity, but it was a unity that kept ratcheting up the tension. That day, Simon Peter preached that the Spirit had been poured out on all flesh. But he soon faced a crisis when Jesus appeared and told him that Gentile believers were joint heirs with Jewish believers and that he (Peter) shouldn't call unclean what God had pronounced to be clean (Acts 10–11). As the Spirit moved outward – from Jerusalem to Samaria to the ends of the earth – each stage created a new crisis . . .
>
> Fragmentation is a crisis. God has called us to unity. But the way we get there is not by finding a better technology to start rebuilding the tower as was done in the first place. Sometimes God fragments what we were doing because it is killing us.
>
> For, in order to achieve the kind of unity we need, we must be unified in doing what's right and pleasing in the sight of God. Sometimes that means a future that looks nothing like the one we planned – seeking unity with people we never thought about. Trying to find our way back to Babel won't get us there.[33]

And, in any case, the contemporary Tower of Babel is collapsing under its own weight. It is an alien world to those of us brought up in a culture of intelligent public discourse that very sadly is rapidly becoming a distant memory. In the words of philosopher John Finnis, what is happening is a 'decapitation of reality'.[34] Yet how many of us really see this to be the case and do something about it?

# Abram and Nimrod

Although there is no trace of it in Genesis, in later Jewish and Islamic literature there are legendary accounts alleging direct confrontations of various kinds between Abram and Nimrod, ranging from discussion to physical aggression.

Some of them are quite intriguing, like this one from the Jewish Encyclopaedia:

The punishment visited on the builders of the tower did not cause Nimrod to change his conduct; he remained an idolater. He particularly persecuted Abraham, who by his command was thrown into a heated furnace; and it was on this account, according to one opinion, that Nimrod was called 'Amraphel' (= 'he said, throw in'; Targum pseudo-Jonathan on Gen. xiv. 1; Gen. R. xlii. 5; Cant. R. viii. 8).

When Nimrod was informed that Abraham had come forth from the furnace uninjured, he remitted his persecution of the worshipper of Yhwh; but on the following night he saw in a dream a man coming out of the furnace and advancing toward him with a drawn sword. Nimrod thereupon ran away, but the man threw an egg at him; this was afterward transformed into a large river in which all his troops were drowned, only he himself and three of his followers escaping. Then the river again became an egg, and from the latter came forth a small fowl, which flew at Nimrod and pecked out his eye. The dream was interpreted as forecasting Nimrod's defeat by Abraham, wherefore Nimrod sent secretly to kill Abraham; but the latter emigrated with his family to the land of Canaan.

Ten years later Nimrod came to wage war with Chedorlaomer, King of Elam, who had been one of Nimrod's generals, and who after the dispersion of the builders of the tower went to Elam and formed there an independent kingdom. Nimrod at the head of an army set out with the intention of punishing his rebellious general, but the latter routed him. Nimrod then became a vassal of Chedorlaomer, who involved him in the war with the kings of Sodom and Gomorrah, with whom he was defeated by Abraham (Sefer ha-Yashar, as mentioned earlier; cf. Gen. 14.1–17).

Nimrod was slain by Esau, between whom and himself jealousy existed owing to the fact that they were both hunters (Targum pseudo-Jonathan on Gen. xxv. 27; Sefer ha-Yashar, section 'Toledot,' p. 40b; Pirke R. El. *loc.cit.*; comp. Gen. R. lxv. 12).[35]

A common element in many of these legends is that Abram was a monotheist and protester against idolatry.

Leaving legend aside, the main contrast between Nimrod and Abram lies in the perennially important matter of how we make our name. This is a vivid and apt way of describing the human search for significance, the hunger for answers to our big questions concerning identity. Is meaning something we and we alone can create, as the inhabitants of Babel thought? Should we today, like them, put our trust in human prowess to make our name? That is one way of living and it is very much to the fore in our age of artificial intelligence. AI might well be regarded as the contemporary equivalent of the Babel project, as it is a human attempt, first of all, to develop machines capable of replicating higher-order human cognitive functions, such as reasoning, learning, problem solving, perception and natural language processing, and then second, and much more speculatively, to construct an artificial super-intelligence – a machine that has superior cognitive capacity to that of humans that is eventually capable of being an all-embracing centre of decision making and control.

Israeli historian Yuval Noah Harari, in his best-selling book *Homo Deus* mentioned earlier, presents a grandiose transhumanist agenda for the twenty-first century: first, to abolish physical death by technical means and then to enhance human happiness. According to him, in order to fulfil that objective 'It will be necessary to change our biochemistry and re-engineer our bodies and minds . . . so that we shall need to re-engineer Homo Sapiens so that it can enjoy everlasting pleasure . . . .'[36] And 'Having raised humanity above the beastly level of survival struggles, we will now aim to upgrade humans into gods, and turn Homo Sapiens into Homo Deus.'[37]

Like the ancient inhabitants of Babel, Harari wishes to reach heaven.[38] But he is hardly likely to get there, since his motivational principle is the same as that of Babel – overweening confidence in human capacity for technology.

Harari echoes the themes of C. S. Lewis's *That Hideous Strength*. Lewis imagines a small university in a fictitious place called Edgestow that sells part of its land to permit the construction of NICE, the tightly policed sinister National Institute for Coordinated Experiments, which engages in social engineering. It gradually transpires that this laboratory has managed to preserve the vocal organs and brain of a certain Alcasan in some state of existence, through which an evil mind speaks to direct the work of the Institute. The idea is that a large body is no longer necessary to preserve the brain and voice so that: 'The individual is to become all head. The human race is to become all Technocracy.'[39] It is one version of the transhumanist vision of life that is designed to be (largely) independent of biology.

The book moves to its climax at a dinner in the Institute when one of the directors gets up to speak. There is a strange atmosphere in the room that soon leads to the audience gazing at the speaker, 'every mouth opened in something between fascination and horror'. The speaker ends a sentence with the words 'as gross an anachronism as to trust to Calvary for salvation in modern war'. This causes irritation but the sentences get rapidly more incoherent, even though those who utter them think they are communicating intelligibly: 'The madrigore of verjuice must be talthibianised...'. The next speaker decants even more gibberish until the whole room descends into a veritable Babel of babbling and eventually violence and murder. The carnage gets even worse when the room is invaded by wild animals that have broken out of the cages where they have been held for purposes of vivisection.

Three of the leaders of the Institute who escape the mayhem go to the room that contains the severed Head. It speaks to them and demands first that they bow to adore it. It then demands another head and one of the leaders is guillotined to provide it . . .

This is Lewis's powerful version of the effect of a supernatural Babel-like confusion of language and behaviour sent to judge those who have rejected all objective values. Some two years before he wrote *Nineteen Eighty-Four*, George Orwell wrote a perceptive review of *That Hideous Strength*. Of Lewis he said:

His book describes the struggle of a little group of sane people against a nightmare that nearly conquers the world. A company of mad scientists – or, perhaps, they are not mad, but have merely destroyed in themselves all human feeling, all notion of good and evil – are plotting to conquer Britain, then the whole planet, and then other planets, until they have brought the universe under their control.

All superfluous life is to be wiped out, all natural forces tamed, the common people are to be used as slaves and vivisection subjects by the ruling caste of scientists, who even see their way to conferring immortal life upon themselves. Man, in short, is to storm the heavens and overthrow the gods, or even to become a god himself. Plenty of people in our age do entertain the monstrous dreams of power that Mr Lewis attributes to his characters [the NICE scientists], and we are within sight of the time when such dreams will be realisable.[40]

It reminds me of Harari's Homo Deus!

There are also important insights into the ideologies of Babylon in one of the most famous of all the prophetic books in the Old Testament – Daniel. It opens with a description of the conquest of Jerusalem by the Babylonian emperor Nebuchadnezzar in 597 BC. He takes Daniel and his three friends captive to Babylon and has them trained to be administrators. One of the first things that happens is the forced replacement of their Hebrew names (with their biblical connotations) by Babylonian names that refer to pagan deities. For instance, Daniel, meaning 'God is my judge', is renamed Belteshazzar, a name that refers to Bel (Marduk), the principal Babylonian deity at the time.

That action of renaming them was a piece of clever social engineering in an attempt to alter the identities of Daniel and his friends by removing any reference to the God of heaven that they could have used in witness. Babylon changes names! But Bel did not make Daniel's name great. The God of heaven did. I have written extensively about the relevance of this to human identity in my book on Daniel entitled *Against the Flow*.[41]

# 2

# From Shem to Abram

With Babel as background, Genesis now gives us a second genealogy of Shem. This time the genealogy contains only the direct line of descent to Abram, the main character in this section of the book. At each step it simply comments in passing that X had other sons and daughters, until it reaches Terah, the father of Abram, Nahor and Haran. We are given only the sketchiest of details about their lives. Haran dies young and leaves his son Lot in the care of Terah. Abram marries Sarai, his half-sister (Gen. 20.12), and Nahor marries Milcah.

Since Genesis gives us such a detailed description of Babel, Abram might be expected to have been one of its citizens. However, this was not the case. Abraham was a native of the ancient Mesopotamian city of Ur, which dates from around 3800 BC and was an important Sumerian city-state from the twenty-sixth century BC. In fact, it was for a time the capital of lower Mesopotamia, while Babylon was only a provincial centre. Abram may therefore have actually lived in what was the capital of the region at the time.

Ur is located at the site of modern Tell el-Muqayyar in southern Iraq, about 225 km south east of Babylon. Once a coastal city near the mouth of the River Euphrates on the Persian Gulf, its site is now well inland on the south bank of the Euphrates, not far from Nasiriyah in modern-day Iraq.

The dating of Abraham's life has proved somewhat problematic. Egyptologist Kenneth Kitchen dates the oppression of the Israelites in Egypt from around 1320 to 1260/1250 and the exodus around 1260/1250, and uses a 645-year period between Abraham and the exodus. This gives a date for the period between Abraham and Joseph from around 1900 to 1600.[1] This would place Abraham during the Isin-Larsa period between 2017 and 1763 BC.

One of the main sources of evidence for these dates is the record in Genesis 14 of Abraham's battle with a coalition of Eastern kings at a time when city-states had their own royal dynasties.

Kitchen points out that the formation of such a coalition was only possible at certain times:

Before the Akkadian Empire, Mesopotamia was divided between the Sumerian city-states, but this is far too early[2] for our narrative (pre-2300). After an interval of Gutian interference, Mesopotamia was then dominated by the Third Dynasty of Ur, whose influence reached in some form as far west as north Syria and Byblos.

After its fall, circa 2000, Mesopotamia was divided between a series of kingdoms, Isin, Larsa, Eshnunna, Assyria, etc., with Mari and various local powers in lands farther north and west. This situation lasted until the eighteenth century, when Hammurabi (1792–1750 BC) of Babylon eliminated most of his rivals.

From circa 1600/1500 onward, Assyria and Babylon (now under Kassite rule) dominated Mesopotamia, sharing with none except briefly Mitanni (ca. 1500 to mid-thirteenth century) within the Euphrates' west bend, and the marginal Khana and Sea-land princedoms were eliminated in due course. Thus, from circa 2000 to 1750 (1650 at the extreme), we have the one and only period during which extensive power alliances were common in Mesopotamia and with its neighbors.[3]

The reader eager to know more about this fascinating historical epoch is strongly encouraged to read Georges Roux's classic book, *Ancient Iraq*.[4]

Although the whole country worshipped a common high-level pantheon, each city-state had its own patron deity. In Ur the patron deity was Nanna, the Sumerian moon-god of time (lunar months), whose Akkadian name was Sin, the father of the sun-god Shamash. The crescent moon was used as a symbol of this god and it was later adopted as the symbol of Islam. The name of the city is derived from the god's name. UNUG$^{KI}$, literally 'the abode [UNUG] of Nanna'. It is noteworthy that Genesis 1 constitutes a protest against such idolatry by describing both the sun and the moon as lights, not deities.[5]

With its position on the Euphrates, Ur was a centre of trade and commerce. It had an advanced culture with impressive architecture. Its central edifice was a large three-storeyed ziggurat, built of sun-dried bricks like Babel and faced with glazed fire-dried bricks that were held together by bitumen. At its top was a shrine, the bedchamber of the local patron god Nanna (Sin). Its base measured 64 by 46 metres, and its height was about 30 metres.[6] What is left of it can still be seen in Nasiriyah, Iraq.

Excavations of the Royal Cemetery at Ur uncovered royal tombs that contained treasures of gold, silver, bronze, and semi-precious stones that demonstrated not only the wealth of the citizens of Ur but also their highly developed civilisation and art. Evidence was found of a custom whereby kings were buried along with a whole retinue of their court officials, servants and women, privileged to continue their service in the next world. Musical instruments from the royal tombs, golden weapons, engraved shell plaques and mosaic pictures, statuary and carved cylinder seals – all are a collection of unique importance, giving evidence of a little-known civilisation.[7]

Stone was rare in the region, so all buildings were constructed of clay often mixed with straw, gravel or potsherds and moulded into bricks that were dried in the sun and then set in gypsum mortar. Wealthier citizens could afford more durable kiln-fired bricks and many of them enjoyed high-quality, comfortable and spacious two-storey homes.[8]

Mesopotamian education was mostly for boys from wealthy homes since tuition was expensive. It centred around literacy, and young people typically spent 12 years learning to write in cuneiform – wedge-shaped marks made on clay by a stylus with a triangular-shaped tip.[9] This writing was already very well developed by Abraham's time. Teachers, who were mainly scribes or priests, also taught history and mathematics in addition to literacy. Older students, depending on their intended profession and what they could afford, would have been able to learn a wide variety of subjects such as geography, zoology, botany, astronomy, engineering, medicine and architecture.[10]

## Abram and Sumerian idolatry

A single statement in the book of Joshua indicates that Abram's immediate ancestors had not preserved a clear vision of commitment to the one true God: 'And Joshua said to all the people, "Thus says the LORD, the God of Israel, 'Long ago, your fathers lived beyond the Euphrates, Terah, the father of Abraham and of Nahor; and they served other gods'"' (Josh. 24.2–3).

Scholars are not sure exactly who is included in the 'they', but it would seem that Abram came from a family that engaged in the worship of idols. This is rather strange in light of the fact that, according to the Genesis chronologies, Abram was 60 when Noah died and he was 110 when Shem died. That means, presumably, that Abraham, and his forebears even more so, knew both Noah and Shem. If that is the case, they may well have learned from Noah and Shem about God's dealings with them, particularly during the time of the Flood. Of Noah it is said that he walked faithfully with God (Gen. 6.9), although his positive influence waned in later life.

More information, specifically about Abram's contact with Noah, may have appeared in the Book of Jashar (Sefer Ha Yashar) that is referred to by Joshua (Josh. 10.12–13) and Samuel (2 Sam. 1.17–18 ). The uncertainty here is that we do not possess a copy of this ancient book, although there is a medieval[11] Hebrew Midrash with this title by an unknown author.[12] It would seem to be a mixture of biblical-type references and legend. Intriguingly, it mentions contact between Abram and Noah:

> Haran [Abram's oldest brother] was forty-two years old when he begat Sarai, which was in the tenth year of the life of Abram; and in those days Abram and his mother and nurse went out from the cave, as the king and his subjects had forgotten the affair of Abram. And when Abram came out from the cave, he went to Noah and his son Shem, and he remained with them to learn the instruction of the Elohim and His ways, and no man knew where Abram was, and Abram served Noah and Shem his son for a long time.
>
> Abram was in Noah's house thirty-nine years, and Abram knew Yehovah from three years old, and he went in the ways of Yehovah until the day of his death, as Noah and his son Shem had taught him; and all the sons of the earth in those days greatly transgressed against Yehovah, and they rebelled against him and they served other elohim [lawmakers and judges], and they forgot Yehovah who had created them in the earth; and the inhabitants of the earth made unto themselves, at that time, every man his elohim; elohim of wood and stone which could neither speak, hear, nor deliver, and the sons of men served them and they became their elohim.[13]

We have no corroboration of these statements. They may represent an attempt to give some background to Joshua 24.2. However, Roux gives us a wealth of useful factual information about the gods of ancient Mesopotamia that has been gained from archaeology – particularly from the decipherment of all kinds of texts detailing epic tales, myths, rituals, hymns, prayers, lists of gods and various other kinds of sacred literature. These texts come mainly from the priestly library of Nippur (the religious centre of Sumer), and the palace and temple libraries of Nineveh and Assur.

Roux explains how Mesopotamian culture was permeated with religion:

> For more than three thousand years the religious ideas promoted by the Sumerians played an extraordinary part in the public and private life of the Mesopotamians, modelling their institutions, coloring their works of art and literature, pervading every form of activity from the highest functions of the kings to the day-to-day occupations of their subjects. In no other antique society did religion occupy such a prominent position, because in no other antique society did man feel himself so utterly dependent on the will of the gods.[14]

It has been suggested that the name of Abram's wife, who was also his half-sister, Sarai (Sarah), is related to the name Sarratu, the wife of the moon-god Sin, whereas Milcah, Abram's niece, may be a name derived from Malkatu, the daughter of Sin. The extent of the family's involvement with idolatry is unclear and no further detail is given in Scripture, though various Jewish legends say that Terah was an idol-maker.

One well-known story says that one day when Terah was absent from his workshop, Abram smashed the idols, leaving only the largest. When his father returned, Abram said that there had been a fight among the idols. His father replied that idols cannot fight since they are lifeless. 'Then why do you worship them?' Abram replied.[15]

The worship of 'other gods' mentioned in the Joshua text rates in the Bible as the number one offence against the one true God, Creator of heaven and earth. That is shown by its prohibition heading the list of the Ten Commandments given to Israel through Moses:

> And God spoke all these words, saying, 'I am the LORD your God, who brought you out of the land of Egypt, out of the house of slavery. You shall have no other gods before me. You shall not make for yourself a carved image, or any likeness of anything that is in heaven above, or that is in the earth beneath, or that is in the water under the earth. You shall not bow down to them or serve them, for I the LORD your God am a jealous God, visiting the iniquity of

the fathers on the children to the third and the fourth generation of those who hate me, but showing steadfast love to thousands of those who love me and keep my commandments.'
(Exod. 20.1–6)

The wording refers explicitly to what we might call crude idolatry, the kind mocked to absurdity with delightful sarcasm by the prophet Isaiah in a passage well worth reading:

All who fashion idols are nothing, and the things they delight in do not profit. Their witnesses neither see nor know, that they may be put to shame. Who fashions a god or casts an idol that is profitable for nothing? Behold, all his companions shall be put to shame, and the craftsmen are only human. Let them all assemble, let them stand forth. They shall be terrified; they shall be put to shame together.

The ironsmith takes a cutting tool and works it over the coals. He fashions it with hammers and works it with his strong arm. He becomes hungry, and his strength fails; he drinks no water and is faint.

The carpenter stretches a line; he marks it out with a pencil. He shapes it with planes and marks it with a compass. He shapes it into the figure of a man, with the beauty of a man, to dwell in a house. He cuts down cedars, or he chooses a cypress tree or an oak and lets it grow strong among the trees of the forest. He plants a cedar and the rain nourishes it. Then it becomes fuel for a man. He takes a part of it and warms himself; he kindles a fire and bakes bread. Also he makes a god and worships it; he makes it an idol and falls down before it. Half of it he burns in the fire. Over the half he eats meat; he roasts it and is satisfied. Also he warms himself and says, 'Aha, I am warm, I have seen the fire!' And the rest of it he makes into a god, his idol, and falls down to it and worships it. He prays to it and says, 'Deliver me, for you are my god!'

They know not, nor do they discern, for he has shut their eyes, so that they cannot see, and their hearts, so that they cannot understand. No one considers, nor is there knowledge or discernment to say, 'Half of it I burned in the fire; I also baked bread on its coals; I

roasted meat and have eaten. And shall I make the rest of it an abomination? Shall I fall down before a block of wood?' He feeds on ashes; a deluded heart has led him astray, and he cannot deliver himself or say, 'Is there not a lie in my right hand?'
(Isa. 44.9–20)

Isaiah does not hesitate to mock the grotesque absurdity of the sight of a human being made in the image of God bowing down to some inanimate physical artefact fashioned by a human being. Yet millions still do precisely that. God prohibits it because it is not an innocent activity. It demeans both humans and God himself.

It is important to realise that in the ancient world (and also today) it was not so much that people *loved* their idols instead of God, although many did. It is rather that they simultaneously *feared* and *trusted* them instead of God as the controllers of their lives and destinies.

Leon Kass says:

We make a mistake when we think of idols in terms of their physical appearance – statues, figurines, icons. In that sense they belong to ancient times we have long outgrown. Instead, the right way to think of idols is in terms of what they represent. They symbolise power. That is what Ra was for the Egyptians . . . what Zeus was for the Greeks, and what missiles and bombs are for terrorists and rogue states today.[16]

In the West the dominant world view of naturalism, with its overweening confidence in the power of the human mind and its attribution of creative powers to nature, is as idolatrous as the philosophies of the ancient Near East. The secular pressure to trust almost anything other than God is everywhere. Of course, inevitably, we all have to exercise trust in institutions and people in order for society to function. But this does not mean that we should put our final trust in them instead of God.

The idolatry of Babylon was seen in the way people went about finding their identity in something other than God. This is highly relevant to our generation, sunk in relativism as it is. The effect of the so-called sexual revolution is that many young people trust in sexual relationships to give them the meaning and identity they long for. Yet this is idolatry and it so often turns into self-destructive desires to be 'liked' on Facebook, serial disappointment, jealousy, resentment and worse. That happens because true fulfilment cannot be found in idols, but only in a relationship with God. That is the message of Abraham.

Idolatry is an expression of the same proud rebellion against God that began in Genesis 3 with the temptation that involved three fundamental human desires: appetite for food, desire for aesthetic satisfaction and intellectual longing for human flourishing. All of these desires are good in themselves since they were created by God. He placed the humans in an environment where those desires could be satisfied and enjoyed in harmony and fellowship with him.

God permitted the first humans to eat of all the trees around them in the garden except for one, telling them that in the day they did eat they would surely die. That tells us at once that God gave them dignity as moral beings. In particular, they possessed the capacity to say yes or no to what God said. They could either choose to trust the Creator and believe his word and obey it, or they could grasp at what they were tempted to think would be gained by asserting their independence of him.

According to Genesis the source of the temptation was a subtle talking snake. The question as to the level at which we should read this goes beyond our remit here.[17] The important thing for us now is that the suggestion was made to the first humans that God's word was not to be trusted; that it was a ploy on God's part to suppress them and prevent them realising their full potential. They were persuaded that, if they wished to be truly free, they should ignore God's single restrictive condition, follow their instinctive desires and go ahead and eat the fruit of the tree of the knowledge of good and evil.

We need to pause here, since it is amazing just how many people misread this and think that God forbade access to the *tree of knowledge*, as if he did not wish them to gain knowledge. However, it was not a tree of knowledge! That concept appears nowhere in Scripture. It was the tree of *knowledge of good and evil* – that is, this tree represented a particular kind of knowledge.

From the beginning God wanted humans to gain knowledge. That is evident from the fact that he placed them in a garden and instructed them to explore it with a view to gaining knowledge of the world – naming the animals was an obvious part of that exercise. On the other hand, the knowledge of good and evil that they acquired through their disobedience turned out to be something no one would wish to possess.

Yet still today a subtle snake-like voice whispers a powerful lie in all-too-willing ears. It insinuates that God, if indeed there is a God, is against their human flourishing and wishes to spoil their enjoyment of what life has to offer.

This question of whether or not to trust and obey God's word is the central issue of the book of Genesis and, indeed, of life itself. It is the most fundamental of life's battles – whether to put our faith in God or in something or someone else, which would be idolatry. The challenge to all of us is what we are going to do about it.

# Part 2

# GENESIS 12.1—15.21

**THE LIFE OF ABRAHAM: STAGE 1**
**SUMMARY**
A.  God's call and promise (12.1-20)
The journey: Haran – Canaan – Egypt – Canaan
God calls Abram to go on a journey to another land and promises that
   he will become a great nation that will bless the world.
Abram leaves with Lot and Sarai (Lot mentioned twice) plus their
   possessions and servants.
The Lord appears to Abram at Shechem and promises him the land.
   Abram builds an altar and moves on and builds another altar. He
   journeys further south.
A famine hits and he enters Egypt. Fearful of what the Egyptians may
   do, he asks Sarai to deny their true relationship.
Pharaoh takes Sarai and enriches Abram, but is afflicted by God.
   Pharaoh learns the truth and expels Abram and Sarai with their
   acquired wealth. They return to where Abram built the last altar.

B.  Abram and Lot (13.1-18)
Abram and Lot separate because of their wealth in order to have
   space for their livestock. Abram gives Lot the choice and he moves
   to Sodom. God repeats the promise of the land to Abram and
   encourages him to measure it.

Abram settles at Mamre. He builds an altar there.

In a battle between multiple warring factions, Lot is captured with the people of Sodom. Abram mounts a successful rescue with the help of local chiefs and rescues Lot and his possessions.

C. Abram and Melchizedek (14.1–24)

As the king of Sodom is travelling to meet Abram, Melchizedek provides Abram with bread and wine and blesses him. The king of Sodom asks Abram for the rescued people and tells him to keep the spoils of war.

Abram refuses, since he is not prepared to be enriched by the king of Sodom.

D. God makes a covenant with Abram (15.1–21)

God appears, calms Abram's fear and promises great reward. Abram raises the problem of his childlessness and is promised his 'very own son' – and descendants as numerous as the stars.

Abram asks how he can know that he will inherit the land of Canaan. In reply, God makes a covenant guaranteeing it unconditionally to him and his descendants. God tells Abram to select certain animals and cut them in pieces, making two separate piles of the pieces.

Abram falls into a deep sleep and God tells him of the future of his nation – descending to another land (Egypt) and being afflicted there for four centuries until they are delivered with great wealth and return to the promised land.

Abram sees a smoking torch and blazing fire pot passing between the two piles of animal pieces – a symbol of God's ratification of the covenant.

**PERVASIVE THEMES**

1 The journey theme – Abram's journeys initially and the prediction of their recapitulation by his descendants.

2 The theme of wealth and how and from whom it is obtained runs right through this stage. There is wealth in terms of material possessions and there is wealth in terms of kinship and having children.

3 The theme of capture and rescue. In A Sarai has to be rescued, in B it is Lot and in D it is the future nation.

4 The theme of kinship. In A it is husband/wife (kinship denied), in B it is uncle/nephew (kinship asserted), in C it is Abraham tithing to a high priest and in D it is child-heir to servant-heir (one kinship asserted, the other denied).

## LITERARY STRUCTURE AND THOUGHT FLOW

In sections A and D we find the common theme of going down to Egypt and returning.[1] In A, Abram goes down with Sarai, and D predicts that Abram's descendants will go down as a nation. The cause in A is famine, and Genesis will later tell us that the cause in D is also a famine.

In A, Pharaoh's house is plagued by God because he takes Sarai. In D, Egypt (unnamed) afflicts Abram's descendants but, as Exodus later tells us, both Egypt and Pharaoh's house are plagued by God, because they will not let Abram's descendants go.

In A, Abram and Sarai leave Egypt in a hurry but with great wealth. In D, we learn that the nation will eventually leave Egypt with great wealth. Exodus later shows they left in a hurry.

In A, God speaks, tells Abram to go to a land he will show him and promises nationhood. When Abram arrives, God speaks and promises the land to Abram's offspring. This is an intensification of the original promise. Yet Abram does not stay in the land but goes to Egypt, where he becomes wealthy as a result of failing to tell the truth that Sarai is his wife. In B, that wealth leads to Lot separating from Abram.

God intensifies the promise yet more by telling Abram that he and his offspring will possess the land for ever and that his offspring will be as uncountable as dust. Then God invites Abram to pace out the land and measure it – another sign of ownership.

After Lot is captured and rescued, Abram is strengthened by the visit of the priest-king Melchizedek to face a crucial decision regarding his attitude to material wealth. Abram, though the victor in the battle and therefore entitled to the spoil, refuses to take any material goods from the king of Sodom.

As if to confirm the rightness of what Abram has done in B and C, in D God promises him great reward. Abram now shows that what he thinks of as reward is not material wealth – that he's already had in plenty – but rather a solution to the problem of his childlessness. God now promises him his very own son. He invites Abram to look at the stars and promises that his offspring will be just as numerous as they are.

To make things even more certain, God commits himself to Abram by making a covenant with him defining in much more detail the territory eventually to be given to Abram's offspring – and the suffering his nation will have to go through in Egypt before they eventually inherit.

This stage therefore records God's steadily increasing commitment to Abram. It is also a progressive account of Abram coming to terms with what true wealth actually is.

# 3

# The call of Abram

## From Ur to Haran

The description of Abram's early life, calling by God and migration to Canaan is sparse. The last few verses of Genesis 11 tell us that a family group led by Abram's father had already set out for unspecified reasons from Ur to travel to Canaan. They got as far as Haran in northern Mesopotamia – and stopped: 'Terah took Abram his son and Lot the son of Haran, his grandson, and Sarai his daughter-in-law, his son Abram's wife, and they went forth together from Ur of the Chaldeans to go into the land of Canaan, but when they came to Haran, they settled there' (v. 31). No reason is given in Genesis as to why Terah (or Abram) left Ur and decided to go to Canaan, nor why they broke their journey in Haran.

Intriguingly, in his defence to the Sanhedrin, the first Christian martyr, Stephen, rehearsed events as follows:

'Brothers and fathers, hear me. The God of glory appeared to our father Abraham when he was in Mesopotamia, *before he lived in Haran*, and said to him, "Go out from your land and from your kindred and go into the land that I will show you." Then he went out from the land of the Chaldeans and lived in Haran. And after his father died, God removed him from there into this land in which you are now living.'
(Acts 7.2–4, emphasis mine)

It seems clear from this that God had already spoken to Abram in Ur, his home city. Yet Genesis says that it was his father who initiated the journey to Canaan. He took his son Abram and daughter-in-law Sarai and his grandson Lot and set off on a journey in the direction of the land

41

of Canaan, presumably following the River Euphrates upstream past Babel until they reached Haran[1] about 600 miles away.

The city of Haran, like Ur, was devoted to moon worship. For some reason the travelling group broke their journey there and settled down. Could it be that Terah was still grieving for the earlier loss of his son Haran, who died in Ur? Some Jewish traditions claim that Terah left Ur because he wished to protect Abram from Nimrod's revenge and because Abram had convinced him of the existence of the one true God. In other words, the situation is not entirely clear. There could have been a mix of reasons, both human and divine, why they left and why they stopped. The same may be true of our own 'journey' in life and it should give us hope that, if we get stuck for some reason, it doesn't necessarily mean that God has lost interest in or finished dealing with us.

In any case, for an undisclosed reason they broke their journey at Haran and remained there for some considerable time. It would be so interesting to know just how much Abram knew about the God of Noah and how much he was influenced by what he heard from his older relatives as well as by the all-pervasive local polytheistic culture. Yet, we know nothing. We are simply told that Terah died in Haran at the age of 205. According to Genesis 11.26, Abraham would have been 135 years old at the time of his father's death.

## The God who speaks

Now the LORD said to Abram, 'Go from your country and your kindred and your father's house to the land that I will show you. And I will make of you a great nation, and I will bless you and make your name great, so that you will be a blessing. I will bless those who bless you, and him who dishonours you I will curse, and in you all the families of the earth shall be blessed.' So Abram went, as the LORD had told him, and Lot went with him.
(Gen. 12.1–4)

Abram's first major discovery was that there is a God who speaks, a God who instructed him to leave Mesopotamia, promising him a whole array of attendant gifts and blessings. These promises are central, not only to Genesis, but to the whole of the Bible's storyline.

God said that he would do seven things for Abram:

1 Show him a land
2 Make of him a great nation
3 Bless him and make his name great
4 Make him a blessing
5 Bless those that bless him
6 Curse those who dishonour him
7 Bless through him all the families of the earth (see Gen. 12.7).

The third of these promises, to make Abram's name great, recalls the motivation for building the city of Babel – 'let us make a name for ourselves'. In fact, God promised to give Abram essentially what the Babel-builders desired, only more so and on very different conditions. Abram was called to trust God to give him real significance and not to trust himself. Furthermore, as we have seen, the New Testament reveals that he was looking for a city with foundations, whose designer and builder was God (see Heb. 11.10). The first and most important 'foundation' of that city is faith in God and not in oneself.

The significance of this epoch-defining call of God is heightened by the fact that it appears in a book that starts with God speaking the universe into existence, and creating beings in his image that could both understand God's words and speak to him.

Dialogue between God and man is central to biblical revelation from its very first page. Robert Alter comments:

Everything in the world of biblical narrative ultimately gravitates towards dialogue – perhaps . . . because to the ancient Hebrew writers speech seemed the essential human faculty: by exercising the capacity of speech man demonstrated, however imperfectly, that he was made in the image of God.

This means, according to Alter, that 'a remarkably large part of the narrative burden is carried by dialogue, the transactions between characters typically unfolding through the words they exchange.[2] A lifelong dialogue started when Abraham heard the voice of God calling him to set out on a journey.

At this point I can imagine some of my scientific colleagues interrupting: 'Surely you, as an academic committed to a rational scientific understanding of the world, don't take seriously the claim that Abram actually heard the voice of God? After all, there is no God anyway and, as far as hearing voices goes, that phenomenon is well known to psychiatric medicine. It is, in fact, the most common kind of auditory hallucination, research having shown that around ten per cent of people hear voices at some time or other.[3] The experience is often associated with trauma, stress and mental health conditions such as schizophrenia, bipolar disorder, the influence of certain drugs or even lack of sleep. Hearing voices, therefore, does not necessarily correspond to any objective form of communication.'

This means we have a choice. Either we relegate the call of Abram to 'voices in the head', or we put aside any initial anti-supernatural prejudice and consider the possibility that the materialistic view of the universe might just be false; that the universe is not a closed system of cause and effect, and that there is a Creator God who can and does communicate from time to time.[4]

In any case, this is not a notion arising from the lunatic fringe of religion. Far from it, as it is the central claim of the Bible that God, the Creator and Upholder of the universe, has revealed himself by speaking. The Bible claims to be the word of God in written form and that Jesus Christ is the Word of God in human form. Abram was not the only one who heard God speak: there is a whole spectrum of prophets right through the centuries of the Old Testament period who proclaimed what God had said to them.

In the New Testament this took on an entirely new dimension with the advent of the Word of God incarnate, Jesus the Son of God. Those who heard him speak were hearing God speak – as he himself carefully explained on one occasion in response to a challenge put to him by one of his disciples:

Philip said to him, 'Lord, show us the Father, and it is enough for us.'
Jesus said to him, 'Have I been with you so long, and you still do not

know me, Philip? Whoever has seen me has seen the Father. How can you say, "Show us the Father"? Do you not believe that I am in the Father and the Father is in me? The words that I say to you I do not speak on my own authority, but the Father who dwells in me does his works. Believe me that I am in the Father and the Father is in me, or else believe on account of the works themselves.'
(John 14.8–11)

That is, the very words Jesus was speaking at that moment were the Father's words – he was speaking directly to the disciples through his Son.

Now clearly this, if true, as I believe, is plainly supernatural and it also applies to the way in which the disciples not only recalled Jesus' words to them but also were later to experience God speaking to them. For, in that same discourse in the Upper Room in Jerusalem, Jesus went on to say:

'I still have many things to say to you, but you cannot bear them now. When the Spirit of truth comes, he will guide you into all the truth, for he will not speak on his own authority, but whatever he hears he will speak, and he will declare to you the things that are to come. He will glorify me, for he will take what is mine and declare it to you. All that the Father has is mine; therefore I said that he will take what is mine and declare it to you.'
(John 16.12–15)

As I hope to show in this book, the story of Abraham is a major stage in the long narrative of God's self-revelation that culminated in Jesus Christ. That narrative is not only coherent but it corresponds to reality and thus satisfies the main criteria that characterise truth.

One of the reasons why I believe that God did speak to Abraham as recorded in Genesis is not because I choose to ignore psychological research on hearing voices – I don't – but because of my conviction that Jesus is the Son of God. That conviction is rational and is based on evidence both objective and experiential.[5] It was Jesus himself who said: '"Your father Abraham rejoiced that he would see my day. He saw it and was glad." So the Jews said to him, "You are not yet fifty years old, and have you seen Abraham?" Jesus said to them, "Truly, truly, I say to you, before Abraham was, I am'" (John 8.56–58).

If we regard science as a set of disciplines geared to investigating natural phenomena by natural means,[6] then science by definition cannot adjudicate either the existence of God or his voice, as they do not fit into a naturalistic world view. However, as I have argued elsewhere, science is not applied naturalism.

Nevertheless, I am sceptical about many contemporary claims of the following sort: 'God spoke to me and said I would get better . . . God told me to marry that person . . . God gave me this message for you . . .' My scepticism is not based on believing that God cannot speak today. It is based on the fact that many such claims turn out to be spurious, because the content of what God is alleged to have said turns out to be false. For more detail on the matter of God speaking today, see Appendix 2.

There is, actually, no scientific reason to deny, and many rational reasons[7] to affirm, that God spoke audibly to Abram, Isaac, Jacob, Moses, Gideon, Samuel, the prophets, and apostles like Peter, James and John, and, perhaps most famously, Paul who heard the voice from heaven as he travelled to Damascus to persecute Christian believers.

Above all, that voice spoke to Jesus in the hearing of others on three signal occasions – at his baptism (Matt. 3.17), at the transfiguration (Matt. 17.5) and a few days before the crucifixion when Jesus prayed: 'Father, glorify your name' (John 12.28).

Centuries earlier the same voice had told Abram to leave Mesopotamia and promised him a whole array of attendant gifts and blessings. These promises are central, not only to Genesis, but to the whole of the Bible's storyline.

The voice said: 'Go!' In Hebrew the command is *lech lecha*[8] (by which it is often known). It can be translated 'go to yourself' or 'go for yourself' and essentially means 'get (yourself) going'. This nuanced ambiguity in meaning has prompted a great deal of comment. Reading it as 'go to yourself' has led to conceiving it as an internal odyssey where Abram travels to the roots of his soul. On the other hand, 'go for yourself' or 'go forth or out' signifies a call to separate from his past background and take a journey with God. I find it good to think of both simultaneously.

Jews regard the *Lech Lecha* as an important fundamental principle. The late Chief Rabbi Lord Jonathan Sacks wrote:

These words are among the most consequential in the history of mankind. With them a new faith was born that has lasted for two thirds of the course of civilisation and remains young and vigorous today. Not only did Abraham give rise to what today we call Judaism. He was also the inspiration of two other religions, Christianity and Islam, both of which trace their descent, biological or spiritual, to him, and which now number among their adherents more than half the six billion people on the face of the earth . . .[9]

That brings us to the key phrase, the first words of God to the bearer of a new covenant: *Lech Lecha*. Is there, already in these two words, a hint of what was to come? For Abraham was to hear these words again in connection with his supreme test in Genesis 22, where he was called upon to offer his son Isaac.

Sacks goes on to cite the famous eleventh-century commentator Rashi:

Travel for your own benefit and good. There I will make you into a great nation; here you will not have the merit of having children. Sometimes we have to give up our past in order to acquire a future . . .

There is, however, a fourth interpretation: 'Go by yourself.' Only a person willing to stand alone, singular and unique, can worship the God who is alone, singular and unique...

*Lech Lecha* [then] means: Leave behind you all that makes human beings predictable, unfree, able to blame others and evade responsibility. Abraham's children were summoned to be the people that defied the laws of nature because they refused to define themselves as the products of nature (Nietzsche understood this aspect of Judaism particularly well). That is not to say that economic or biological or psychological forces have no part to play in human behaviour. They do. But with sufficient imagination, determination, discipline and courage we can rise above them. Abraham did. So, at most times, did his children . . .

*Lech Lecha* in this sense means being prepared to take an often lonely journey: 'Go by yourself.' To be . . . a child of Abraham is to have the courage to be different, to challenge the idols of the age, whatever the idols and whichever the age. In an era of polytheism, that meant seeing the universe as the product of a single creative will – and therefore not meaningless but coherent, meaningful.

In an era of slavery it meant refusing to accept the status quo in the name of God, but instead challenging it in the name of God. When power was worshipped, it meant constructing a society that cared for the powerless, the widow, orphan and stranger. During centuries in which the mass of humankind was sunk in ignorance, it meant honouring education as the key to human dignity and creating schools to provide universal literacy. When war was the test of humanity, it meant striving for peace. In ages of radical individualism like today, it means knowing that we are not what we own but what we share; not what we buy but what we give; that there is something higher than appetite and desire – namely the call that comes to us, as it came to Abraham, from outside ourselves, summoning us to make a contribution to the world.[10]

Christians, who count among the children of Abraham, would do well to listen to Jonathan Sacks. We need to be reminded to get ourselves going in more senses than one.[11] For Jesus' call to his disciples was just as radical as God's call to Abram:

'Do not think that I have come to bring peace to the earth. I have not come to bring peace, but a sword. For I have come to set a man against his father, and a daughter against her mother, and a daughter-in-law against her mother-in-law. And a person's enemies will be those of his own household. Whoever loves father or mother more than me is not worthy of me, and whoever loves son or daughter more than me is not worthy of me. And whoever does not take his cross and follow me is not worthy of me. Whoever finds his life will lose it, and whoever loses his life for my sake will find it.'
(Matt. 10.34–39)

48

This is a challenge that permits no compromise. Jesus insists that commitment to him must be of such quality and depth that all other loves seem like hate by comparison.

And again:

> Then Jesus told his disciples, 'If anyone would come after me, let him deny himself and take up his cross and follow me. For whoever would save his life will lose it, but whoever loses his life for my sake will find it. For what will it profit a man if he gains the whole world and forfeits his soul? Or what shall a man give in return for his soul? For the Son of Man is going to come with his angels in the glory of his Father, and then he will repay each person according to what he has done. Truly, I say to you, there are some standing here who will not taste death until they see the Son of Man coming in his kingdom.'
> (Matt. 16.24–28)

Yet though the Lord expects radical commitment, he does not expect it to be an irrational 'leap of faith' with no evidence base. One of the early apostles, Peter, when describing his motivation in following Christ, said that he was called by his glory and virtue (see 2 Pet. 1.3). Just as Abraham saw the glory of God and responded by following God's call, so centuries later did Peter, followed by millions of others including me.

# 4

# From Haran to Canaan

So Abram went, as the LORD had told him, and Lot went with him.
Abram was seventy-five years old when he departed from Haran.
And Abram took Sarai his wife, and Lot his brother's son, and all
their possessions that they had gathered, and the people that they
had acquired in Haran, and they set out to go to the land of Canaan.
(Gen. 12.4–5)

We may think of this journey as a small-scale migration, consisting of
a caravan in the ancient sense. It comprised Abram, his wife Sarai, his
nephew Lot, whose father had died, and a largish group of servants,
herders and so on whom they had 'acquired'[1] in Haran. It is evident that
Abram was a wealthy man. Indeed, his possessions are mentioned in
the text before his people, which may well indicate a value priority in
his mind at that time. The matter of possessions figures prominently in
this section and it will not be long before Abram's attitude to the relative
values of people and possessions will be put to the test.

We are told that Abram left Haran when he was 75. That was 60
years before the death of his father, which means that his father would
have been alive during a good deal of Abram's early life. It is, therefore,
somewhat strange that Genesis records Terah's death so early on in the
narrative, although that is in keeping with a repeated structural feature
of Genesis, that in its major sections less important individuals are
discussed first of all and in less detail – like discussing Ishmael before
Isaac, and Esau before Jacob.

In any case, Genesis tells us that Abraham lived for a total of 175 years
(25.7). Sarah was ten years younger (17.17) and lived to the age of 127
(23.1). For comparison, Isaac lived 180 years, Jacob 147 years, Joseph 110
years, Moses 120 years.

According to Scripture, lengthy lifespans were much more common in the ancient world than they are today. Genesis records unusually high ages in the time before the Flood – like the 969 years of Methuselah's life. At the time of the Flood God makes the following statement: 'My Spirit shall not abide in man for ever, for he is flesh: his days shall be 120 years' (Gen. 6.3). This is often taken to imply a limit to longevity, but scholars are divided as to whether it may indicate the length of time until the Flood would come, so that it was a limitation not on lifespan, but on the time available for building the ark. In any event lifespans, according to the biblical record, markedly declined after the Flood – perhaps another indicator of an accumulation of genetic damage after the Fall.

Psalm 90.10 says: 'The years of our life are seventy, or even by reason of strength eighty; yet their span is but toil and trouble; they are soon gone, and we fly away.' Interestingly, this psalm is attributed to Moses, who nevertheless lived to 120!

This is not the place to evaluate evidence for a decline in longevity in ancient times. The interested reader might consult an article by Dr James Tour, a world-renowned chemist and researcher in nano-materials at Rice University, Texas, that attributes the decline in longevity after the Flood to mutation accumulation and genetic entropy.[2]

Abraham clearly had a very strong constitution and, since up to 90 or 100 is not an uncommon lifespan today,[3] perhaps we can get some better physical feeling for the proportions of Abraham's life by scaling it down in our imagination by, say, a factor of 90/175, which is roughly one half, so that we might think of him in contemporary terms as leaving Haran at an age of around 38, with his wife Sarai of 33, to embark on their life's great adventure.

The drawback with this way of looking at it is that it is a purely physical perspective. When he left Haran, although he may well have had the physique of a present-day 38-year-old, he had already had 75 actual years' experience – an old head on young shoulders! His approach to things may therefore not have been quite that of a 38-year-old today, so the comparison may be misleading and should not be pressed too far.

Stephen, in his speech in Acts 7, said that Abram's leaving Haran was when 'God removed him from there'. Accordingly, the next verses of Genesis say:

Now the LORD said to Abram, 'Go from your country and your kindred and your father's house to the land that I will show you. And I will make of you a great nation, and I will bless you and make your name great, so that you will be a blessing. I will bless those who bless you, and him who dishonours you I will curse, and in you all the families of the earth shall be blessed.'
(Gen. 12.1–3)

There is a marginal note in the ESV text indicating that a possible translation of the Hebrew of the first phrase here is as a pluperfect: 'Now the Lord *had said* . . ', which would support the idea mentioned above that the Lord had spoken to Abram earlier, presumably in Ur.

Might it have been that the journey was undertaken for the same reason as that undertaken centuries later from the same region: the journey of the Magi to Bethlehem? After all, the Babylonians in ancient times were very knowledgeable about the stars, and Abraham may have been interested in astronomy, as some of the Jewish legends suggest. I like to think of him as a man full of curiosity and questioning, wanting to find out where the journey would take him, with an inner conviction that it would take him somewhere important.

Does all this mean that Abraham was the driving force to get his father moving from Ur to Haran in the first place? If so, he must have been a remarkably convincing man. Had Terah originally shared Abram's vision and then lost it in Haran? There is so much here that we don't know, although one would imagine that very strong motivation was needed to break with culture and background and set out on a journey into the unknown.

Terah may never have had that motivation, but Abram appears to have done, although the length of time he seems to have taken to get going might indicate that he lost a sense of urgency until the passing of his father got him back on track. We just don't know, however much we would like to. In any case, God did not give up on Abram. It may even be that God appeared to him again and impelled him to a fresh start. The order of the narrative in Genesis 12 might favour that understanding. God is faithful, even if initial response to his call is hesitant.

Abram's initial steps on his journey show fuzziness as to exactly when it was that he first sensed God calling him – Ur? Haran? There are elements of ambiguity, hesitancy, even uncertainty, in which Abram's humanity is evident as he matured in his understanding of God's call. That I find very encouraging as I reflect on my own experience of God's call on my life.

And that is encouraging because it is the way it happens to many of us. We sense God's call upon our lives, but are uncertain of what it all means and how we should proceed. Not all is clear at the beginning, but there is enough to get us moving even if it is by fits and starts. One of the most important things for us to grasp from the story of Abraham is that we also can be involved in the great project that he started – involved as his spiritual children, travelling on the greatest journey of all.

God was the great initiator of the project: he appeared and spoke to Abram. God was the sovereign author of this great plan for the redemption of the world through the seed of Abraham.

Leon Kass suggests that Abram obeyed the voice because he was an ambitious man who wished to have a great name and power. That may, of course, have been part of his motivation – after all, he was human – yet I am nevertheless inclined to think that there must have been something deeper than that: a desire to find something more, an inner longing to find a greater narrative in which to frame his life. In any case, with any of us, our response to God's call is a complex mixture of his voice and our desires, not all of them quite as they should be. Yet the wonderful thing is that we gradually learn to recognise what is really right and good as our lives become more attuned to God's ways through our experience.

In fact, it would seem that Genesis deliberately sets the promise to Abram to make his name great against the background of Babylon's attempt to make *its* name great, in order to differentiate between two ways of living: Babylon's way or Abram's. For there is an important sense in which our lives are ruled either by a desire to create our own name and identity, or we learn to trust God and are content to leave those matters to him. The difference between these two ways of living is what the biblical narrative is all about.

Abram would learn in due course that trusting God necessarily involved his leaving behind his country, his kindred and his home. God was calling him to something entirely new that meant he had to break with his culture, family and all that had shaped his life up to that point.

This is not the first time that 'leaving' is discussed in Genesis. At the beginning of the book it is said that marriage involves a man leaving his father and mother and cleaving to his wife. In order to create the stable new marital units that are the building blocks of society, there must be a definite leaving of parents. Psychologists and psychiatrists tell us about the damage and even marriage break-up that may result from failure to move away from immediate parental influence. I can testify to the importance of both leaving my own home and my wife's leaving hers.

Abram had, in that sense, left his father and mother, but now he was being called to leave much more. Leaving father and mother does not necessarily mean leaving one's culture and native land – indeed, for most of history, it has normally involved neither. Yet Abram was called by God to leave all that had shaped him up to that point.

Kass suggests that God insisted on this radical break to set Abram free from pressure to conform. In order to go further with God, he had to step out of his box, be willing to be different and refuse to allow assimilation to his background culture. Abram had to become 'his own man' – or, more accurately and much better, 'God's own man'. That would make him a uniquely influential pioneer.

Geographical moves were important for Abraham. At a much lower level, they are important to many of us, including me – first when I left Northern Ireland to move to Cambridge. Next, when, just after my marriage, I moved to Cardiff in Wales and settled in as a lecturer. Then came a move to take my young family to Germany and do research for a year. All of those moves fitted into a conventional university career path, yet I gradually learned to appreciate that behind them there was the providential guiding hand of God so that they formed part of something even more important – my spiritual journey.

One way of thinking about Abraham's spiritual journey, common among Jewish scholars, is in terms of the series of 'tests' that he underwent. Through them God trained him for his unique role in salvation history. He was the founding patriarch of a nation that God chose not only to be a vehicle of witness to the world, but also to carry the human lineage of the Messiah. Opinions vary as to how many of these tests there were.

Some think twelve. Many Jewish scholars agree with the twelfth-century Jewish philosopher and Torah scholar, Ramban, who thought that there were ten. Finally, Leon Kass lists eleven, as follows:[4]

1  Abraham called to leave home: the promise of Seed
2  Sarah in trouble in Egypt
3  Abraham in trouble with Lot – Lot leaves him
4  Lot in trouble – Abraham rescues him
5  Hagar in trouble with Sarah
6  Abraham and the covenant of circumcision
7  Abraham hosts three men/angels/God?
8  Lot and Sodom in trouble – Abraham argues justice
9  Sarah in trouble in Gerar
10 Trouble with Ishmael
11 Abraham called to sacrifice Isaac the promised Seed.

As Kass indicates, most of the incidents have to do with family troubles. This is striking, because they appear here essentially for the first time in Scripture.

The Genesis account also frames Abraham's life in terms of one of the so-called seven great themes of literature: the journey.[5] His journey, like all human journeys, has multiple facets – moral, spiritual and intellectual, as well as geographical.

Whatever the precise timing of it, God's call of Abram must rank as one of the pivotal events in world history. Jonathan Sacks wrote:

All other civilisations rise and fall. The faith of Abraham survives . . . What made Abrahamic monotheism unique is that it endowed life with meaning. That is a point rarely and barely understood . . . We make a great mistake if we think of monotheism as a linear development from polytheism, as if people first worshipped many gods and then reduced them to one. Monotheism is something else entirely. *The meaning of a system lies outside the system. Therefore the meaning of the universe lies outside the universe.* Monotheism, by discovering the transcendental God, the God who stands outside the universe and creates it, made it possible for the first time to believe that life has a meaning, not just a mythic or scientific explanation.[6]

Sacks' statement that the meaning of a system lies outside the system repackages Wittgenstein's assertion that

All propositions are of equal value. The sense of the world must lie outside the world. In the world everything is as it is and happens as it does happen. In it there is no value – and if there were, it would be of no value. If there is a value which is of value, it must lie outside all happening and being-so. For all happening and being-so is accidental. What makes it non-accidental cannot lie in the world, for otherwise this would again be accidental. It must lie outside the world.[7]

God, the source of all ultimate meaning, called to Abram. It was the first great 'follow me' call in history. What led up to it? Were there hidden years of questioning as to whether there existed something more than nature, of increasing doubts about the rationality of worshipping the moon, as hinted at in the rabbinic writings? Maybe he had seen through the vacuous polytheism of the day and, reflecting on the glory of the heavens and the wonders of life, had started to wonder if there was some reality behind it that was worthy of the name 'God'.

Such ideas fit in with statements of the Jewish-Roman historian Josephus (c. AD 37–100). Basing himself on the writing (in Greek) of an early third-century BC Babylonian historian and astronomer called Berossus, Josephus wrote:

Abraham, endowed with great sagacity, with a higher knowledge of God and greater virtues than all the rest, was determined to change the erroneous opinions of men. He was the first who had the courage to proclaim God as the sole Creator of the universe, to whose will all the heavenly bodies are subject, for they by their motions show their dependence on Him. His opposition to astrology provoked the wrath of the Chaldeans, and he had to leave their country and go to Canaan.[8]

Fourth-century AD Roman historian Eusebius cited a second-century BC text, *Concerning the Jews of Assyria,* written by the earliest Greco-Roman historian Eupolemus, which said that Abraham 'surpassed all men in nobility and wisdom, who was also the inventor of astronomy and the Chaldaic art, and pleased God well by his zeal towards religion'.[9]

An important piece of additional biblical information about Abram's call is to be found in the book of Acts. One of the things I learned from David Gooding is the importance of literary structure – not as an end in itself, but as a way of supporting and enhancing the message of a book. For example, in the book of Acts, the beginnings and endings of the various sections often echo each other in what is called a chiastic structure – from the Greek letter *chi* that resembles an X. For instance, if a section had four parts, the structure would be in the form XYYX – the first and last and the two middle parts having elements in common and/ or in contrast.[10]

We find this feature in the second section of Acts. It highlights a similarity and a contrast between Abraham and Saul of Tarsus (Paul). That section begins with the trial and stoning of Stephen who, as we mentioned above, began his defence by saying: 'The God of glory appeared to our father Abraham . . .' It ends with Saul seeing a great light from heaven that blinded him until he reached Damascus. Both Abraham and Saul saw the glory of God; both were sent on journeys, but in opposite directions. Abraham was sent out from the Gentile world to learn to trust God and witness for him. Saul was instructed to continue his journey to Damascus to meet a man called Ananias, who had been told by God that Saul was 'a chosen instrument of mine to carry my name before the Gentiles' (Acts 9.15). So Abraham was called *out* and Paul was sent *back* into the Gentile world as God's missionary ambassador. True pilgrimage involves journeying in both directions.

Paul's gospel outreach to the Gentile world was a major fulfilment of God's promise to Abraham to bring blessing to the world. Here is what Paul wrote to the Galatian churches:

Know then that it is those of faith who are the sons of Abraham. And the Scripture, foreseeing that God would justify the Gentiles by faith, preached the gospel beforehand to Abraham, saying, 'In you

shall all the nations be blessed.' So then, those who are of faith are blessed along with Abraham, the man of faith.
(Gal. 3.7–9)

# Arrival in the land

When they came to the land of Canaan, Abram passed through the land to the place at Shechem, to the oak of Moreh. At that time the Canaanites were in the land. Then the LORD appeared to Abram and said, 'To your offspring I will give this land.' So he built there an altar to the LORD, who had appeared to him. From there he moved to the hill country on the east of Bethel and pitched his tent, with Bethel on the west and Ai on the east. And there he built an altar to the LORD and called upon the name of the LORD. And Abram journeyed on, still going towards the Negeb.
(Gen. 12.5–9)

The roughly 900 km journey from Haran to Shechem[11] lacks any detailed narrator comment. We are simply told that the land was occupied by a Canaanite population, another group descended from Noah's grandson, Canaan – the son of Ham, who was cursed by Noah for his behaviour. Leon Kass comments: 'Canaanites are Dionysiac, earth-worshipping, fertility obsessed, and licentious. They are an orgiastic people in their celebrations.'[12] Not the easiest kind of culture in which to survive. Yet there is no talk here of dispossessing the Canaanites by force. Indeed, (moderately) peaceful co-existence seems to characterise most of the narrative. The mention of the Canaanites flags up the fact that tension might lie in wait for Abram and his clan even though the Canaanites were distantly related to him.

Throughout history, land has been and still is an extremely important commodity. That was particularly true in the ancient Near East. It was living the dream to have a piece of land, however small, that you could call your own, on which you could raise a family, teach them your skills and, in the end, pass on the land as an inheritance. It gave life lasting meaning.

What now happened to Abram was in an altogether different and unprecedented category: 'Then the LORD appeared to Abram and said, "To your offspring I will give this land."' This was no mere piece of land for a smallholding. This was a very big deal indeed – Abram was to be given land enough to support not merely a family but a nation.

It was an extraordinary development. It had never happened before and it has never happened since. To no other individual has God ever directly promised a land in this way. All through history nations have taken or lost territory by occupation, migration, force and war. However, Paul taught that God is ultimately responsible for governments. In Romans 13.1 he wrote: 'Let every person be subject to the governing authorities. For there is no authority except from God, and those that exist have been instituted by God.' The usual Christian understanding of this statement is that God, in his sovereignty over history, permitted people like Nero to rule – he did not directly appoint them nor explicitly give them the territories of the Roman empire.

Then again, at the individual level, there are many of us who see Paul's statement in Acts 17 as characterizing our own experience:

> And he made from one man every nation of mankind to live on all the face of the earth, having determined allotted periods and the boundaries of their dwelling place, that they should seek God, in the hope that they might feel their way towards him and find him. (Acts 17.26–27)

More than that, many who own the plot of land on which their home stands would gratefully see in the obtaining of it the guiding hand of God.

However, Abram's experience is at a completely different level. He, unique in history, was told directly by God that this land was for the nation to which he would give rise and from which the Messiah would come. No other person or nation was granted that role of carrying the human line of God become flesh – Jesus Christ our Lord.

Yet the strange thing about it all is that Abram himself did not receive any inheritance in the land during his lifetime. Stephen, in his speech in Acts 7.5, said of God: 'Yet he gave him no inheritance in it, not even a foot's length, but promised to give it to him as a possession and to his offspring after him, though he had no child.' Even the latter would be complicated. Stephen continued:

And God spoke to this effect – that his offspring would be sojourners in a land belonging to others, who would enslave them and afflict them for four hundred years. 'But I will judge the nation that they serve,' said God, 'and after that they shall come out and worship me in this place.'
(Acts 7.6–7)

The Feast of Passover, initially celebrated on the day that Israel left Egypt to travel to the promised land under Moses' leadership, is regarded as the beginning of the free nation of Israel. After wandering for 40 years (unnecessarily!) Joshua led them across the Jordan into the land to settle.

That, however, was far from the end of the story, as we are all aware. For centuries this 'promised land' has been and still is the subject of endless bitter and sometimes violent disputes and wars between those who claim Abram as their progenitor in one sense or another: Jews, Christians and Muslims. And not only the land, but many different parts of it, large and small, have been subject to dispute between the same groups, none more so than in Jerusalem itself.

The constant war and wrangling over possession of the land for nearly 4,000 years raises an obvious question: was this really what Abram was originally promised? Might we have missed something? After all, how could a godly person not feel ashamed of what has happened? Indeed, some might even dare think, should not God himself feel ashamed of it also? Why did it all turn out this way?

That this question is justified is clear from the letter to the Hebrews. It carries forward Stephen's point that Abraham did not receive the promise, by adding even more enigmatically that his descendants did not really do so either:

These all died in faith, not having received the things promised, but having seen them and greeted them from afar, and having acknowledged that they were strangers and exiles on the earth.

For people who speak thus make it clear that they are seeking a homeland. If they had been thinking of that land from which they had gone out, they would have had opportunity to return. But as it is, they desire a better country, that is, a heavenly one. Therefore God is not ashamed to be called their God, for he has prepared for them a city.
(Heb. 11.13–16)

Hebrews 11 goes on to survey the history of Israel at the time of the Judges, Samuel and King David, when men and women who trusted God did remarkable exploits, even though they were often terribly mistreated, persecuted and murdered. They were heroes of faith in God. Yet the chapter ends by saying: 'And all these, though commended through their faith, did not receive what was promised, since God had provided something better for us, that apart from us they should not be made perfect' (vv. 39–40).

This gives a radically different perspective. The thing promised that these faithful people did not receive, or only received in part, was an earthly homeland. The writer to the Hebrews interprets their attitude as that of men and women who feel themselves to be strangers on planet earth and not simply strangers wandering away from a promised land on earth. Here the talk is of a heavenly country and city of which God is not ashamed, by contrast with the sorry history of the nation on earth.

It brings us back to our question: why did all of this happen in the way that it did? This is such an important issue that Appendix 1 will be devoted to it in order not to interrupt the flow of the main narrative, to which we now return.

Abram, as he journeyed, had of course no idea of this complex future. The promise of a nation, which God had made to him earlier, and now the remarkable promise of a land, would have resonated with his deepest longings and, no doubt, that fact amplified their authenticity for him as the Lord appeared to him and confirmed to him that he had arrived at his appointed destination.

At least Abram now knew that he was in the land of promise and he celebrated the Lord's appearance to him by building an altar to the Lord and worshipping him.

By contrast with Nimrod, the beginning of whose kingdom was building cities, Abram did not build a city to try to reach heaven. Because heaven had reached down to him, Abram began by building altars, first at Shechem and then, after moving further south, at Bethel, where he 'called upon the name of the Lord'.[13] He had real contact with heaven, whereas Babel did not.

These altars showed that Abram thought of his direct dealings with God as permanent and solid and his tent dwelling as temporary and transient. The text employs words typical of a nomadic life – 'pulling up his stakes' in verse 8, and the word for 'journey' in verse 9 is derived from another word for 'pulling out' stakes.

The word 'altar' in English is derived from the Latin *altus*, meaning 'high'. It denotes a raised structure on which religious rites, including offerings and sacrifices of various kinds, are performed.[14] The first mention of an altar in Genesis occurs after the Flood: 'Then Noah built an altar to the Lord and took some of every clean animal and some of every clean bird and offered burnt offerings on the altar' (Gen. 8.20). In Hebrew the word is *misbeach*, which is derived from *zabah*, meaning 'to slaughter for food or sacrifice'.

The use of the word in connection with Abram is only the second time it has appeared in the Bible. At this stage we are not told whether or not Abram made offerings. The emphasis is on speaking to God: Abram 'called upon the name of the Lord'.

Genesis records the building of four altars by Abraham. The first three occur at the beginning of the narrative. The first was at Shechem, where the Lord appeared to him and promised that he would give the land to his offspring. Little did the man realise that the 'offering' on the fourth and final altar would be his firstborn offspring, Isaac . . .

The second altar was built between Bethel (meaning 'house of God') and Ai (meaning 'heap of ruins'). The concept of the house of God is not to be confined to a place where God dwells, but also denotes the rule and government of God – as in the idea of a royal house that rules a nation. Using a little imagination, living between those two cities aptly reminds us of the tension in which believers in God live – between allowing God to rule over their lives or being pulled into ruinous lifestyles that could destroy them. There will be plenty of examples of that tension in what follows.

The third altar was built at the Oaks of Mamre in Hebron, where Abram settled and where he and subsequent patriarchs were eventually buried in the cave of Machpelah.

The implied contrast between the permanency of an altar that was set up to record dealings with the Almighty, and the transience of nomadic life should prompt us to evaluate our own lives, even though they may be very different from that of Abram. For the culture in which we live can easily make us think that our homes, towns and employment are the tangible, permanent things, whereas relationship with God, if that even makes sense, is intangible, ill defined, fleeting and temporary. Sadly, for some people that is what it is – nothing more than unsatisfying, intermittent church attendance. That is the thinking characteristic of secular Babel.

How, then, can we mould the contours of our lives in order to move God up – or even onto – the scale of what we count as permanent? One way is to spend more time in prayer, to cultivate fellowship with his people and above all to allow him to speak to us through his Word. For it was Abram's experiences of God speaking to him that he came to look upon as the solid and permanent things in his life. It is worth trying to identify particular times in our lives when we had a real sense that the Lord was speaking to us.

I am of course aware that such experiences are, by definition, subjective and many of us, including myself, are very hesitant about saying things like 'The Lord spoke to me', and even more hesitant about statements like 'The Lord told me to tell you'! Nevertheless, in all due humility, we must not take understandable scepticism and hesitation to such an extreme that we rob ourselves of the conviction that the Lord can and does speak to us through his Word. After all, he has promised to reveal himself to us. A promise confirmed by my own experience.

Abram did not settle in Bethel but kept moving south towards the Negev, every step taking him away from the promised land. One wonders why. Is there a possibility that he was vaguely aware that this matter of inheritance would be very difficult? That the actual inheriting of the land by his offspring would be delayed for centuries? Certainly part of that delay would soon be communicated to him, as we shall see when we reach Genesis 15. Even then, as we know from subsequent history, their occupation of the land would only be temporary and subsequently intermittent, until the State of Israel was set up in 1948.

# 5

# From Canaan to Egypt

Famine forced Abram to cross the frontier of the promised land and go down to Egypt, exactly as it would force his grandson Jacob and his children to do in later years. It was a risky step and Abram feared for his safety. He put self-preservation (and material prosperity) above his marriage relationship and, rejecting honesty and truth, he asked Sarai his wife to say she was his sister. Abram would prosper as a result, but God would plague Pharaoh's house until he sent Abram and Sarai away – as a later pharaoh would do to the nation.

> Now there was a famine in the land. So Abram went down to Egypt to sojourn there, for the famine was severe in the land. When he was about to enter Egypt, he said to Sarai his wife, 'I know that you are a woman beautiful in appearance, and when the Egyptians see you, they will say, "This is his wife." Then they will kill me, but they will let you live. Say you are my sister, that it may go well with me because of you, and that my life may be spared for your sake.'
> (Gen. 12.10–13)

This is the first time in the Bible that we meet a reference to famine. The fact is that this world is constituted in such a way that food can run short. And it did, in stark contrast with the plenty of the garden of Eden. The famine brought Abram (briefly) to Egypt. Much later a famine would bring his grandson Jacob and his family to Egypt, where they would remain for more than four centuries until Moses led them back to Canaan.

Abram discovered that responding to the call of God did not exempt him from hazards and difficult decisions. He had left the lush plains of Mesopotamia and may have expected the promised land to be a paradise like Eden. God's call had been so clear, so what was the meaning of this famine? The narrative records no cry of Abram to God about what he should now do, nor is there any record of God intervening to tell him. That silence tells us something about the nature of God's guidance that is easily overlooked by Christians today. For there are some who think that God micro-manages our lives and will instruct us in detail at every point about what we should do next.[1]

That is clearly not the case – and for a very good reason. Parents who insist on making every decision and doing everything for their children risk leaving them immature and lacking in character. All (healthy) children need to learn to tie their own shoelaces, and parents must love their children enough to give them space to grow up and develop their own character and convictions. This means that they must be allowed to make mistakes.

That is what God does for us. His guidance consists much more in giving us moral principles that should form our character – who we are – than in giving directions as to what we should do. Abram and the rest of us must make our own decisions and mistakes, and learn from them.

In this case, Abram decided not to wait and starve – as he thought – so he left Canaan, promised land though it was, and pressed on south towards the then powerful empire of Egypt. We are told he 'went down to Egypt'. This going down was very different from the *lech lecha* of his call to 'get going' in Genesis 12. It may seem in retrospect to have been a move in the wrong direction – a spiritual decline. Yet it was also a *lech lecha* in the sense of going into himself and learning about the weaknesses in his own character. Jonathan Sacks comments:

'Going' has the connotation in Torah of moving towards one's ultimate purpose – of service towards one's Creator. And this is strongly hinted at by the phrase, 'Go to yourself' – meaning, towards your soul's essence and your ultimate purpose, that for which you were created . . .

Abraham's removal to Egypt was not an interruption but an integral part of the command of 'Lech Lecha' – to journey towards that self-fulfillment which is the service of G-d.

And as Abraham's destiny was the later destiny of the children of Israel, so it is ours. Our exile, like his, is a preparation for (and therefore part of) redemption. And the redemption which follows brings us to a higher state than that which we could have reached without exile.[2]

It is encouraging to think that a wrong move in life could, in God's hands, have the same effect for us.

Kass gives us more insight into Egyptian culture:

It boasts the fertility of the Nile, technology, architecture, administration; people who have sophisticated magical powers to manipulate certain kinds of phenomena. It has nature worship, but the human being has no special dignity in the cosmos. One man, Pharaoh, believed to be a god, rules despotically over all the others, primarily in his own interest.[3]

Kass sums up the Egyptians as 'rationalist technocrats'.

Abram hoped to find in Egypt food for his family and people, and pasture for his flocks. Yet he hesitated at the frontier. He became afraid that his wife's beauty could endanger his life, should she come to the attention of the powerful men of Egypt. What is striking about this is that Sarai was no longer a young woman, and the suggestion has been made that she retained her beauty because she lived at a time when people lived much longer than today and aged less rapidly.[4]

Sarah's beauty was later the subject of much praise in rabbinic tradition. She was regarded as one of the most beautiful women in the world – the others being Eve, Rahab, Abigail and Esther. Indeed, some thought that only Eve was more beautiful.

The very first recorded words of a human being in the Bible were spoken by Adam to his newly created wife Eve. He welcomed her with the words: 'This at last is bone of my bones and flesh of my flesh; she shall be called Woman because she was taken out of Man.' The narrator then goes on to supply the biblical definition of wife/marriage that is cited both by Jesus and Paul in the New Testament: 'Therefore a man shall leave his father and his mother and hold fast to his wife, and they shall become one flesh' (Gen 2.24).[5]

By vivid contrast, Abram's first words in the Genesis narrative, also directed to his wife, are concerned with requesting that, if asked, she should deny that she was 'flesh of his flesh', and say instead that she was his sister. It was a half-truth, as she actually was his half-sister.

On this issue Leon Kass says:

God cares for Sarai . . . but especially for Sarai as Abram's wife . . . The attentive reader may learn from this story that, though one may choose a wife, *one cannot choose what wife means*, that a wife is not transmutable into a sister or a concubine when it suits one's purpose.'[6]

True affirmation of relationships is one of life's most important lessons. Abram will one day have to learn what it means to be a father, but in order to do that he must first learn the meaning of 'wife'. This is another foundation principle of God's future city – witness the metaphor used in Revelation 21.2: 'And I saw the holy city . . . coming down out of heaven from God, prepared as a bride adorned for her husband.' This city is a holy city – its values are rooted in the character of God, and Abram had to learn those values at the practical level of marriage. And so do those of us who are married!

Those of us who are husbands reading this, including myself, should ask ourselves: what does 'wife' mean to me? How do I express that meaning? Looking back over the past year, how have I treated her? How has our relationship developed? Have I been inattentive or neglectful? What would she say if I asked her to tell me what she thought 'wife' meant to me?

Some of us may have to admit that we struggle here. Do we need to repent, say that we are sorry and prove it by doing something about it?

What is more, Abram seemed to have little sense that his mission in life was meant to be a joint venture with Sarai. And what about us men today who may well be involved in ministry, having a vision and sense of calling? Do we, for instance, consult our wives about the invitations we accept, or do we simply charge ahead without it occurring to us that our wives could help us here and, by being really involved, have a heightened sense of companionship in the ministry? And what do we ask our wives to do? Is it always consonant with our high calling to serve the Lord as joint heirs of his kingdom?

It is difficult to imagine Abram and Sarai praying together about the problem of Egypt. But then experience prompts me to ask those of us who are husbands: when was the last time we prayed and read Scripture with our wives? And wives, do you encourage your husband to do this with you? Spending even just a little time doing that is infinitely better than spending no time at all.

I sometimes liken a Christian marriage to a triangle with the Lord at the apex. On occasions when I have been involved in marriage ceremonies in an official capacity I have sometimes presented the couple with a triangle, one of the simplest of musical instruments. I encourage them to hang it in a prominent place in their home and sound it when tension starts to rise as a reminder to get together before the Lord and sort it out, as it is well nigh impossible to pray and fight at the same time!

If you are in leadership, what about the men/women you have the privilege and responsibility to lead – how do they treat their wives/husbands? It is for wives to ask how they should treat their husbands in light of Scripture. Their influence, as we see from the Abraham story, is critical. How should we think and behave in the contemporary world, to protest against the devaluation and even redefinition of marriage? I cited Kass above – 'one cannot choose what wife means' – yet that is precisely what many are doing under the influence of postmodern relativism.

Kass says that giving rise to and maintaining a godly nation is dependent on the right kind of women. He writes:

> It is no wonder that Abraham, to begin with, does not understand this truth. Rarely do great men, with great dreams, like to acknowledge their dependence, least of all on the seemingly weaker sex. Strong men are not easily domesticated. Ambitious men do not readily accept the need for those who will replace them. Proud men are not given to yielding to their wives. Before he can become a founder, and even a proper father, he must become a proper husband and appreciate Sarah as a wife.[7]

We men need to heed such words, however much they may sting.

God had promised Abram a prosperous future. That future clearly depended on his thriving and so, imagining a threat to him through Sarai, he decided to put his own self-preservation, well-being and material wealth above honesty, truth and the integrity of his marriage. And he did so even though the whole prospect of fathering a great nation depended entirely on that marriage.

All of us are aware that money can very often be a source of tension in marriages, but it is hard to see by what mental contortions Abram managed to persuade himself to make his own well-being his chief value and allow himself to risk prostituting his wife by asking her to go along with the deceitful half-truth that she was his sister. Sad to say, once more there is no record of either Abram or Sarai calling on God for help.

Well-being, which could be considered the opposite of famine, has become one of the major idols of our day, as billions of hits on Google will readily demonstrate. The craving for well-being is responsible for a great deal of suffering and misery as people put themselves first. It has also become a major subject of academic study, with millions hanging on every word the pundits say.

For that reason, Christians should be at the forefront of shaping concepts of well-being. It is, first of all, good to know that there is an established correlation between a living faith in God and well-being. Former President of the Royal College of Psychiatrists, Andrew Sims, writes:

> The advantageous effect of religious belief and spirituality on mental and physical health is one of the best-kept secrets in psychiatry and medicine generally. If the findings of the huge volume of research on this topic had gone in the opposite direction and it had been found that religion damages your mental health, it would have been front-page news in every newspaper in the land.[8]

However, it is all too common to encourage the pursuit of well-being by rejecting God-given norms and cutting moral corners. That often includes setting aside the sacred commitment of marriage and selfishly breaking vows in the name of 'love'. That proceeds from a destructive idolatry of the self.

At a fundamental level, the well-known *Times* columnist Matthew Parris, an atheist, is convinced of the positive value of Christianity in promoting well-being. In a widely discussed article he wrote: 'As an atheist I truly believe that Africa needs God: missionaries, not aid money, are the solution to Africa's biggest problem – the crushing passivity of the people's mindset.' Parris explains:

> Travelling in Malawi refreshed another belief, too: one I've been trying to banish all my life, but an observation I've been unable to avoid since my African childhood. It confounds my ideological beliefs, stubbornly refuses to fit my worldview, and has embarrassed my growing belief that there is no God.
>
> Now a confirmed atheist, I've become convinced of the enormous contribution that Christian evangelism makes in Africa: sharply distinct from the work of secular NGOs, government projects and international aid efforts. These alone will not do. Education and training alone will not do. In Africa Christianity changes people's hearts. It brings a spiritual transformation. The rebirth is real. The change is good.
>
> I used to avoid this truth by applauding – as you can – the practical work of mission churches in Africa. It's a pity, I would say, that salvation is part of the package, but Christians black and white, working in Africa, do heal the sick, do teach people to read and write; and only the severest kind of secularist could see a mission hospital or school and say the world would be better without it.

Parris concludes:

> Those who want Africa to walk tall amid 21st-century global competition must not kid themselves that providing the material means or even the knowhow that accompanies what we call development will make the change. A whole belief system must first be supplanted.

And I'm afraid it has to be supplanted by another. Removing Christian evangelism from the African equation may leave the continent at the mercy of a malign fusion of Nike, the witch doctor, the mobile phone and the machete.[9]

Removing the God dimension from his life at this point left Abram at the mercy of the temptation to look after himself at the expense of his marriage. The low moral tone of the conversation he had with Sarai leads us to wonder just how much he had understood God's commitment to him in helping him see the project through. It is very easy to think anachronistically of Abram, as if he were from a 'decent Christian heritage', whereas Scripture tells us that his background was in pagan idolatry. However, we need to put against that the fact that marriage in Mesopotamian culture was mostly monogamous and usually involved protective contracts between the families.[10]

What is disturbing is that even though God had promised him offspring, Abram showed no concern about protecting his wife Sarai, the potential mother of the new nation. Abram clearly expected the Egyptians to take Sarai because of her outstanding beauty. He was right. They did.

When Abram entered Egypt, the Egyptians saw that the woman was very beautiful. And when the princes of Pharaoh saw her, they praised her to Pharaoh. And the woman was taken into Pharaoh's house. And for her sake he dealt well with Abram; and he had sheep, oxen, male donkeys, male servants, female servants, female donkeys, and camels.
(Gen. 12.14–16)

There is a wonderful Jewish legend that Abram locked Sarai in a box in order to smuggle her into Egypt. The tax officials said he had tax to pay on the contents of the box. They asked if it was vessels, to which Abram replied that he would pay tax on vessels. Was it silk? they asked, to which Abram replied that he would pay tax on silk, and so on. They finally insisted on opening the box and, according to the Genesis Rabbah 40.5, the whole of Egypt was lit up with her beauty when they opened it. The tax officials then said that she was only suitable for a king. In this legend Abram comes across as being prepared to pay any amount to protect Sarai. The story may well have been concocted to present him in a somewhat better light than Genesis does.

The fact is that Abram had put Sarai in a very dangerous position. Pharaoh's desire for a beautiful and exotic addition to his harem posed an obvious potential threat to the identity of the seed God had promised Abram. And, ironically, Abram profited from it all on a grand scale as Pharaoh lavished his wealth on Abram for Sarai's sake. How did Abram manage to live with his conscience which must surely have needled him about neglecting his wife?

Perhaps it was his fear that drove Abram to suppress his conscience, abandon his responsibility of care for Sarai and allow others to come dangerously close to her. Without telling Abram, God, in his faithfulness to his promise, intervened by afflicting 'Pharaoh and his house with great plagues because of Sarai, Abram's wife' (Gen. 12.17).

It was rather an ironic start for a man who was to be a blessing to the nations of the world!

Jewish tradition insists that nothing indecent happened between Sarai and Pharaoh, and there are various stories. For instance, there is one about an angel with a whip who thrashed Pharaoh every time he approached Sarai. She, so the story goes, constantly protested to Pharaoh that she was Abram's wife.[11]

Be that as it may, Pharaoh eventually discovered the truth, forthrightly rebuked Abram for deceiving him and told him in no uncertain terms to get out:

So Pharaoh called Abram and said, 'What is this you have done to me? Why did you not tell me that she was your wife? Why did you say, "She is my sister", so that I took her for my wife? Now then, here is your wife; take her, and go.' And Pharaoh gave men orders concerning him, and they sent him away with his wife and all that he had.
(Gen. 12.18–20)

It was profoundly embarrassing for Abram to be deported in this way. We might hope that he was thoroughly ashamed. His failure to acknowledge that Sarai was his wife had increased his wealth and, one would suppose, his (superficial) sense of well-being. It is sad that it is possible for men to have a totally false sense of well-being that derives from neglect of their marriage. The letter to the Hebrews, after describing the heroes and heroines of faith, gets down to some practical matters of marriage and money: 'Let marriage be held in honour among all . . . Keep your life free from love of money . . . "The Lord is my helper; I will not fear; what can man do to me?"' (Heb. 13.4–6). This quote is from Psalm 118.6, where the context is David's fear of encroaching enemies.

We will also be embarrassed if and when we allow ourselves to be shamed by non-believers who catch us out for having shoddy standards and messing up in our dealings with them.

One of the main lessons of the story is that, for our own sakes, we need to avoid pretence of two kinds: pretending to be what we are not, and pretending not to be what we are. Also, how easily we make false assumptions about the moral convictions of others, especially if they do not share our world view.

Another positive lesson is that if God could use someone who got it as wrong as Abram did, he can use us. That reflects the nature of his grace and it is important for us to remind ourselves of it, especially when we, like Abram, make a bad mistake on our own journey and are ruefully forced to identify with him.

Abram clearly had no idea that, in certain respects, Pharaoh had higher moral standards than he did. One wonders how much he really knew of Egyptian culture. Did he know, for instance, of the moral code that can be gleaned from the Egyptian 'books of the dead' that were buried with a dead person, in which they had earlier recorded oaths that they had behaved well, not deceived or stolen, not committed adultery and so on?

When dealing with others we should always be aware that, according to Genesis, all men and women are created in the image of God as moral beings. As Paul puts it in Romans 2.14–16, morality is written in the human conscience. That is, we are hard-wired for morality, all of us, irrespective of our particular world view. Although the Fall has damaged us, we are nevertheless able to distinguish good from evil. And non-Christians, having that same capacity, will have every right to judge us if our lives seem inconsistent to them. The litany of Christian leadership scandals in recent years is a shame on the name of Christ, and the world has every right to protest against it.

Not surprisingly, therefore, Pharaoh unceremoniously deported Abram, although it does not seem that he tried to take back the wealth he had showered upon him. Nor is there any hint of Abram offering to return it.

Standing with the truth would surely have served Abram much better at the beginning. He failed to do so and had to be censured in a very embarrassing way. Yet, when a non-Christian colleague, friend or acquaintance remonstrates with us, it is not the end of the world. After all, it is better that an unbeliever puts us right than that we are not rebuked at all. Open admission that we were in the wrong can do a great deal more for our credibility than pious talk.

Of course, not all powerful men are as morally scrupulous as Pharaoh was on this occasion. When offered easy pickings of a sexual nature, many will take them without compunction – often with disastrous consequences.

We note in passing that Josephus says that Abram was held in high regard by the intellectual elite in Egypt. He consulted with them about many issues and was instrumental in introducing them to the arithmetic and astronomy he had learned in Mesopotamia. In fact, Josephus suggests that one of the reasons Abram went to Egypt was to search out their knowledge and philosophy.[12] It is possible that Josephus was subtly implying that the Egyptians owed their skills in these areas to the Hebrews. Finding evidence for Josephus's claims is another matter – there is none.

That is a great pity, since one of the obvious questions that is left hanging regarding many of the incidents in the Abraham narrative is this: here is a man who is held out as a pioneer of faith in God and the founder of a nation called to witness to the world the existence of the one true God, yet what can we say about his own personal witness to God to the world outside his family and entourage? Did he, for example, communicate anything positive to the Egyptians about God, or did his behaviour entirely preclude any credibility he had? We just don't know for certain, even though there are legends that assert it.

At this stage Abram could not have had any idea that the issue of going down to Egypt was to play a portentous role in the life of the nation that he was to father. It would be triggered by the unconscionable sale of his great-grandson Joseph by his brothers as a slave to Egypt. It would be a famine that subsequently brought Abram's grandson Jacob and his family to Egypt to live with Joseph, who had saved the country from disaster and built up vast reserves. Yet all of this was eventually forgotten and Abram's descendants became Egyptian slaves. Some 400 years later their descendants would be delivered by God through Moses. Once more God would plague the house of Pharaoh, not just to let Sarai go, but to let the nation descended from her go. Once more, not Sarai and Abram alone, but the nation descended from them, would come out of Egypt – and with great wealth that had been given to them by the Egyptians.

In this way, history would be repeated at a higher level. This is a phenomenon, recognised by Jewish commentators in the Midrash,[13] that recurs in Genesis, where a particular narrative becomes a prototype of something that happens later. Another example of this, on an even greater timescale, is the way in which the subsequent experience of Abraham and Isaac on Mount Moriah foreshadows the events of Calvary. We shall consider this in due course.

Although Abram and Sarai did escape from Egypt with their lives and considerably augmented wealth, what they did there had other less palatable consequences. Abram had failed the test of want provoked by the famine. On the one hand his failure paradoxically led to material plenty; on the other it must have badly marred his witness to the world, as mentioned above, to say nothing of how it affected his relationship with Sarai who, ironically, was the one person indispensable to the fulfilment of his dreams. It also led to the introduction of an Egyptian woman, Hagar, into Abram's home as part of the wealth they had been given by Pharaoh. We shall hear much more about her role in the narrative as we proceed.

This leads me to observe that it is not only marital relationships that can get compromised through fear. Another relationship that gets marginalised or outright denied through fear is the most important relationship of all – that between us and the Lord. In this regard, it is instructive to read (and re-read) the apostle Peter's encouragement to all believers not to be afraid to witness:

Now who is there to harm you if you are zealous for what is good? But even if you should suffer for righteousness' sake, you will be blessed. Have no fear of them, nor be troubled, but in your hearts honour Christ the Lord as holy, always being prepared to make a defence to anyone who asks you for a reason for the hope that is in you; yet do it with gentleness and respect, having a good conscience, so that, when you are slandered, those who revile your good behaviour in Christ may be put to shame. For it is better to suffer for doing good, if that should be God's will, than for doing evil.
(1 Pet. 3.13–17)

Notice the context – fear. Abram was afraid of the famine. Then he became afraid of Pharaoh, and that led to fear of doing the right thing by Sarai and hence to failure to admit to his true relationship with her. Paul wrote to the Christian community at Corinth about the relationship of the believer to the Lord Jesus:

I wish you would bear with me in a little foolishness. Do bear with me! For I feel a divine jealousy for you, since I betrothed you to one husband, to present you as a pure virgin to Christ. But I am afraid that as the serpent deceived Eve by his cunning, your thoughts will be led astray from a sincere and pure devotion to Christ. For if someone comes and proclaims another Jesus than the one we proclaimed, or if you receive a different spirit from the one you received, or if you accept a different gospel from the one you accepted, you put up with it readily enough.
(2 Cor. 11.1–4)

Paul compares loyalty to Christ with faithfulness in betrothal and marriage. The issue is spiritual and theological faithfulness. It is possible for someone to remain sexually faithful to their spouse but to stray from a solid theological commitment to the Lord and become compromised with doctrines that may eventually lead to spiritual shipwreck. It is also possible for the reverse to happen – people remain outwardly orthodox in doctrine, but are privately unfaithful to their spouses.

The major lesson Abram had to learn was that the God who appeared to him was holy. Truth, honesty and the sanctity of the marriage bond matter to him. He does not approve when we pretend to be what we are not; nor does he approve when we pretend not to be what we are.

It can be painful to learn that God does not need lying, cheating, dishonesty, theft, compromise and double dealing for the attainment of his objective to see us flourish. How easily we get tempted to try to save ourselves from inconvenience and hassle by evasion and deceit – only to find that none of it works.

Abram was on a steep learning curve – having to be taught the importance of these things by an Egyptian monarch who worshipped the sun! As a result, Abram left Egypt a humbler and wiser man. He had learned that his own stratagem of telling a half-truth had not saved him from the results of his own stupidity and deviousness. God had saved him. Abram would fail again, but he had at least made some progress in the right direction by recognising that fact.

The prophet Isaiah later wrote words that remind us of Abram's experience:

'Ah, stubborn children,' declares the LORD,
'who carry out a plan, but not mine,
and who make an alliance, but not of my Spirit,
   that they may add sin to sin;
who set out to go down to Egypt,
   without asking for my direction,
to take refuge in the protection of Pharaoh
   and to seek shelter in the shadow of Egypt!
Therefore shall the protection of Pharaoh turn to your
   shame,
   and the shelter in the shadow of Egypt to your
   humiliation.'
(Isa. 30.1–3)

The contemporaries of Isaiah were looking to Egypt and not to the Lord. Isaiah put his finger on what Abram had failed to do at the border of Egypt and at many other times in his life – he did not look to 'the Holy

One of Israel' or consult the Lord. As a result he did not learn how the Lord would have helped him without his having to be economical with the truth and resorting to underhand methods.

What about us? Have we ever stood at a mental border-crossing, tempted to 'go down to Egypt' for help when we thought our resources were running out as a consequence of some kind of 'famine'? Or have we ever paused at a border, knowing that to cross it would involve compromise? On the internet, for instance, where it may only take a couple of clicks to do yourself moral damage?

Has God ever saved us from the consequences of our own stupidity, waywardness and even obstinacy? What did we learn from that experience? Or are we still not listening?

As far as we know, Abram built no altars in Egypt!

We need, however, to be careful here to avoid a false deduction. What Isaiah meant by going 'down to Egypt' for help is the general principle of acting in our own wisdom and strength without consulting the Lord and looking to him for help. This should not be taken to mean that the Lord would never actually guide people to Egypt, for the issues involved in going to Egypt are not always the same. The fundamental principle is not whether we travel to or from a country, but whether we are following God's guidance in so doing.

For instance, God told Jacob at the time of famine to go down to Egypt with his entire family, to settle where his son Joseph had become a ruler. Also, it was God who eventually called Israel out of Egypt. The Lord told Joseph and Mary to take the infant Jesus to Egypt in order to escape the murderous wrath of Herod, and he alerted Joseph and Mary that it was time to return ('Out of Egypt I called my Son' – see Matt. 2.13–23).

Prototypes once more.

We should also recall that Scripture has positive things to say about Egypt. The prophet Isaiah anticipates a day when Egypt will be a blessing: 'In that day Israel will be the third with Egypt and Assyria, a blessing in the midst of the earth, whom the LORD of hosts has blessed, saying, "Blessed be Egypt my people, and Assyria the work of my hands, and Israel my inheritance"' (Isa. 19.24–25).

# 6

# Abram and Lot

## From Egypt to Bethel – the test of wealth

Abram returns to Bethel and calls 'upon the name of the Lord'. The possessions gained by dubious means in Egypt lead to tension between the herdsmen of Abram and Lot, and eventually to separation. Abram gives Lot the choice as to where to live. Lot chooses the plain of Jordan near Sodom, because it is like the 'garden of the Lord'. Abraham stays in the land occupied by Canaanites. This raises the question of the implications of such choices for location, business, family, children and culture.

God did not abandon Abram because of his denial of his wife. Abram retraced his steps and went back to where the disastrous move started. The narrator reminds us that the altar was 'where his tent had been at the *beginning*, between Bethel and Ai, to the place where he had made an altar at the *first*'. That double emphasis reminds us of the wise advice of C. S. Lewis, who once said that if we take the wrong turn at a crossroads, the only way to make progress is to retrace our steps back to the crossroads and take the right turn. That is the meaning of repentance: returning to bow at the altar of God.

Abram's experience of Egypt had been less Bethel (house of God) and more Ai (heap of ruins). Getting back to the house of God was a positive step that doubtless involved Abram's rueful repentance.

Now he had to face some new challenges that had arisen because of his material wealth. God nowhere says that material goods are bad and that it is wrong or unspiritual to have them, though he does warn of the dangers of setting our trust and hope in them and failing to share them (1 Tim. 6). Wealth can get such a grip that it destroys relationships and takes men and women away from God so that they lose their vision. One wonders if it might have been wealth that side-tracked Abram's father from completing the pilgrimage to the promised land in the first place.

So Abram went up from Egypt, he and his wife and all that he had, and Lot with him, into the Negeb. Now Abram was very rich in livestock, in silver, and in gold. And he journeyed on from the Negeb as far as Bethel to the place where his tent had been at the beginning, between Bethel and Ai, to the place where he had made an altar at the first. And there Abram called upon the name of the LORD. And Lot, who went with Abram, also had flocks and herds and tents, so that the land could not support both of them dwelling together; for their possessions were so great that they could not dwell together, and there was strife between the herdsmen of Abram's livestock and the herdsmen of Lot's livestock. At that time the Canaanites and the Perizzites were dwelling in the land.
(Gen. 13.1–7)

From this and later indications it seems that Abram was a nomadic livestock farmer – a cattle man. In that connection it is interesting that the moon-god Nanna, worshipped in Ur, was regarded as a patron deity of cattle men.

Over the years Abram's companion in travel, his nephew Lot, had amassed large herds and become wealthy in his own right – no doubt helped by Abram. Pressure for pasture space led to tension between his herdsmen and those of Abram. That, in turn, inevitably meant that trouble developed between the two men.

Such tensions are very common in families, believers very much included. There is often someone in a family who thinks (maybe correctly) that they have had a raw deal, especially when it comes to parental inheritance allocation, or favouritism in general – a topic that is particularly prominent in the later account of Joseph.[1]

The Genesis narrator remarks in passing that the Canaanites and Perizzites were still in the land. Perhaps that is meant as a hint to the reader that the moral quality of the negotiations between Abram, Lot and their herdsmen was likely to be scrutinised by the locals.

Once more, the issue had to do with Abram's personal relationships – not with his wife this time, but his nephew. Abram, the older man, took the initiative in trying to sort it out:

Then Abram said to Lot, 'Let there be no strife between you and me, and between your herdsmen and my herdsmen, for we are kinsmen. Is not the whole land before you? Separate yourself from me. If you take the left hand, then I will go to the right, or if you take the right hand, then I will go to the left.'
(Gen. 13.8–9)

This time, Abram rises to the challenge – at least to a certain extent. Magnanimous in the confidence that God has given him the land, he gives Lot the choice on the principle that they are brothers. Abram recognised the importance of kinship in connection with his nephew – the very thing he denied in connection with his wife.

This is an important principle that comes under the spotlight near the beginning of Genesis, when Cain has murdered his brother Abel and, when called to account, cynically says: 'Am I my brother's keeper?'

In 1 Corinthians 6 Paul remonstrates with the church at Corinth, where Christians are failing to recognise the implications of the fact that they are brothers and are taking each other to court.

When one of you has a grievance against another, does he dare go to law before the unrighteous instead of the saints? Or do you not know that the saints will judge the world? And if the world is to be judged by you, are you incompetent to try trivial cases? Do you not know that we are to judge angels? How much more, then, matters pertaining to this life! So if you have such cases, why do you lay them before those who have no standing in the church? I say this to your shame. Can it be that there is no one among you wise enough to settle a dispute between the brothers, but brother goes to law against brother, and that before unbelievers? To have lawsuits at all with one another is already a defeat for you. Why not rather suffer wrong? Why not rather be defrauded? But you yourselves wrong and defraud – even your own brothers!
(1 Cor. 6.1–8)

Nowadays many of us live in increasingly litigious societies, particularly in the West. We need to pause and ask ourselves: do we always have to get our rights? Some people think so, with the result that both in families and in the Church brothers and sisters go to law with each other without any thought of the potential hurt and damage that is highly likely to ensue. Their wrangling usually only succeeds in undermining the credibility of the Church. Some of us have witnessed the tragedy of whole families tearing themselves to pieces over a disputed inheritance, or even over what they imagined their parents' intentions were. A sense of unfairness, if allowed to become rancorous, can be deadly.

Conflict resolution is an important pastoral skill and the Church needs men and women who know how to adjudicate wisely and fairly between disputing parties. And if there are none such to be found, says Paul, why not suffer wrong and be defrauded? That can be hard to do, but there are some things that we just have to let go for the sake of the testimony.

And that seems to have been Abram's attitude here. We cannot help noticing that Lot did not defer to Abram as the man who had been a father to him and, presumably, had helped make him rich. Nor is there any record of them bringing the matter before the Lord. The key factor was kinship – they were brothers.

Abram decided, therefore, to let Lot choose the pasture he wanted:

And Lot lifted up his eyes and saw that the Jordan Valley was well watered everywhere like the garden of the LORD, like the land of Egypt, in the direction of Zoar. (This was before the LORD destroyed Sodom and Gomorrah.) So Lot chose for himself all the Jordan Valley, and Lot journeyed east. Thus they separated from each other. Abram settled in the land of Canaan, while Lot settled among the cities of the valley and moved his tent as far as Sodom. Now the men of Sodom were wicked, great sinners against the LORD.
(Gen. 13.10–13)

Lot chose to settle near Sodom because the region around it looked like the garden of the Lord – an echo of Eden. It was lush grazing for his herds and he could see that it looked like a good business choice. From a commercial perspective it probably was – but there are other perspectives that are much more important for a believer in God, which we are led to think Lot actually was (2 Pet. 2.7).

However, Eden as such no longer existed. It had been invaded by a poisonous defection from God that was very much resident in the cities at the heart of this Eden-like landscape.

One wonders just how much Lot initially knew about what the narrator informs us at this point: that the men of Sodom had a reputation for sexual depravity. It is hard to imagine that Lot knew nothing, as such a reputation could not have remained secret. As he moved nearer to Sodom, he must have had more than a glimmer of its potentially destructive cultural and moral influence on him and his family. It may even be that his wife came from that region, as Jewish tradition suggests.

There is a lesson here. It was very dangerous to move near to Sodom. It still is. These days, Sodom is only a click or two away in cyberspace from any of us and there is a multi-million-dollar industry engaged in attempting to draw us into its orbit.

Reflecting about this in the light of the eventual tragic consequences of his decision for Lot and his family, we might well be inclined to think that this was one situation Abram should not have let go. He would later act swiftly to rescue Lot from physical captivity. Was not moral captivity even worse?

That makes one wonder what Abram would have done if Lot had demurred and given him the first choice of grazing land.

We also notice that although Paul advised letting some things go, like certain financial disputes between believers, he did not suggest that the Corinthians should let sexual transgressions go. On the contrary, he insisted that the church should discipline offenders and expel them in certain cases. In addition, Paul did not regard matters of fundamental doctrine as things that should simply be let go – witness 1 Corinthians 15 on the resurrection. Similarly, Peter did not let the deception perpetrated by Ananias and Sapphira go (see Acts 5.1–11).

Jesus taught that we should not judge, that we be not judged. He warned us to get the mote out of our own eyes before we try to take the plank out of someone else's. But at the same time he told us to beware of false prophets. You cannot do that without judging. We do have to make judgements, and the point is that we need to be sure we are seeing clearly so our judgements are fair.

We also need wisdom to discriminate between what we should let go, even if it hurts us, and what we should confront, even if we find it painful.

Abram does not seem to have judged the issue here carefully enough and it is not hard to imagine that he later regretted letting it go.

Not long afterwards, as we shall see, God tested Abram on this issue in two different ways.

# From Bethel to Mamre

God renews and augments his promise to Abram of land and posterity. Abram moves to Mamre near Hebron and builds another altar there.

It must have been a strange feeling for Abram to find himself without Lot, alone after all those years of living and working together. In terms of immediate family, only his wife Sarai was with him now. She was still childless and getting no younger. With Lot gone, Abram had no potential heir of any kind. Lot must have known that, in accordance with the customs of the time, he would have been the prime candidate to inherit Abram's fortune. Yet there is no record that Abram made any attempt to persuade him to stay, and Lot decided to strike out on his own. Already wealthy, he may have felt that he did not want or need to be beholden to the ageing Abram and his dreams any more. He wanted to be his own man and make his own way in the world.

What now? God appears once more and speaks to Abram about the extent of his inheritance and the number of his progeny:

The LORD said to Abram, after Lot had separated from him, 'Lift up your eyes and look from the place where you are, northwards and southwards and eastwards and westwards, for all the land that you see I will give to you and to your offspring for ever. I will make your offspring as the dust of the earth, so that if one can count the dust of the earth, your offspring also can be counted. Arise, walk through the length and the breadth of the land, for I will give it to you.' So Abram moved his tent and came and settled by the oaks of Mamre, which are at Hebron, and there he built an altar to the LORD. (Gen. 13.14–18)

Abram now does what Lot failed to do. Standing on the commanding heights between Bethel and Ai, by contrast with Lot down in the plain, he allows the Lord to direct his eyes to a spectacular panoramic view of the promised land.

In keeping with the legal proceedings connected with land conveyancing at the time, God then instructed Abram to take a lengthy journey and pace out the land, even though his descendants would not occupy it for centuries to come. Abram once more built an altar to record the fact that the Lord had made such great promises to him. By so doing, Abram made plain that he took these appearances of God as something of permanent value. He wished to have something tangible by which to remember not only that they had happened, but where they had happened.

Abram's two tests so far, coping with famine and want on the one hand and coping with wealth and plenty on the other, may well face us at some time or other. Paul has wise words to say as he responds to the generosity of the church at Philippi:

> I rejoiced in the Lord greatly that now at length you have revived your concern for me. You were indeed concerned for me, but you had no opportunity. Not that I am speaking of being in need, for I have learned in whatever situation I am to be content. I know how to be brought low, and I know how to abound. In any and every circumstance, I have learned the secret of facing plenty and hunger, abundance and need. I can do all things through him who strengthens me. Yet it was kind of you to share my trouble.
> (Phil. 4.10–14)

Paul had known times of want and extreme privation. He had also experienced times of plenty. The secret of Paul's ability to cope with both was his relationship with the Lord. Abram had yet to take that on board properly, but had at least made a start. And, though he had no idea as yet, there was another major test just beyond his horizon.

# The battle of the kings: the test of responsibility

Lot is caught up in a war between a coalition of Babylonian kings and a coalition of Canaanite kings, and is captured. Abram rescues Lot. The king of Sodom tries to get Abram to take the spoil for himself but give up the rescued people to him. Abram is strengthened for the encounter by the sudden intervention of the king-priest Melchizedek.

The narrative now moves to a surprising political level, involving what appears to be an international conflict resulting from an invasion of Canaan by Babylonian forces, which had led to the subjugation of the Canaanites for 12 years. At length, the local kings – petty monarchs each in charge of a single city and its surroundings – rebelled against their Babylonian oppressors and went into battle against them in the Vale of Siddim just south of the Dead Sea:

> Then the king of Sodom, the king of Gomorrah, the king of Admah, the king of Zeboiim, and the king of Bela (that is, Zoar) went out, and they joined battle in the Valley of Siddim with Chedorlaomer king of Elam, Tidal king of Goiim, Amraphel king of Shinar, and Arioch king of Ellasar, four kings against five. Now the Valley of Siddim was full of bitumen pits, and as the kings of Sodom and Gomorrah fled, some fell into them, and the rest fled to the hill country. So the enemy took all the possessions of Sodom and Gomorrah, and all their provisions, and went their way. They also took Lot, the son of Abram's brother, who was dwelling in Sodom, and his possessions, and went their way.
> (Gen. 14.8–12)

Lot had moved to Sodom and, when the local Canaanite coalition was defeated by the Babylonian group, the king of Sodom fled and Lot was captured, and all his possessions were taken. However, one of the escapees from the conflict went and told Abram the Hebrew[2] what had happened.

Abram was once more presented with a decision regarding whether or not he still had responsibility for Lot as 'his brother's keeper'. The matter of moral responsibility appears early on in Genesis in the context of the temptation and Fall in the garden of Eden. Adam blamed Eve for the disaster and Eve blamed the serpent. Neither of them had initially consulted God. As a result sin entered the world, and death through sin, with all its devastating consequences. Subsequently, up to this point in

Genesis, there is little evidence of people taking real moral responsibility for their actions, but rather the exact opposite, if we think of Cain and Lamech and the vast majority of Noah's generation.

That was about to change. Although the text does not tell us whether God said anything about it or not, Abram's conscience must have told him that he was at least partly to blame for Lot's captivity, since he had encouraged him to take the pick of the land without giving him any advice about potential negative consequences.

The narrator then says:

> Then one who had escaped came and told Abram the Hebrew, who was living by the oaks of Mamre the Amorite, brother of Eshcol and of Aner. These were allies of Abram. When Abram heard that his kinsman had been taken captive, he led forth his trained men, born in his house, 318 of them, and went in pursuit as far as Dan. And he divided his forces against them by night, he and his servants, and defeated them and pursued them to Hobah, north of Damascus. Then he brought back all the possessions, and also brought back his kinsman Lot with his possessions, and the women and the people. (Gen. 14.13–16)

Abram, deciding that he was his brother's keeper, took action and set out with an expeditionary force to rescue Lot. We earlier noted that Abram had acquired not only possessions in Haran but people. Robert Alter translates that Abram had *bought* them, which would imply that they were slaves. However, Alter at once points out that 'as subsequent stories in Genesis make clear, this was not the sort of chattel slavery later practiced in North America. These slaves had certain limited rights, could be given great responsibility, and were not thought to lose their personhood.'[3]

The number of such people had grown substantially so that the text speaks of 318 men who were born in Abram's house. They had been trained to form a small but efficient standing army. Abram and his band, supported by his local friends Aner, Eshcol and Mamre and, presumably, their own men (Gen. 14.24), mounted a night attack, routed the Babylonian oppressors, chased them out of the region and rescued

Lot. It was a remarkable victory against what one would imagine were considerable odds. It reminds us of the later victory of Gideon over the Midianites with his army of 300 (Judg. 7). God was clearly involved (Gen. 14.20).

Abram's standing in the region must have been greatly enhanced. Was he beginning to be a blessing to the world?

Before we move on, we note that this is the first occasion in the Bible where a believer is actively involved in battle, and readers will be aware that the matter of the morality of war in the Old Testament is much discussed – in particular in connection with the invasion of Canaan to take possession of it under the leadership of Joshua.

The first thing to point out is that there is a clear discontinuity between the Old and New Testament on this issue. Christ stated the specifically Christian position when he was put on trial by the Roman political and military governor Pilate: 'My kingdom is not of this world. If my kingdom were of this world, my servants would have been fighting, that I might not be delivered over to the Jews. But my kingdom is not from the world' (John 18.36).

Consistent with this the apostle Paul later taught:

For though we walk in the flesh, we are not waging war according to the flesh. For the weapons of our warfare are not of the flesh but have divine power to destroy strongholds. We destroy arguments and every lofty opinion raised against the knowledge of God, and take every thought captive to obey Christ, being ready to punish every disobedience, when your obedience is complete.
(2 Cor. 10.3–6)

However, although there is discontinuity between the Old and the New Testament, there are important continuities. In particular, there is only one God – not two, with one in the Old Testament and one in the New Testament. Nor are there two sets of moral commandments. Each of the Ten Commandments, in one form or another, apart from the Sabbath law, is repeated in the New Testament for Christians.

There is no indication in Genesis that Abraham discussed with God the matter of Lot's capture and what he should do about it. It would appear that he simply decided to do it, although it may be relevant that immediately after his victory he met Melchizedek, who blessed him in the name of God.

The driving out of the Canaanites is a different matter since, as we shall see in Chapter 11, God told Abraham the moral principle behind it when he informed him that the nation he would father would be in Egypt for four centuries: 'And they shall come back here in the fourth generation, for the iniquity of the Amorites is not yet complete' (Gen. 15.16).

In other words, the return of Israel to Canaan to take possession would be an instrument in God's hand to judge the Amorites at the precise time when it was morally deserved. That is spelled out in detail in Deuteronomy: 'Every abominable thing that the LORD hates they have done for their gods, for they even burn their sons and their daughters in the fire to their gods' (Deut. 12.31; 18.10). That is, the tribes that were to be displaced went in for a particularly cruel and brutal form of idolatry that not only violated the first three of the Ten Commandments, but also involved that most horrific of all pagan rites: child sacrifice, one of the most degrading practices ever to exist.

Therefore, the invasion of Canaan was not based on any sense of Israel's moral superiority. Moses explicitly told them of the dangers of such an attitude:

> Do not say in your heart, after the LORD your God has thrust them out before you, 'It is because of my righteousness that the LORD has brought me in to possess this land,' whereas it is because of the wickedness of these nations that the LORD is driving them out before you.
> (Deut. 9.4)

Readers interested in a comprehensive analysis of this topic are referred to Paul Copan's excellent book *Is God a Moral Monster?*[4]

# 7

# Abram and Melchizedek

The Genesis narrator now tells us the sequel to Abram's military success: 'Then he brought back all the possessions, and also brought back his kinsman Lot with his possessions, and the women and the people' (Gen. 14.16). The narrative order in this list is rather striking, and presumably deliberate: (1) possessions, (2) Lot and possessions, (3) Women, (4) people. Things first, people last. It raises the obvious question: do people matter more than things? Abram will have to decide.

> After his return from the defeat of Chedorlaomer and the kings who were with him, the king of Sodom went out to meet him at the Valley of Shaveh (that is, the King's Valley). And Melchizedek king of Salem brought out bread and wine. (He was priest of God Most High.) And he blessed him and said, 'Blessed be Abram by God Most High, Possessor of heaven and earth; and blessed be God Most High, who has delivered your enemies into your hand!'
>
> And Abram gave him a tenth of everything. And the king of Sodom said to Abram, 'Give me the persons, but take the goods for yourself.' But Abram said to the king of Sodom, 'I have lifted my hand to the LORD, God Most High, Possessor of heaven and earth, that I would not take a thread or a sandal strap or anything that is yours, lest you should say, "I have made Abram rich." I will take nothing but what the young men have eaten, and the share of the men who went with me. Let Aner, Eshcol, and Mamre take their share.'
>
> (Gen. 14.17–24)

We are now given an intriguing bird's-eye view of the dramatic dynamics of the developing situation. The narrative depicts the king of Sodom on his way to meet Abram, who by this time was a major power-broker in the region. We are not told whether Abram knew the king was coming, although presumably Abram realised that, by bringing Lot home, he would inevitably have to negotiate with the ruler of the dangerous territory of Sodom.

Abram may well also have been concerned at what might happen, not only to Lot, but to himself, although his success in defeating a coalition of kings would have meant he had little to fear from the one king of Sodom. Nevertheless, Lot would have to be rescued again . . .

Just at this juncture, as if out of nowhere, a mysterious royal figure intercepted Abram: Melchizedek. The impression given by the narrator is that his appearance was no coincidence, but rather a divinely orchestrated intervention. We are told that this Melchizedek was king of Salem and priest of the Most High God. He laid on a welcome spread of bread and wine for Abram and his battle-weary men – although when a king laid on 'bread and wine', it is likely to have been a right regal banquet rather than a snack. Melchizedek showed his superiority by blessing Abram in the name of God, the Possessor of heaven and earth.[1] Abram then in turn honoured him by giving him a tenth of all the spoil.

The king of Sodom may have arrived in time to catch part of Abram's discussion with Melchizedek. There are different ways of understanding what happened next. One is that, even though Abram had retrieved the king of Sodom's property, the king, lacking the grace and magnanimity of Melchizedek, curtly ordered Abram to give him the people and keep the spoil for himself. The other, in the words of Matthew Henry, is:

> Observe the king of Sodom's grateful offer to Abram, Give me the souls, and take thou the substance. Gratitude teaches us to recompense to the utmost of our power, those that have undergone fatigues, run hazards, and been at expense for our service and benefit.[2]

Both interpretations raise the question of relative values. How important are material possessions?

On the first interpretation, would Abram let the people (lit. 'lives'), including Lot, go back under the influence of Sodom? That might have been the attractive thing to do, since they were not Abram's 'people', apart from Lot, who had left him anyway. Furthermore, having to look after additional people might have been a much greater hassle than getting more goods. Was this a chance for Lot to move back in with Abram?

And what would victory in battle do to Abram's character and vision? Was this success in war what God had meant by saying that he would make Abram's name great?

In any event, it was not hard to see that if Abram let the king of Sodom make him rich, an unpleasant payday would inevitably arrive, as Lot, who did compromise with Sodom, eventually found out when it was sadly too late.

As the goods were spoils of war, according to convention at the time they could have been claimed by Abram, and in fact he did claim a tenth of them, which he gave to Melchizedek and also the proportion rightly due to his local supporters, Aner, Eshcol and Mamre.

However, Abram himself insisted on maintaining his independence, not only personally but nationally, and gave the rest to the king of Sodom, retaining nothing for himself. In light of this, one cannot help thinking that Abram could have profited from a conversation with Melchizedek earlier on, before he went to Egypt . . .

Resisting the temptation to be made rich by others is an important life principle – especially for those in the public eye who may be more exposed to such allurements by dint of their position and influence. Entrapment by means of money, sex or power to create dependence is widespread, and not only in politics. Even Christian institutions and individuals may sometimes be guilty of stooping to buy 'loyalty' in subtle ways, as (far too) many scandals involving large sums of money or possessions have shown in recent times. It is a real temptation for the wealthy to use their wealth to create dependence and facilitate manipulation.

Matthew Henry's comment is apposite:

Abram generously refused this offer. He accompanies his refusal with a good reason, Lest thou shouldest say, I have made Abram rich: which would reflect upon the promise and covenant of God, as if He would not have enriched Abraham without the spoils of Sodom. The people of God must, for their credit's sake, take heed of doing any thing that looks mean or mercenary, or that savours of covetousness and self-seeking. Abraham can trust the Possessor of Heaven and earth to provide for him.[3]

And if Abraham could learn to do that, so surely can we.

The New Testament letter to the Hebrews draws our attention to the meaning of the name Melchizedek: 'king [*melekh*] of righteousness [*tsadiq*]': or 'my king [*melchi*] is righteous'. Also, the name of the city over which he ruled, Salem (*shalom*), means 'peace'. Salem is, of course, part of the name of Jerusalem. No comment is made as to whether these two cities are the same, although they may well have been, as the King's Valley is mentioned in 2 Samuel 18.18 as the place near Jerusalem where the tomb of Absalom was situated.

The juxtaposition of the name of the king and that of his city serve to remind us that moral integrity is essential to harmony. It is as if we are being given a strong hint that there is no true peace without righteousness. That is surely a message that should be blazoned across the world today, where, again and again, disastrous attempts are made to resolve conflicts (or build utopias) without regard to moral considerations.

The theme of righteousness is foundational to biblical thought. The root of the Hebrew word for it is an Aramaic term meaning 'straight, even, speaking the truth' and so it refers to moral characteristics of uprightness, integrity, truthfulness, justice and transparency in thought, word and deed, both privately and publicly.

This incident in Abram's life has to do with the relationship of peace to righteousness. Abram tried to restore peace and harmony by resolving a bitter conflict between his herdsmen and those of Lot. They decided to separate – a tactic that worked initially. Then Lot was captured by a coalition of warlords, and that led to Abram getting mixed up in international strife and having to use force to rescue Lot.

That done, the next issue for Abram would not be so much peace but righteousness. Would he find the courage to do the right thing? Up to this point Abram had signally failed. He had been duplicitous in regard to his wife in Egypt. By not doing the right thing by her, his wealth had increased a great deal and had become a problem. He had also failed to steer Lot away from seductive Sodom.

Did Abram talk over matters of peace and righteousness with Melchizedek? Did the latter explain to him that not all sources of wealth are righteous: that the only safe thing in the end was to realise that God, the Possessor of heaven and earth, was the ultimate source of true wealth? Did Melchizedek also warn Abram that the king of Sodom was about to tempt him with a glittering offer that had the potential to increase his wealth even more?

We saw earlier that Abram had grown up in a glorious civilisation and culture that took particular pride in its magnificent cities. Was it that Abram had thought about cities and their organization, had seen the problems of city rule in trying to preserve peace and control crime and corruption? Was it that he had begun to wonder whether there was an ideal kind of city that was both righteous and peaceful? And now he meets a king of righteousness who reigns in a city of peace. Was this another pointer from God that moved Abram forward in his quest for a city that had foundations whose builder and maker was God?

Melchizedek was an important figure. He was the first person in the Bible to be called a priest – a person who deals with sacred things on behalf of others. He predated by a long time the Israelite Levitical priesthood that would eventually be established at the time of Moses at God's instigation.

Melchizedek's designation as 'priest of the Most High God' uses a term for God (El Elyon) that appears here for the first time in the biblical text. It occurs four times in this short section. Both Melchizedek and Abram say that the Most High God is the possessor of heaven and earth. Scholars tell us that El is the word for the supreme god of the Canaanites and therefore suggests that Melchizedek was a pagan priest. Translator Robert Alter adds that the two terms El Elyon 'are also plain Hebrew words that mean "God the Most High" and elsewhere are used separately or (once) together as designations of the God of Israel. Whatever Melchizedek's theology, Abram elegantly co-ops him for monotheism by using El Elyon in its orthodox Israelite sense (verse 22) when he addresses the king of Sodom.'[4]

However, it is easy to read this text under the influence of the widespread evolutionary assumption that polytheism was the primitive state of religion and that monotheism, a higher form of religion, must have come later. I do not find this convincing. Theodorus van Baaren, Professor of the Science of Religions at the University of Groningen, says: 'There exists no historical material to prove that one system of belief is older than the other.'[5]

Records of monotheism in other cultures go back to the time of Pharaoh Akhenaten in Egypt, around 1300 BC. Here, for example, is part of the Great Hymn to Aten: 'O sole god, like whom there is no other! Thou didst create the world according to thy desire, Whilst thou wert alone: All men, cattle, and wild beasts . . . The lord of all of them, wearying (himself) with them, The lord of every land, rising for them . . .'[6]

It surely could well be that Melchizedek was a monotheist directed by the true God of Israel to help a fellow believer. If that was indeed the case, it is fascinating to think that Abram discovered that there existed another person who had independently come to believe in the God of heaven. Maybe that awesome discovery turned Melchizedek's act of hospitality into an unexpectedly rich feast of the fellowship of believers. In any case, it is hard to imagine that their conversation was a brief and casual chat, but rather a deep meeting of minds.

As with so much of Scripture, how we wish we had more information. It is hard to go any further than this based on the Genesis text alone. However, Melchizedek is mentioned once more in the Old Testament text, this time by King David in one of his most famous psalms – Psalm 110:

The LORD says to my Lord:
  'Sit at my right hand,
until I make your enemies your footstool.'
. . .
The LORD has sworn
  and will not change his mind,
'You are a priest for ever
  after the order of Melchizedek.'
(Ps. 110.1, 4)

Up to this point in Scripture the only order of priests was the Levitical priesthood instituted by Moses. So what was David talking about when he referred to another, more ancient order? More importantly, perhaps, to whom did David's words apply?

Jewish expositors appear to have real difficulty with the statement with which the psalm begins. Its meaning seems to have remained obscure and unsettled until one day, around a thousand years later in Jerusalem, Jesus of Nazareth got into a discussion with some scholars about the identity of the Messiah:

> Now while the Pharisees were gathered together, Jesus asked them a question, saying, 'What do you think about the Christ? Whose son is he?' They said to him, 'The son of David.' He said to them, 'How is it then that David, in the Spirit, calls him Lord, saying, "The Lord said[7] to my Lord, Sit at my right hand, until I put your enemies under your feet"? If then David calls him Lord, how is he his son?' And no one was able to answer him a word, nor from that day did anyone dare to ask him any more questions.
> (Matt. 22.41–46)

The logic is compelling. Jesus elicited from the Pharisees, a conservative group of Jewish religious scholars, that they believed the Messiah to be a descendant of David – a son of David. They also did not dispute Jesus' assertion that David was speaking of Messiah, calling him 'my Lord'. He therefore pressed the point: how could David call Messiah (his son) his Lord? That would have contradicted all Jewish beliefs about priority and rank. The rank of Messiah was clearly indicated by God's invitation recorded in the psalm that Messiah should sit at his right hand. They could not answer. Jesus' question put a complete stop to all further enquiry.

It also became clear later, when Jesus appeared before the high priest, how the Jewish authorities understood the idea of sitting at God's right hand. They demanded Jesus' crucifixion for blasphemy when he explicitly told them that he himself would one day occupy that position.

Over the years I have asked a number of Jewish acquaintances the same question about Psalm 110, and the answers have usually been unsatisfactory evasions like 'our rabbis are still working on it'.

Some expositors accuse Christians of misinterpretation in that they correctly recognise the first word translated 'Lord' in the statement to be *Yahweh* (God). However, they, again correctly, point out that the second word translated 'Lord' is *Adonai*. The word means 'my master' or 'my lord'. It may be used both of humans and God. It is used as a term of polite respect (in modern Hebrew, for 'sir') and in connection with leadership roles, as for example by Joseph when he says that God had made him lord over Pharaoh's house (Gen. 45.8). It is used for the first time to address God by Abram in Genesis 15.2 and it frequently occurs thereafter to describe God with respect, as sovereign ruler and almighty master.

Psalm 110 speaks of Messiah sitting at the right hand of God. Jesus' argument shows from the Old Testament that the promised Messiah would turn out to be human – yes, a descendant of Abraham and David, but more than human, destined to sit at God's right hand. There is a hint here of the doctrine of the Trinity.

Peter took up this argument for another purpose at the climax of his Pentecost sermon in Acts 2.34–35 when he made the self-evident but powerful observation that, since David did not ascend into the heavens, he could not have been talking about himself, but about the Messiah, when he said: 'The LORD said to my Lord, Sit at my right hand, until I make your enemies your footstool.' This allowed Peter confidently to announce the most earth-shattering good news the world has ever heard: 'Let all the house of Israel therefore know for certain that God has made him both Lord and Christ, this Jesus whom you crucified' (v. 36).

Three thousand people responded and the Christian Church came into being.

# The provision of divine help: Jesus as our High Priest

Whoever Melchizedek actually was in historical terms, and in spite of the brevity of the Genesis record of his encounter with Abram, he is of pivotal importance in the wider biblical narrative. For when explaining the nature of the assurance that believers may have in Christ, the letter to the Hebrews says:

We have this as a sure and steadfast anchor of the soul, a hope that enters into the inner place behind the curtain, where Jesus has gone as a forerunner on our behalf, having become a high priest for ever after the order of Melchizedek.

For this Melchizedek, king of Salem, priest of the Most High God, met Abraham returning from the slaughter of the kings and blessed him, and to him Abraham apportioned a tenth part of everything. He is first, by translation of his name, king of righteousness, and then he is also king of Salem, that is, king of peace. He is without father or mother or genealogy, having neither beginning of days nor end of life, but resembling the Son of God he continues a priest for ever. (Heb. 6.19—7.3)

Here, citing Psalm 110, Jesus is called a High Priest 'after the order of Melchizedek'. In the biblical account there are two orders of priests, that of Aaron and Levi, instituted in Exodus to take charge of Israel's worship and service in connection with the tabernacle – and the prior one of Melchizedek, although Genesis 14 makes no mention of Melchizedek being the founder of a priestly order.

So what then is this strange 'order of Melchizedek'? Hebrews understands it as follows. It tells us that Melchizedek 'is without father or mother or genealogy, having neither beginning of days nor end of life'. It may seem at first glance that Melchizedek slipped into this world from an eternal parallel realm – an extremely odd claim to make.

However, the simplest way to understand it is as most scholars actually do. They observe that Genesis is a book where all the prominent figures are given a genealogy, their death is described and their age at death is recorded. Yet no such details are provided for the important figure of Melchizedek – a very striking omission. How can we explain this?

Surely not by thinking literalistically and imagining that Melchizedek didn't actually have a father or a mother? It would rather seem, in light of what Hebrews says, that Genesis deliberately doesn't mention his parents, nor does it record any beginning or end to Melchizedek's life. What could conceivably be the point in doing that?

Well, as far as Scripture is concerned, Melchizedek suddenly appears at a point where his ministry is needed and then disappears. Therefore, as Hebrews informs us, he can function as a thought model or prototype to help us understand what it means that Jesus is an eternal High Priest, available to help in all times and places of need.

In other words, the order of Melchizedek is vastly different from that of Levi – the latter contained thousands of priests through the generations, the former only two: the original Melchizedek and the Lord Jesus, the Messiah.

I am sure that many of us when facing a testing decision have had the experience of someone coming alongside us and giving us crucial advice. Yet mostly our experience is that we wish someone would suddenly appear and do that – but it doesn't happen. That is especially the case when we suddenly wish that perhaps our parents or a trusted friend were available, but they passed away years ago – if only they were alive still. That is the idea here. Melchizedek did just that for Abram, and the Lord Jesus will do it for us. For he is alive still. His life is indissoluble.

You ask me: do you really believe that – as a scientist in the twenty-first century? Come on! This is simply an obscure text of uncertain provenance in an ancient religious document framed in pious language that comforts because of its elevated ideas, whereas in practice it amounts to nothing more than illusory psychological self-deception, utterly irrelevant to the contemporary world...

Yes, I do really believe it as a scientist in the twenty-first century, both as an objective fact out there and as something relevant to everyday life.

Let us first ascertain the facts. The first one is Melchizedek's exalted status. That status is highlighted by the fact that Abram was blessed by him and not the other way round, and that Abram gave him a ten per cent tithe from his spoils. Hebrews says:

> See how great this man was to whom Abraham the patriarch gave a tenth of the spoils! And those descendants of Levi who receive the priestly office have a commandment in the law to take tithes from the people, that is, from their brothers, though these also are descended from Abraham. But this man who does not have his descent from them received tithes from Abraham and blessed him who had the promises. It is beyond dispute that the inferior is blessed by the superior. In the one case tithes are received by mortal

men, but in the other case, by one of whom it is testified that he lives. One might even say that Levi himself, who receives tithes, paid tithes through Abraham, for he was still in the loins of his ancestor when Melchizedek met him.

(Heb. 7.4–10)

As described in the books of Exodus and Leviticus, Moses later instituted a priesthood based on Abram's great-grandson, Jacob's son Levi. The Levitical priests were given the right to exact a ten per cent tithe from their fellow Israelites, from which they lived. Yet their ancestor Abram paid a tenth to another priest who was not (obviously!) from the tribe of Levi.

To Western ears, arguing that Levi also effectively paid the tithe because he was still in the loins of Abram sounds quaint. However, it is nonetheless perfectly valid in Hebrew thought as evidence that the priesthood of Melchizedek is superior to that of the later priesthood of Levi. That is important because the Levitical priesthood proved inadequate, as is indicated in the next verse: 'Now if perfection had been attainable through the Levitical priesthood (for under it the people received the law), what further need would there have been for another priest to arise after the order of Melchizedek, rather than one named after the order of Aaron?' (v. 11).

It is perhaps difficult for Christians to understand how revolutionary the suggestion of introducing a new priesthood would have seemed to Jews after centuries of familiarity with the God-given Levitical system set up by Moses. It must have appeared to be a shocking and unacceptable affront to one of their core beliefs when the Christian apostles claimed it. How could such a change be legal, let alone correct?

To get across the necessity of a new order of priesthood, the writer to the Hebrews proceeds very carefully, taking account of the precise details in order to establish the legality of the appointment of Melchizedek from a biblical perspective. A change in the law was a pre-requisite:

For when there is a change in the priesthood, there is necessarily a change in the law as well. For the one of whom these things are spoken belonged to another tribe, from which no one has ever served at the altar. For it is evident that our Lord was descended from Judah, and in connection with that tribe Moses said nothing about priests.

This becomes even more evident when another priest arises in the likeness of Melchizedek, who has become a priest, not on the basis of a legal requirement concerning bodily descent, but by the power of an indestructible life. For it is witnessed of him,

'You are a priest for ever,
    after the order of Melchizedek.'

For on the one hand, a former commandment is set aside because of its weakness and uselessness (for the law made nothing perfect); but on the other hand, a better hope is introduced, through which we draw near to God.
(Heb. 7.12–19)

The change was so important that God sealed it by adding a solemn oath:

And it was not without an oath. For those who formerly became priests were made such without an oath, but this one was made a priest with an oath by the one who said to him:

'The Lord has sworn
    and will not change his mind,
"You are a priest for ever."'

This makes Jesus the guarantor of a better covenant.

The former priests were many in number, because they were prevented by death from continuing in office, but he holds his priesthood permanently, because he continues for ever. Consequently, he is able to save to the uttermost those who draw near to God through him, since he always lives to make intercession for them.

For it was indeed fitting that we should have such a high priest, holy, innocent, unstained, separated from sinners, and exalted above the heavens. He has no need, like those high priests, to offer sacrifices daily, first for his own sins and then for those of the people, since he did this once for all when he offered up himself. For the law appoints men in their weakness as high priests, but the word of the oath, which came later than the law, appoints a Son who has been made perfect for ever.

Now the point in what we are saying is this: we have such a high priest, one who is seated at the right hand of the throne of the Majesty in heaven.
(Heb. 7.19—8.1)

Readers who are interested in more detailed analysis of this rich text might wish to consult David Gooding's excellent exposition, *An Unshakeable Kingdom*.[8] It is sufficient for our purposes here to note that the point of the mention of Melchizedek in the New Testament is to give authentication – particularly, but not only, to Jewish people – that a different order of priesthood relating to the Messiah was not a Christian innovation but had been clearly predicted in the Old Testament (Ps. 110). We can therefore accept that our High Priest is the risen and ascended Lord Jesus who 'ever lives to make intercession for us'.

This means that just as Melchizedek was there at the right time to support and strengthen Abram in his encounter, so the Lord Jesus is there to do the same for us. The letter to the Hebrews encourages us to come to him for help:

and since we have a great priest over the house of God, let us draw near with a true heart in full assurance of faith, with our hearts sprinkled clean from an evil conscience and our bodies washed with pure water. Let us hold fast the confession of our hope without wavering, for he who promised is faithful.
(Heb. 10.21–23)

In order to appreciate the practical implications of all this we need to set it in the original context of the letter to the Hebrews. It was written to Christian believers of Jewish heritage who were under increasing pressure from Jewish authorities to give up what those authorities held to be the blasphemous claim that Jesus was Messiah, the Son of God, and turn back to the old Jewish ways and priesthood. That pressure had turned ugly:

> But recall the former days when, after you were enlightened, you endured a hard struggle with sufferings, sometimes being publicly exposed to reproach and affliction, and sometimes being partners with those so treated. For you had compassion on those in prison, and you joyfully accepted the plundering of your property, since you knew that you yourselves had a better possession and an abiding one. Therefore do not throw away your confidence, which has a great reward. For you have need of endurance, so that when you have done the will of God you may receive what is promised. For,

> 'Yet a little while,
> and the coming one will come and will not delay;
> but my righteous one shall live by faith,
> and if he shrinks back,
> my soul has no pleasure in him.'

> But we are not of those who shrink back and are destroyed, but of those who have faith and preserve their souls.
> (Heb. 10.32–39)

The writer encourages these beleaguered Christians to stand firm in their faith in Jesus as Messiah the Son of God. They have had to face something very similar to Abram – a choice between their material possessions and Christ. They have shown their mettle by holding on to their faith in the Lord Jesus as Messiah, but the pressure has clearly ramped up and the writer urges them again to be confident as they, like Abraham, have been promised an eternal reward.

In great detail the writer compares and contrasts the old Jewish system instituted by Moses, with its two-party covenant, priests, sanctuary, sacrifices and ritual, with what Jesus has brought in: a new priesthood, a new sanctuary, a new sacrifice – all of which are infinitely superior to the old in every way. If only these beleaguered believers could grasp this, the temptation to abandon the new and revert to the old would lose its appeal.

Hebrews tells us that there was and still is today a superbly adequate resource to help us maintain our faith in the Lord. Sadly, in my experience, this important issue is all too seldom discussed among Christian believers, who are left unaware of the protection available to them. Believers usually readily understand that the Lord Jesus made provision for the guilt of their sins on the cross, that he rose for their justification and that he sent the Holy Spirit to indwell them and develop their new life to change their character and empower their public witness.

But many people are not so sure about the stability of their own faith in God – is there any provision for maintaining that? Some think that faith is a gift given by God to those whom he arbitrarily chooses, so that one either has it or one doesn't – and nothing can be done about it. That view can easily promote an unbiblical determinism. It does not sit well with the fact that God will one day judge people for not believing, as it is hard to see how it can be morally justifiable to condemn people for not doing what they couldn't do – that is, believe.

Others think very differently. They hold that one of God's gracious gifts to all men and women as creatures made in his image is the capacity to believe and thus form genuine relationships, in particular by opening their hearts and minds to put their whole trust in Christ, thereby receiving the magnificent gift of salvation as something that they could never merit or deserve. Since I have written a book on these issues,[9] I shall content myself at this point by saying that I believe Scripture teaches the latter view of those I have just outlined. We shall later see some more evidence for this in Abraham's life and experience.

What, then, can be said about the maintenance of our faith? I believed in Jesus yesterday and I believe in him today, but will I still believe in him tomorrow? After all, I don't know what might happen tomorrow to threaten or even imperil my faith in Christ. Perhaps I am a young person at school and some classmates, or teachers even, ridicule my Christian commitment. Or they try to force me into looking at something very questionable on the internet, or get me involved in online gambling or drugs, or join in bullying another pupil, or making false and horrible statements about someone on

Facebook. The list of pressures on young people is endless. How can they find the strength and courage to face these kinds of things tomorrow and come through with their faith in Jesus intact?

Not only young people, but adults. The Christian students who think they will be done down in the eyes of their professors if they even casually admit to church attendance. The temptation to join in questionable activities because everyone is doing it and Christian standards are old fashioned. The colleagues at work who cut corners to improve the bottom line and ask you to join in for 'the sake of the company', with the unspoken threat of losing your job or being passed over for promotion if you don't.

How are you going to stand for truth tomorrow with all of this awaiting you? It can be very daunting.

Long ago, Melchizedek was sent by God to minister to Abram as a high priest. The New Testament tells us that, in a similar way, Jesus now acts as our High Priest. In particular, he supports us with *his* prayers.

Let us watch him as he helps Peter in this way. At the Last Supper in Jerusalem, Jesus said to him:

> 'Simon, Simon, behold, Satan demanded to have you, that he might sift you like wheat, but I have prayed for you that your faith may not fail. And when you have turned again, strengthen your brothers.' Peter said to him, 'Lord, I am ready to go with you both to prison and to death.' Jesus said, 'I tell you, Peter, the cock will not crow this day, until you deny three times that you know me.'
> (Luke 22.31–34)

Peter clearly thought his commitment to Jesus was strong, and asserted his readiness – as did all the others – to go with Jesus to prison and death, if necessary (see Mark 14.31). Jesus knew otherwise. He told Peter several things in advance in order to prepare him for an ordeal he did not expect.

Jesus told him that behind the scenes Satan (= the Accuser) was homing in on the disciples. He had, apparently, requested permission to 'sift them as wheat'. This shows that he, although powerful and dangerous, cannot simply do what he likes. 'Sifting wheat' is an odd metaphor in the context, since it speaks of a violent shaking, but one that is designed to do good work in separating valuable grain from all the husks and useless things that come with it. But it was what was going to happen to Peter – a profound shaking.

Jesus predicted that, far from standing by him, Peter would deny him three times over. Luke describes what happened after the arrest of Jesus in the garden of Gethsemane:

> Then they seized him and led him away, bringing him into the high priest's house, and Peter was following at a distance. And when they had kindled a fire in the middle of the courtyard and sat down together, Peter sat down among them. Then a servant girl, seeing him as he sat in the light and looking closely at him, said, 'This man also was with him.'
> (Luke 22.54–56)

She was right. Peter was now under pressure to stand with the truth. 'But he denied it, saying, "Woman, I do not know him."' (Luke 22.57)

He got a second opportunity. 'And a little later someone else saw him and said, "You also are one of them." But Peter said, "Man, I am not."' (Luke 22.58)

Failed again. Yet he got a third chance: 'And after an interval of about an hour still another insisted, saying, "Certainly this man also was with him, for he too is a Galilean." But Peter said, "Man, I do not know what you are talking about."' (Luke 22.59–60)

Failed again, for the third and final time.

> And immediately, while he was still speaking, the cock crowed. And the Lord turned and looked at Peter. And Peter remembered the saying of the Lord, how he had said to him, 'Before the cock crows today, you will deny me three times.' And he went out and wept bitterly.
> (Luke 22.60–62)

David Gooding takes up the story:

> Peter got up and in great distress fled out into the cover of the night. But now the darkness would never swallow him up completely:

the link between Christ and him had been maintained, and Peter's faith in the truth of the word of Christ was actually at this moment stronger than ever. He had proved Christ's word to be true. And if Christ had been right about the denial, right too even about the detail of the cock crowing, he would be right in regard to the rest of his prophecy (see 22:31–32): Peter would turn again and strengthen his brethren. The memory of that assured statement saved Peter from ruinous despair. The intercessions of the king-priest had secured for Peter that his faith did not fail (see 22:32). They will do the same for every believer on every battlefield of life.[10]

This is how our great High Priest saves a man even in spite of himself. This was where, a few weeks later, Peter got the courage to stand in front of a large crowd in Jerusalem and accuse them of doing something similar to what he himself had done – denying the holy one, Jesus the Messiah.

We should note exactly what Jesus prayed for – Peter's faith. He did not pray for Peter's testimony, nor his control of his tongue, nor for his nerve. Only his faith. In fact, the other things did fail. Yet Peter's faith did not, as we have just seen.

According to the Gospel of John, chapter 17, Jesus' statement that he had already prayed for Peter was followed by what is often called Jesus' high priestly prayer, in which he committed himself to pray for all who believed in him:

'Holy Father, keep them in your name, which you have given me, that they may be one, even as we are one. While I was with them, I kept them in your name, which you have given me. I have guarded them, and not one of them has been lost except the son of destruction, that the Scripture might be fulfilled. But now I am coming to you, and these things I speak in the world, that they may have my joy fulfilled in themselves. I have given them your word, and the world has hated them because they are not of the world, just as I am not of the world. I do not ask that you take them out of the world, but that you keep them from the evil one. They are not of the world, just as I am not of the world. Sanctify them in the truth; your word is truth. As you sent me into the world, so I have sent them into the world. And for their sake I consecrate myself, that they also may be sanctified in truth.

'I do not ask for these only, but also for those who will believe in me through their word . . .'
(John 17.11–20)

I am one of those – and so are many of you, my readers. He prays for us.

This wonderful provision is reinforced in the letter to the Hebrews, which encourages believers to hold on to their faith because Jesus their High Priest will intercede for them as he did for Peter. Praying that we might hold on and be kept from the evil one is the heart of our High Priest's ministry. We should be thankful for it every day.

The king of Sodom was an evil man and no doubt Melchizedek's intervention saved Abram from his dangerous clutches. The ill-gotten riches of Sodom could so easily have become a root of all kinds of evil for Abram. In any case, there was no need for Abram to take them, since God was the possessor of everything in heaven and on earth.

Thinking about the king of Sodom, who was all geared up to tell Abram what to do with the spoils of war and the people he had rescued, reminds me of the occasion when someone in a crowd said to Jesus, 'Teacher, tell my brother to divide the inheritance with me.' Jesus declined and gave a solemn warning to all his hearers: 'Take care, and be on your guard against all covetousness, for one's life does not consist in the abundance of one's possessions' (see Luke 12.13–15).

The word translated 'abundance' here means 'excess'. Jesus is saying that life does not consist in what we have *above and beyond what we need*. He drives the point home by telling a parable about a rich man who was planning how to store his vast wealth for years to come when God suddenly told him that his life had run its course: '"Fool! This night your soul is required of you, and the things you have prepared, whose will they be?" So is the one who lays up treasure for himself and is not rich towards God' (Luke 12.20–21). The man's excess goods could not buy him a further hour of life. Nor could worry about them do any good – a point Jesus also made in Matthew 6. That context is also relevant to Abram's story. Abram had put a great deal of work into building up livestock and material possessions, as well as hiring many servants and retainers.

As we shall see below, Abram needed to learn that there was no future in possessing an abundance of goods if you had no heir to leave them to. What shall it profit a man if he gains the whole world and loses his own soul? Life trumps goods.

It appears reasonable to think that Melchizedek effectively challenged Abram's attitude to goods, but also the motivation behind all his acquisition. Think of it as follows. As we have seen, one possible translation of Melchizedek's name is 'my king is righteous'. If we put the ideas of rule, righteousness and attitude to goods together, we are immediately reminded of our Lord's teaching in the Sermon on the Mount in Matthew 6 on the matter of motivation for our daily work. Jesus says that we are not to worry:

> '"What shall we eat?" or "What shall we drink?" or "What shall we wear?" For the Gentiles seek after all these things, and your heavenly Father knows that you need them all. But seek first the kingdom of God and his righteousness, and all these things will be added to you.' (Matt. 6.31–33)

Why does Jesus say that 'the Gentiles seek after all these things'? Don't we all? Well, yes, and we all certainly need them to live. God our heavenly Father recognises that. However, those who do not know God – and, alas, many who do – make these material things their prime goal in life and their main motivation for working. Jesus' disciples are told that their goal should be different. They should seek first the kingdom of God and his righteousness, and the things would be added. In other words, for the believer, material things are by-products of work, not its goal. What is the goal?

It is to seek the kingdom of God. The word 'kingdom' here does not mean a realm ruled by God; it means God's rule itself. So seeking the kingdom of God means actively seeking God's rule in my life – living out the fundamental Christian confession that Jesus is Lord. It means living righteously by his standards. Here we have it in one word: Melchizedek – my king is righteous. As Paul puts it elsewhere: 'For the kingdom of God is not a matter of eating and drinking but of righteousness and peace and joy in the Holy Spirit. Whoever thus serves Christ is acceptable to God and approved by men' (Rom. 14.17–18).

Melchizedek's very name constituted a challenge to Abram to live righteously and experience the invigorating rule of the Lord that made life meaningful and worthwhile. If he or we lose that goal and make the by-products into our goal – well, the incident with Pharaoh shows what happens.

In any case, what use was wealth compared with 'lives'? More possessions could not fill the son-shaped vacuum in Abram's heart that had caused him so many years' heartache. The older he got, the more any hope of producing new life faded. He refused to be enriched by the king of Sodom, even though he had rescued him and his people from the invaders from the East.

What is left hanging by this incident is: did Abram accede to the king of Sodom's request to give him the people? The succeeding chapters will show that Lot and his family went back to Sodom – moving from one form of captivity to another. In any case, what could Abram have done with a large population of citizens of the kind that gave Sodom its horrific reputation?

Presumably, the point is not that Abram kept the people, but that he resolutely refused to increase his wealth by his rescue.

It is important to balance this by recalling that Scripture makes it clear there are good uses to which wealth can be put. Paul gave advice to the wealthy Christians in the prosperous city of Ephesus through his young protege Timothy, as follows:

As for the rich in this present age, charge them not to be haughty, nor to set their hopes on the uncertainty of riches, but on God, who richly provides us with everything to enjoy. They are to do good, to be rich in good works, to be generous and ready to share, thus storing up treasure for themselves as a good foundation for the future, so that they may take hold of that which is truly life. (1 Tim. 6.17–19)

Abraham was looking for the city with foundations and he was learning about what they were. This matter of having a healthy attitude towards wealth was one of them – using it, if God has given it to us, to lay 'a good foundation for the future', investing money, energy and time in God's kingdom in a thousand different ways.[11]

How shall we know how to do that? Just as Abraham was advised by Melchizedek, so we have the privilege of approaching a much greater High Priest, the Lord Jesus, and consulting him about investment opportunities in the world to come.

I cannot help wondering if Lot was with Abraham as he went to meet the king of Sodom. Did Lot meet Melchizedek? If he did, it is clear that he learned nothing from the encounter. Lot missed the opportunity and, placing himself at the centre of his own world, headed back to Sodom, invested his wealth there and lost everything in the fire of God's judgement, as we shall see later on.

We all know, don't we, just how easy it is to invest in Sodom – our time with questionable films on television and the internet, our money on visiting questionable places where we place ourselves in moral danger with the company we keep. The sex industry is a multi-billion-dollar commercial juggernaut. We need a powerful High Priest to avoid its destructive intentions. And the good news is that there is one who ever lives to help us in time of need.

# 8

# Justification by faith

God speaks once more to Abram and promises him great reward. Abram is concerned about his childlessness. God once more promises him his own physical heir, and offspring as numerous as the stars. Abram believes God and his faith is counted as righteousness. God confirms this promise with a covenant, but predicts that Abram's seed will spend a long time as slaves in Egypt before eventually coming out with great wealth and attaining the promised inheritance.

> After these things the word of the LORD came to Abram in a vision: 'Fear not, Abram, I am your shield; your reward shall be very great.' But Abram said, 'O Lord GOD, what will you give me, for I continue childless, and the heir of my house is Eliezer of Damascus?' And Abram said, 'Behold, you have given me no offspring, and a member of my household will be my heir.' And behold, the word of the LORD came to him: 'This man shall not be your heir; your very own son shall be your heir.' And he brought him outside and said, 'Look towards heaven, and number the stars, if you are able to number them.' Then he said to him, 'So shall your offspring be.' And he believed the LORD, and he counted it to him as righteousness. (Gen. 15.1–6)

Abram had plenty of material wealth, but he didn't have a son and heir with whom to share the blessings that God had showered upon him. He had already been 25 years in the land and God had already spoken to him three times about his offspring, yet he and Sarai were still childless even though his household was no doubt full of the children born to his servants.

God recognised his as yet unspoken turmoil. His first words to Abram were 'Fear not'. Abram is the first but by no means the only person in

Scripture to be told by the Lord not to be afraid. Hearing God's voice say 'Fear not' has brought comfort to untold millions – because God has the capacity to bring peace and calm into troubled hearts and minds.

And now for the first time in the Genesis record Abram addresses God. Their conversation reveals a great deal about Abram's state of mind. God's mention of reward – an everyday term for wages paid for work done – gave Abram an opportunity to speak about what was troubling him.

Conversations with another person on delicate issues are very often easier to conduct and more productive if the other person mentions something related to the topic that you can pick up on rather than you diving in without warning. You may need to wait. Waiting for the Lord's timing – 'waiting on the Lord' – is an important biblical discipline.

Abram expressed to God his heart's deepest concern. What use to him were material possessions as compensation – if that was what God had in mind – when he had no children and therefore no future? He then referred to an ancient law that allowed a servant to be legally adopted as the heir of a childless couple. Under this regulation, Abram's chief steward Eliezer, who came from Damascus, could inherit. Abram could see that happening and it was not an outcome he desired. He was full of fears for the future, particularly that life, in terms of having children, seemed to be irretrievably passing him by.

God told him once again that he would have a son of his very own. He invited Abram to step outside his tent and turn his eyes to the myriad stars that shone in the brilliant night sky. 'Count them if you can,' said God, 'for your offspring will be as numerous as that.' Some Jewish traditions hold that Abram was trained in astronomy – a subject that was of importance and well developed in Mesopotamia at that time. He may well have been fascinated by the night sky for many years. And now the Creator of that sky was addressing him!

On a clear night, at most 5,000 individual stars can be seen with the naked eye, as well as objects like the fuzzy outline of the Andromeda Galaxy, with its estimated 100 billion stars, 2.5 million light years away!

What was Abram to say? He had been promised a child at least four times that we know of during the many years of his nomadic existence up to this point. Could he really go on believing such promises in the absence of any corroborating evidence? We know little of his thought processes, but we do know the conclusion to which he came. He decided, in spite of all appearances, to put his trust in what God had said.

Earlier in Genesis we learn that sin entered the world when human beings trusted the words of a creature rather than those of the Creator. As a result, distrust of God became a mighty river through history, poisoning the minds of millions. Now one man, Abram, demonstrates the attitude that reverses the flow. He believes what God says. He humbly accepts it in spite of all evidence to the contrary. The author of Genesis spells out the far-reaching implications of it by commenting that his faith was counted to him as righteousness.

We have already seen the importance that God attached to training Abram in righteousness – that is, in right living, doing what was upright and virtuous. At this important juncture in his life, the right thing to do was to put his trust in God. We saw earlier that the Hebrew root word for faith, *aman*, conveys the notion of trust and firmness, particularly trust in a person. This short statement connecting Abram's faith in God and righteousness lies at the heart of the central biblical doctrine of justification[1] by faith. The parallel statement in Habakkuk 2.4 is: 'the righteous shall live by his faith'. It uses for 'faith' the Hebrew word *emunah*, which is related to *aman*.

Abram's faith in God is the key to understanding the significance of his life and its application to others. In order to appreciate it fully, we need first of all to think about what faith itself means.

## What is faith?

The account of the call of Abram in Genesis 12 does not explicitly use the word 'faith'. In keeping with Hebrew narrative style, instead of telling us what was in the man's mind, it describes what he did: 'So Abram went, as the LORD had told him' (v. 4). Of course, he would only have done so if he had believed what he heard the voice say to him. His faith is evidenced, as all faith in God ought to be, by the action that springs from it.

However, the letter to the Hebrews in the New Testament makes explicit reference to Abram's faith in connection with God's call to him:

By faith Abraham obeyed when he was called to go out to a place that he was to receive as an inheritance. And he went out, not knowing where he was going. By faith he went to live in the land of promise, as in a foreign land, living in tents with Isaac and Jacob, heirs with him of the same promise. For he was looking forward to the city that has foundations, whose designer and builder is God. (Heb. 11.8–10)

The passage gives us an insight into the nature of Abram's faith. First of all, where it was placed: it was faith in God. Second, its content: he believed God's call and promise of offspring and land.

I highlight this, since it is often naively assumed that when the word 'faith' is used in the Bible it is always talking about the Christian faith – faith in Christ for forgiveness, salvation and eternal life. Clearly, Abram knew none of these things as he started his journey. However, he must have become aware of a bigger dimension as his knowledge of God grew, since the Lord Jesus himself said about him: 'Your father Abraham rejoiced that he would see my day. He saw it and was glad' (John 8.56). God must have shown Abraham more than is recorded in Genesis.

What Abram did was to believe what God disclosed to him about his offspring and the land they would inherit. That is the key to understanding the way in which his story is applied in the New Testament. Genuine faith in God trusts/accepts/relies on/believes what God reveals of himself at a particular time, and acts upon it. In Abram's case it was initially about responding to God's call to go on a journey with a goal and a promise.

Third, Abram's faith was evidence based. That evidence consisted, in the first place, of the fact that God appeared to him, revealing his glory and speaking to him, making detailed promises of what would happen in the future – evidence that was gradually confirmed as God's promises proved true.

Centuries later, Jesus revealed his glory to Paul and spoke to him – an experience that anchored his faith in Christ. That evidence was soon amplified by Paul's coming to see that Jesus' fulfilment of Scripture made the Christian claim that he was God incarnate by far the most plausible explanation of all that had happened through him.

Since Abraham is presented to us in the New Testament as the paradigm example of what it means to trust God, it will be worth spending time at this point trying to understand precisely what faith is as such. Unfortunately, we have to do this, since a posse of misguided atheists (once called the New Atheists) has sadly but very effectively spread far and wide the fallacious idea that faith as such is a purely religious concept that means 'believing where there is no evidence'. However, believing where there is no evidence, far from characterizing what faith usually means, is a definition of *blind* faith or credulity – and it can be both delusional and very dangerous.

Here are some influential examples of this view. Bertrand Russell said:

We may define 'faith' as the firm belief in something for which there is no evidence. When there is evidence, no one speaks of 'faith'. We do not speak of faith that two plus two is four or that the earth is round. We only speak of faith when we wish to substitute emotion for evidence.[2]

Richard Dawkins said:

Faith is a state of mind that leads people to believe something – it doesn't matter what – in the total absence of supporting evidence. If there were good supporting evidence then faith would be superfluous, for the evidence would compel us to believe it anyway.[3]

In order to understand what is going on here we need to realise that the word 'faith' has at least two meanings in English – and many other languages.

First, we speak of the Christian faith or the Jewish faith and so on. By that we mean faith in an objective sense – a collection of things to be believed, a set of teachings about facts and experience. This, of course, also applies to philosophies of all kinds, since atheism, naturalism, pantheism and so on are all belief systems in which their adherents have faith – although my experience is that many such people are in complete denial about this and make statements like 'Atheists have no faith'.

Second, there is faith in the subjective sense – my faith or belief – in facts and in people: in God, in Christianity, in global warming, in my spouse, in science, in a bank or a football team and endless other things – including the fact that two plus two equals four and that the earth is round!

When someone is called 'a person of faith' it usually means that they are adherents of a particular religious tradition. It does not normally refer to the obvious yet frequently overlooked fact that everyone exercises faith every day in a myriad different ways – just think what would happen if people did not place their faith/trust in maps, traffic lights, electric appliances, or doctors, surgeons, pilots, lawyers and so on. In that important sense, *everyone* is a person of faith. Faith, as such, is not a religious concept.

In English the word 'faith' derives from the Latin *fides* from which we derive 'fidelity'. In the New Testament the noun used for the same concept is *pistis*, derived from the verb *peitho*, meaning 'persuade'. These words all convey the notion of trustworthiness – that is, one is persuaded that there is evidence on which trust is rationally and worthily based.

In the Old Testament, the Hebrew word for 'believed' (used here in Genesis 15 for the first time) is a derivative of *aman*, a word that has the following range of meanings: to 'be firm', 'endure', 'be faithful', 'be true', 'stand fast', 'trust', 'have belief', 'believe'.[4]

Most people are familiar with the adverbial form of *aman*, amen, that prefaces many well-known statements of Jesus: 'Amen, Amen (= Truly, truly) I say to you'. It is an emphatic assertion of the reliability of or agreement with a statement. These words are all related to the Hebrew *emet* for 'truth'.

All of this shows that Russell's and Dawkins' attempts to define faith are seriously misleading, indeed fallacious. They define *blind* faith and that alone and, by doing so, they promote the absurd idea that all faith is like that. That leads to confusion, as Dawkins contradicts himself by saying: 'If there were good supporting evidence then *faith* would be superfluous, for the evidence would compel us to *believe* it anyway.' He is using faith and belief in his own idiosyncratic and, if I dare say it, irrational way, presenting them as two different concepts, which they never are, either in the Bible or in ordinary language – only in Dawkins' errant imagination.

The upshot of all this is that, whenever we see the word 'faith', we need to ask two questions: (1) Where is the faith placed (in what or in whom)? and (2) What are the grounds, the evidence, on which that faith is based?

To avoid the misconceptions of Bertrand Russell and Richard Dawkins, we need only look at faith as explained in the New Testament. For example, the statement of authorial intention we find towards the end of the Gospel of John:

> Now Jesus did many other signs in the presence of the disciples, which are not written in this book; but these are written so that you may believe that Jesus is the Christ, the Son of God, and that by believing you may have life in his name.
> (John 20.30–31)

Here, John says that his book contains a number of signs. A sign (Greek *semeion*, from which we get the word 'semiotics', the study of signs and symbols) is a pointer that helps us understand something, and these signs are deliberately chosen to present evidence on the basis of which we might believe two facts and experience a third:

Fact 1: Jesus is the Christ (Messiah).

Fact 2: Jesus is the Son of God.

Experience: receiving life in his name (compare John 1.14, 3.16, 5.24 and so on).

Putting it another way, if the Christian apostles thought that it was a virtue to believe without evidence, then the gospels could never have been written, as they claim to be that evidence!

Yet some, like the philosopher A. C. Grayling, object, pointing to the fact that Jesus himself said: 'Blessed are those who have not seen and yet have believed.'[5] Yes, indeed, he did – in fact in the paragraph immediately preceding the one we have just quoted. Here it is in its context:

> Eight days later, his disciples were inside again, and Thomas was with them. Although the doors were locked, Jesus came and stood among them and said, 'Peace be with you.' Then he said to Thomas, 'Put your finger here, and see my hands; and put out your hand, and place it in my side. Do not disbelieve, but believe.' Thomas answered

him, 'My Lord and my God!' Jesus said to him, 'Have you believed because you have seen me? Blessed are those who have not seen and yet have believed.

(John 20.26–29)

Now I am well aware of Aristotle's famous first sentence in his *Metaphysics*:

All men naturally desire knowledge. An indication of this is our esteem for the senses; for apart from their use we esteem them for their own sake, and most of all the sense of sight. Not only with a view to action, but even when no action is contemplated, we prefer sight, generally speaking, to all the other senses. The reason of this is that of all the senses sight best helps us to know things, and reveals many distinctions.[6]

However, it seems to have escaped Grayling's attention that sight is not the only way of gaining knowledge. Jesus did not say: 'Blessed are those *who have had no evidence* and yet have believed.' He said: 'Blessed are those *who have not seen* and yet have believed.' That is entirely different. For seeing something with our physical eyes is only one kind of evidence. I have never seen Jesus in that sense like Thomas did. But, like millions of others, I have ample evidence on the basis of which to trust him. By the way, I have never seen atoms, X-rays or Mongolia either, but there is ample evidence available to leave me in no doubt about their existence. Also, a person blind from birth has never seen a chair, but that does not mean she has no evidence that chairs exist – the evidence of touch.

In light of Grayling's serious misunderstanding, we stress once more that the biblical concept of faith in God is neither credulous nor blind, but is a personal commitment based on evidence. It is also an active stance that leads to action and not merely a passive and subjective mental assent to the existence of God. Of course, this should not be taken to mean that the person making that commitment necessarily knows everything about its nature. This is the case in many, if not most, of life's faith commitments: to marriage, to a new job, to a surgeon to perform an operation or to a pilot to fly a commercial aircraft. It is not possible to know everything. In fact, it is not usually possible even to articulate in detail just what we do know. The key thing is that we have an adequate basis for our trust.

All of this gives the lie to the common notion that faith is ignorant and superstitious and has no evidential basis in reality.

## What is justification by faith?

Abraham's experience of justification by faith is explained in detail in the New Testament, particularly in the writings of Paul. It is relevant to all believers in Christ:

> But the words 'it was counted to him' were not written for his sake alone, but for ours also. It will be counted to us who believe in him who raised from the dead Jesus our Lord, who was delivered up for our trespasses and raised for our justification.
> (Rom. 4.23–25)

This statement brings together two key biblical concepts: righteousness and justification. In order to understand the role they play in the life of Abraham and in the rest of Scripture, we need now to think about their precise meaning

The English word 'righteous' derives from an older word, 'rightwise', meaning 'in a straight way'. The Greek word used in the New Testament, *dikaios*, means a person who observes *dike* = custom, rule, right. It therefore designates someone who is upright, a person of moral integrity. The word can also mean 'judgment' in a legal sense.

The Greek verb *dikaioo*, related to it, is translated by the English 'to justify'. The equivalent Hebrew word is *tzadaq*. They both mean 'to declare righteous' or 'to confer a righteous status on'. They do not mean 'to make righteous'.

This vital distinction is evident in the Old Testament in the following: 'If there is a dispute between men and they come into courts and the judges decide between them, acquitting the innocent and condemning the guilty . . .' (Deut. 25.1). The righteous were righteous to start with, so the judge was responsible for declaring innocent parties righteous, to acquit them, to declare them not guilty. The judge did not *make* them righteous, since they were so already.

A similar example in the New Testament is found in Luke 7.29. Compare the following translations:

1 English KJV: 'And all the people that heard him, and the publicans, *justified God*, being baptised with the baptism of John' (my emphasis).
2 ESVUK: 'When all the people heard this, and the tax collectors too, they *declared God just,* having been baptized with the baptism of John' (my emphasis).

The people did not make God just: that would be absurd. Nor did they, equally absurdly, acquit God of guilt. What they did was to *declare God to be just*, to confess that he was right and, by implication, that they were wrong and needed to repent.

Furthermore, in ordinary conversation, when we ask someone to justify something, we are not asking them to *make* it right but to *declare* why it was or is right. Of course, doing or making things right is important – but justification, declaring things or people right or righteous, is neither of them.

However, as many readers will know, there has been ongoing theological controversy about whether the act of justification simply refers to the conferment of righteous status on someone or whether it also contains an element of actually making them ethically righteous in terms of moral regeneration. This was one of the main Reformation issues between Roman Catholics and Protestants.

This is first and foremost a linguistic question. Eminent scholar C. E. B. Cranfield, in his highly acclaimed commentary on Romans, writes:

While it should be freely admitted that the Protestant position has sometimes been stated misleadingly or seriously distorted so that Catholics have had good reason to be suspicious and alarmed (a good many Protestants have put far too little emphasis on sanctification . . .) there seems to us to be no doubt that *dikaisun* as used by Paul means simply 'acquit', 'confer a righteous status on', and does not in itself contain any reference to moral transformation.[7]

Cranfield says that this conclusion is forced upon him by the linguistic evidence and it is also borne out by the structure of Paul's argument in his epistle to the Romans.

Having said this, it is clear both from the life of Abraham and Romans that *both* justification *and* moral transformation (sanctification) are of paramount importance. It is getting the relationship between the two clear – justification first and sanctification following – that is crucial to the gospel message.

It is for such reasons that many people find the notion of justification by faith somewhat difficult to understand. That underlines the importance of playing close attention to the way in which the New Testament uses the life of Abraham to unpack the concept.

At the beginning of his letter to the Romans Paul flags up the central importance of faith and righteousness to the gospel message of salvation:

For I am not ashamed of the gospel, for it is the power of God for salvation to everyone who believes, to the Jew first and also to the Greek. For in it the righteousness of God is revealed from faith for faith, as it is written: 'The righteous shall live by faith.'
(Rom. 1.16–17)

What gives the gospel message its saving power is that it originates with God, who confers a righteous status on all those who believe in him. The person who puts their faith/trust in God through Christ is declared righteous before God. Thereafter, ongoing trust in the indwelling power of the Holy Spirit becomes the source of the development of moral quality in their lives. What starts in faith continues to grow through faith.

At this point we may run up against a difficulty arising from the common notion that the way to achieve a righteous status with God (to get right with God) is to merit or earn it by keeping the moral law, as, for instance, laid down in the Ten Commandments by Moses. The idea – and it is a sticking point for many people – is that surely we can make up any shortfall in our moral status before God by putting renewed effort into the quality of our behaviour. This appeals strongly to intuition in a world where so much in everyday life, from school through college to the workplace, is merit based. We get what we earn, do we not?

The reason for this is that one of the most important lessons about Abraham is that he was justified by faith *without the law of Moses even being in existence*, and when that law came, it did not annul what God had promised that Abraham would receive by faith. Paul explains this in Galatians:

This is what I mean: *the law, which came 430 years afterwards, does not annul a covenant previously ratified by God, so as to make the promise void.* For if the inheritance comes by the law, it no longer comes by promise; but God gave it to Abraham by a promise ... And if you are Christ's, then you are Abraham's offspring, heirs according to promise.
(Gal. 3.17–18, 29, emphasis mine)

The book of Romans is devoted to spelling this out in detail and, since the issue is of such importance, it will help us to have a thumbnail sketch of the first major argument in that book (chapters 1–3):

Paul is not ashamed of the gospel.

Why? Because it is the power of God unto salvation.

This implies that people need to be saved, then?

Yes, it does, because they are all guilty sinners.

What constitutes them as guilty?

Three things mainly: the evidence of creation, the moral law in their consciences and the testimony of Scripture. These combine to condemn all of us without exception as falling short of God's standards.

Paul deduces:

Now we know that whatever the law says it speaks to those who are under the law, so that every mouth may be stopped, and the whole world may be held accountable to God. For by works of the law no human being will be justified in his sight, since through the law comes knowledge of sin.
(Rom. 3.19–20)

Paul says that yes, the standards set in the moral law have a very real function: through them comes the knowledge of sin. It has been well said that if we are inclined to think we are not sinners, we should try hard to live with the Ten Commandments and the Sermon on the Mount for a month, and then think again! The law certainly measures how far short we fall, but it can no more save us than we can be cured of a fever by swallowing the thermometer showing us how ill we are! Nor can our law keep saving us either.

What then can put us right with God and save us? Paul continues:

> But now the righteousness of God has been manifested apart from the law, although the Law and the Prophets bear witness to it – the righteousness of God through faith in Jesus Christ for all who believe. For there is no distinction: for all have sinned and fall short of the glory of God, and are justified by his grace as a gift through the redemption that is in Christ Jesus whom God put forward as a propitiation by his blood, to be received by faith.
> (Rom. 3.21–25)

This is simply wonderful news. God does something we could never merit nor do for ourselves. If we repent (turn from) our sins and trust him, he confers a righteous status upon us. He acquits us of the guilt incurred by all our sins. This is a revolutionary message and a particularly difficult one for the religious mind that thinks in terms of merit and desert. In that sense, Abraham trumps Moses.

Paul now turns to the Old Testament to establish a *legal* precedent in order to establish this crucial principle for Jews and anyone else who finds it problematic. We should note that Paul is not spiritualising nor allegorising here, but is looking at an actual historical example of faith in action.

> What then shall we say was gained by Abraham, our forefather according to the flesh? For if Abraham was justified by works, he has something to boast about, but not before God. For what does the Scripture say? 'Abraham believed God, and it was counted to him as righteousness.' Now to the one who works, his wages are not counted

as a gift but as his due. And to the one who does not work but believes in him who justifies the ungodly, his faith is counted as righteousness. (Rom. 4.1–5)

We note that Paul takes Abraham to be an historical person, 'our forefather', and regards Scripture as authoritative in speaking about Abraham. He quotes the inspired text where God revealed the terms on which he justified Abraham.

It needs to be stated clearly that the act of receiving salvation does not contribute to that salvation in the sense of doing something (working) to earn it – any more than accepting a legacy is working to merit it. Faith is an action, certainly, but it is not a meritorious work. Faith in God and meritorious work done for God are conceptual opposites.

It is not even the case that we have the faith to do the works that will grant us acceptance. For if our works were adequate, God would be obliged to give us justification, which would no longer be an act of grace, any more than it would be an act of grace for an employer to give an employee at the end of the month the wages she has earned.

Paul is crystal clear here and is at pains to ensure that we do not misunderstand him, even though what he says sounds highly counter-intuitive in a merit-based culture. Abraham did not merit salvation, since it is 'to the one *who does not work but believes* in him who justifies the ungodly, his faith is counted as righteousness'. That is what brings peace with God and leads to peace and security by which we rejoice in hope of the glory of God (Rom. 5.1).

Abram was clearly not working when he gazed up at the stars and humbly believed what God said to him! There was nothing to boast of: his justification before God was an undeserved gift of God's free grace to be accepted in humility and gratitude. He certainly did not earn it.

And that is why the Lord Jesus referred twice to people who had trusted him as children of Abraham: 'And ought not this woman, a daughter of Abraham whom Satan bound for eighteen years, be loosed from this bond on the Sabbath day?' (Luke 13.16), and Jesus said to Zacchaeus: 'Today salvation has come to this house, since he also is a son of Abraham. For the Son of Man came to seek and to save the lost' (Luke 19.9–10).

This establishes what Paul summarises in Ephesians:

> For by grace you have been saved through faith. And this is not your
> own doing; it is the gift of God, not a result of works, so that no one
> may boast. For we are his workmanship, created in Christ Jesus for
> good works, which God prepared beforehand, that we should walk
> in them.
> (Eph. 2.8–10)

God is interested in righteous behaviour. The secret of salvation, however,
is that although it is not based on what we do – we cannot merit it, it is a
gracious gift received by faith – it leads to good works. Zacchaeus proved
by his behaviour that he had genuinely trusted God. So did Abraham –
so that without the law, Abraham learned to fulfil it in his life.

# 9

# God's covenant with Abram

Abram believed God regarding his offspring. God now speaks to him about his inheritance: 'And he said to him, "I am the LORD who brought you out from Ur of the Chaldeans to give you this land to possess." But he said, "O Lord God, how am I to know that I shall possess it?"' (Gen. 15.7–8).

Children were a private matter between Abram, Sarai – and God. The inheritance of land, however, raised all kinds of other concerns and doubts in Abram's mind. There were warring factions all around, constantly contesting for land – the Babylonians were not far off and the Canaanites, thanks to Abram's rescue of Lot, were once more likely to come snapping at his heels. How could he be sure that this part of God's promise would be fulfilled? He wanted evidence on which to base his trust. Blind faith would not do.

The answer God gave him was to make a covenant[1] in the form of a formal, official, binding commitment on God's part to give him the inheritance.

Throughout history covenants have been agreements, usually set down in legally formalised documents, that are instruments designed as security for the signatories. How often these days do we hear a woman say that she wishes her partner would give her the certainty of a marriage certificate in order to stabilise their relationship – or vice versa. And in a world where trust is being steadily eroded, the lawyers make millions in drawing up covenants between people because, in the end, they find it difficult to trust one another.

Abram already had God's word that he would receive the inheritance. Yet in response to his ongoing nervousness and uncertainty about the matter, God gave him a further level of assurance in the shape of a covenant in perpetuity. We understand only too well the need for covenants among human beings and for treaties among nations, but the idea of God binding himself in a covenant with a human being is nothing short of staggering. It shows at the very least that God takes very seriously the need we his creatures have for certainty.

Abram would never forget the dramatic circumstances of its enactment. Genesis tells us what God instructed Abram to do:

> He said to him, 'Bring me a heifer three years old, a female goat three years old, a ram three years old, a turtle-dove, and a young pigeon.' And he brought him all these, cut them in half, and laid each half over against the other. But he did not cut the birds in half. And when birds of prey came down on the carcasses, Abram drove them away.
>
> As the sun was going down, a deep sleep fell on Abram. And behold, dreadful and great darkness fell upon him. Then the LORD said to Abram, 'Know for certain that your offspring will be sojourners in a land that is not theirs and will be servants there, and they will be afflicted for four hundred years. But I will bring judgement on the nation that they serve, and afterwards they shall come out with great possessions. As for yourself, you shall go to your fathers in peace; you shall be buried in a good old age. And they shall come back here in the fourth generation, for the iniquity of the Amorites is not yet complete.'
>
> When the sun had gone down and it was dark, behold, a smoking firepot and a flaming torch passed between these pieces. On that day the LORD made a covenant with Abram, saying, 'To your offspring I give this land, from the river of Egypt to the great river, the river Euphrates, the land of the Kenites, the Kenizzites, the Kadmonites, the Hittites, the Perizzites, the Rephaim, the Amorites, the Canaanites, the Girgashites and the Jebusites.'
> (Gen. 15.9–21)

This all sounds very strange to contemporary ears and we therefore need to unpack it. To begin with, the ritual described here is associated with the making of a covenant, a process that is common today. A covenant is normally a formal agreement drawn up by a lawyer or

128

notary between two parties, each of which has conditions to fulfil, as for example the contract signed by both the seller and the buyer of a house.

One way of making a covenant in the ancient Near East was to cut animals in half and make two piles of the halves with a space between them. The 'signatories' to the covenant would walk between the heaps of animal parts as an indication that they were solemnly bound to keeping the covenant under penalty of having done to them what had been done to the animals. It was easy to get the point – if you don't keep the covenant you will be cut into pieces! Such a covenant is known in Hebrew as *Berit bein Ha Betarim*, which means 'the covenant between the parts'. General opinion has it that the Hebrew for covenant, *berit*, is derived from *barah*, 'to cut'.

The prophet Jeremiah refers to this ritual:

> The men who transgressed my covenant and did not keep the terms of the covenant that they made before me, I will make them like the calf that they cut in two and passed between its parts – the officials of Judah, the officials of Jerusalem, the eunuchs, the priests and all the people of the land who passed between the parts of the calf. And I will give them into the hand of their enemies and into the hand of those who seek their lives. Their dead bodies shall be food for the birds of the air and the beasts of the earth.
> (Jer. 34.18–20)

The reader should note that this text from Jeremiah cannot be referring[2] to the covenant God made with Abram, since Jeremiah's covenant explicitly says that the people ratified the covenant by walking between the pieces, whereas in Genesis 15 the striking thing is that Abram did not walk between the pieces.

On that occasion God alone walked, so to speak, between the pieces, his presence indicated by the moving firepot and the flaming torch. There was no ratification on Abram's part since he didn't have any conditions to fulfil. In fact the man fell asleep before the ceremony began! These circumstances conveyed the fact that God's promise to Abram was an unconditional act of grace – Abram's descendants were guaranteed to receive the inheritance (Gal. 3.18). It is this principle that lies at the heart of the gospel.

The form of this covenant is actually very familiar to us in everyday life in the form of a last will or testament. It involves a single party making a formal commitment to others – for example, to leave after their death a certain specified sum of money to named relatives. In this case only the testator has to sign the testament; the beneficiaries do not, as they do not have to fulfil any conditions in order to receive the benefits. They get the benefits simply by identifying themselves as the person or persons named in the document.

For this reason it is called a one-party, or unilateral, covenant even though two parties are actually involved. The key point is that *only one party has conditions to fulfil*. That was the case with the first covenant mentioned in Genesis – God's covenant with Noah never to flood the earth again, signified by a rainbow (Gen. 9.15–17). It is also the case with the second covenant in Genesis, that with Abram in Genesis 15.

Let us consider exactly what happened, as the narrative contains some unexpected elements. For instance, one might have expected that a ceremony representing the conferment of great blessings and privileges to Abram – offspring and land – would be a joyous occasion filled with great celebration.

Nothing of the sort. The institution of this covenant involved sacrifice – an indicator of what would eventually be necessary to bring the blessing of Abram to the world through Christ. Furthermore, the making of this covenant was enveloped with a sense of threat, darkness and sheer horror.

Abram dutifully brought the animals God had requested and he cut them in two (apart from the birds), placing the parts in two separated heaps as the ritual required. The smell of the slaughtered animals attracted birds of prey – vultures, probably – and Abram was forced to drive them away, as they threatened to make the covenant ritual impossible by stealing the animal parts.

Night was drawing on and Abram, far from taking part in the covenant ritual, fell into a deep sleep filled with a profound sense of dread and darkness as God announced to him the grim news that, yes, he would have offspring, but instead of immediately inheriting the promised land they would migrate to another land. There they would endure oppression for four centuries, before they eventually returned with great wealth[3] to take possession of the land of promise when the wickedness of the Amorites who occupied it at that time had reached its zenith.

In other words, Israel's taking possession of the land would coincide precisely with and be part of the execution of God's providential judgement of the Amorites. This is an important moral point. God would not intervene to expel the current inhabitants of the land until his justice determined that they deserved it. However, when he did intervene he would use Israel's fighting men to carry out the judgement. Long before that, Abraham would himself lead a small private army to battle against a confederation of kings to rescue his captured nephew Lot (see Gen. 14). That raises the whole issue of the morality of such warfare, which we will consider when we come to this incident – albeit briefly, since I have discussed it elsewhere.[4]

God assured Abram that he personally would live to a good old age, but nothing could disguise the fact that he would not live to enjoy the inheritance he had been promised.

Egypt is not explicitly mentioned in the text as the land of oppression, but one cannot help wondering if Abram's mind was triggered by the mention of coming out of the land of oppression with great wealth to think of Egypt and his own experience there.

Looking back from our vantage point in history we surely know something of what Abram's experience of darkness foreshadowed: the evil of antisemitism, the bitter enemy of Abram's race that expressed itself in the unspeakable horror of a whole series of devilishly cruel genocidal attempts throughout the centuries to wipe out the nation of Israel, starting with the pharaoh 'who did not know Joseph' (Gen. 1.8).

The oppression of Abraham's descendants culminated in the twentieth-century Shoah (Holocaust) – a litany of indescribable horrors carried out in concentration camps like Auschwitz, Treblinka, Sobibor, Mauthausen and many other centres, which were deliberately set up to carry out industrial-scale slaughter of men, women and children. Those camps will forever symbolise unimaginable depths of human depravity. It is not without reason that the word 'Holocaust', meaning 'whole burnt offering', was chosen to describe what happened. I made several visits to

Auschwitz during the period of the Cold War and am not ashamed to say that I wept each time, overwhelmed by the sheer scale of the evil that haunted its gas chambers.

Nobel laureate Elie Wiesel captured its awfulness with eyewitness realism and authority:

> Never shall I forget that night, the first night in camp, which has turned my life into one long night, seven times cursed and seven times sealed. Never shall I forget that smoke. Never shall I forget the little faces of the children, whose bodies I saw turned into wreaths of smoke beneath a silent blue sky. Never shall I forget those flames which consumed my faith forever. Never shall I forget that nocturnal silence which deprived me, for all eternity, of the desire to live. Never shall I forget those moments which murdered my God and my soul and turned my dreams to dust. Never shall I forget these things, even if I am condemned to live as long as God Himself. Never.[5]

And we must never forget that darkness either.

And yet, as I write these words, I fear that anti-Semitism is once more rearing up its ugly head in Europe and elsewhere. What a tragic irony, since it was Israel that gave birth to our only hope of conquering such evil.

The rapid onset of the pitch darkness characteristic of the Middle East finally swallowed up that awesome day. Abram became aware of a smoking pot and a flaming torch processing between the animal pieces as God ratified his covenant to give named tracts of land to Abram's offspring.

It was a lot for anyone to take in. Yet subsequent history has confirmed the prediction contained in the terms of the covenant, which therefore becomes part of the evidence for the truth and reliability of Scripture.

Before we continue with Abram's story, we might do well to pause and allow all of this to sink into our minds and hearts. What do we now think of the fact that we who believe in the Lord Jesus are children of Abraham and heirs according to the promise? What does that really involve and how should it impact our lives and our witness to the gospel?

Before we investigate that question, in order to understand it better we shall compare and contrast the covenant God made with Abram with later covenants.

# 10

# The new covenant

## Two covenants – the old and the new

The covenant with Abram was a one-party, or unilateral, covenant or testament. The covenant made much later at Sinai between God and Israel was a two-party, or bilateral, covenant. Influential Dutch-American systematic theologian Louis Berkhof wrote of the need for English readers to bear these differences in mind when they see the word 'covenant' in the Bible. He warns that 'the true sense is often missed if readers suppose that the word must refer to a reciprocal 'agreement' or 'contract.' The issue is important because misunderstandings along this line can have some serious consequences for theology.'[1]

For this distinction between one- and two-party covenants is precisely what differentiates between what is called the old covenant made at Sinai – a two-party covenant made much later than this one with Abram, which was a one-party covenant – and what we call the new covenant, also a one-party covenant, instituted by the Lord Jesus Christ in an upper room in Jerusalem just before he was crucified.

The difference between these covenants has led to much confusion. It has also been the cause of a great deal of tension, not only between Jews and Christians, but also between various traditions within the general Christian tradition.

In order to understand this we need to recall that the covenant at Sinai had as its basis the law of Moses. Here are some of the key statements from the book of Exodus:

Now therefore, if you will indeed obey my voice and keep my covenant, you shall be my treasured possession among all peoples, for all the earth is mine.
(Exod. 19.5)

Then he took the Book of the Covenant and read it in the hearing of the people. And they said, 'All that the LORD has spoken we will do, and we will be obedient.' And Moses took the blood and threw it on the people and said, 'Behold the blood of the covenant that the LORD has made with you in accordance with all these words.' (Exod. 24.7–8)

The people explicitly and consciously covenanted to keep *all* – emphasised – of the words. Blood was sprinkled on them to indicate the solemnity of breaking their side of the agreement. However, they soon discovered that what they had taken on was impossible: they could not keep God's laws and broke their side of the covenant agreement.

What God then did was to institute a system of animal sacrifices and offerings to teach the people (elementary) lessons on the need for repentance and sacrifice to cover their guilt and restore fellowship with God. However, this, in the nature of things, could only be a temporary patch, as the problem, crudely put, did not lie between animals and God but humans and God. The fact was that the blood of goats and bulls could never take away sin.

Speaking of that system of animal sacrifices Hebrews says that

it can never, by the same sacrifices that are continually offered every year, make perfect those who draw near. Otherwise, would they not have ceased to be offered, since the worshippers, having once been cleansed, would no longer have any consciousness of sins? But in these sacrifices there is a reminder of sins every year. For it is impossible for the blood of bulls and goats to take away sins.

Consequently, when Christ came into the world, he said,

'Sacrifices and offerings you have not desired,
    but a body have you prepared for me;
in burnt offerings and sin offerings
    you have taken no pleasure.
Then I said, "Behold, I have come to do your will, O God,
    as it is written of me in the scroll of the book."'

When he said above, 'You have neither desired nor taken pleasure in sacrifices and offerings and burnt offerings and sin offerings' (these are offered according to the law), then he added, 'Behold, I have come to do your will.' He does away with the first in order to establish the second. And by that will we have been sanctified through the offering of the body of Jesus Christ once for all.
(Heb. 10.1–10)

Hebrews is not in any way introducing a novel Christian idea at this point. It is citing the Old Testament, which recognised that there was a major problem with the Sinai covenant.

Here is how Hebrews argues from Jeremiah that the Old Testament predicted there would be a new covenant. It had to do with the fact that the covenant made at Sinai was a two-party covenant between God and the people – and the people broke their side of the conditions they had covenanted to fulfil.

For if that first covenant had been faultless, there would have been no occasion to look for a second. For he finds fault with them when he says:

'Behold, the days are coming, declares the Lord,
when I will establish a new covenant with the house of
    Israel
and with the house of Judah,
not like the covenant that I made with their fathers
on the day when I took them by the hand to bring them out
    of the land of Egypt.
For they did not continue in my covenant,
and so I showed no concern for them, declares the Lord . . .'
(Heb. 8.7–9, cited from Jer. 31.31–34)

Standing back from this for a moment to gain perspective, we have the following historical order:

1 Covenant with Abram – a one-party covenant ratified by God alone.

2 Covenant with Israel – a two-party covenant ratified by God and Israel.
3 The new covenant – ratified by Christ alone.

One obvious and important question is: why, if covenant 2 above did not negate covenant 1, was there need for covenant 3? We shall discuss this question in the next section, which is on the new covenant.

First, however, we see how Abram's security and that of believers in Christ lies in the priority of God's covenant 1 with Abram over covenant 2. That, in turn, depends on the legal convention that a covenant/testament once ratified cannot subsequently be annulled.

Paul is at pains to point out the implications of this in a detailed forensic analysis:

> To give a human example, brothers: even with a man-made covenant, no one annuls it or adds to it once it has been ratified. Now the promises were made to Abraham and to his offspring. It does not say, 'And to offsprings', referring to many, but referring to one, 'And to your offspring', who is Christ. This is what I mean: *the law, which came 430 years afterwards, does not annul a covenant previously ratified by God, so as to make the promise void.* For if the inheritance comes by the law, it no longer comes by promise; but God gave it to Abraham by a promise . . . And if you are Christ's, then you are Abraham's offspring, heirs according to promise.
> (Gal. 3.15–18, 29, emphasis mine)

Paul focuses on an important technical detail in the covenant – that the word 'offspring' (seed) is in the singular. He takes this to be an indicator that even in the original promise there was reference to its supreme fulfilment in one special seed – Christ. That promise was made long before the law of Moses, which has no power to invalidate the original promise.

Why is this of any relevance apart from within the story itself? Because it has far-reaching, and I mean far-reaching, implications for those of us who are believers in Christ: 'And if you are Christ's, then you are Abraham's offspring, heirs according to promise.'

There is more. For not only was faith in God's promise of descendants the ground for Abram and subsequent believers being accounted righteous before God, but the inheritance itself was gifted to Abram on the same basis – faith alone. It was not earned by effort to keep the law either.

Paul explains this in Romans 4:

For the promise to Abraham and his offspring that he would be heir of the world did not come through the law but through the righteousness of faith. For if it is the adherents of the law who are to be the heirs, faith is null and the promise is void. For the law brings wrath, but where there is no law there is no transgression. That is why it depends on faith, in order that the promise may rest on grace and be guaranteed to all his offspring.
(Rom. 4.13–16)

Note that Paul says the promise to Abraham and his offspring involved becoming 'heir of the world' – although the inheritance initially given to Abraham appeared to be restricted to a certain tract of land in the Middle East. Yet there had already been a hint of something far more extensive – 'in you *all the nations of the world* will be *blessed*'.

What has it to do with us? Everything. We cited, just above, Paul's statement that if we are Christ's we are included: 'And if you are Christ's, then you are Abraham's offspring, heirs according to promise' (Gal. 3.29). We need to pause and let this sink in. It is telling us that those of us who trust Christ, and are therefore offspring of Abraham by sharing his faith, are, from a legal perspective, irrevocably inheritors of the world. God has committed himself to guaranteeing it. Yes, it amplifies the original promise. But I imagine few of us would object if, having agreed with a builder a certain price for a three-bedroom house with a single garage and a small garden, he in the end for the same price actually constructed for us a four-bedroom house with a double garage and a large garden.

The upshot of all of this is that nothing less than world inheritance is an integral part of this covenanted promise of God to those who trust him. I wonder just how seriously we are inclined to take this. Certainly in New Testament times there were those who had forgotten the promise of future inheritance and were living as if this world was the only world that existed. Paul had to remind the Corinthian church: 'Do you not know that the saints will rule the world?' (see 1 Cor. 6).

We know little about what will be involved in that rule, except that the Lord himself gave us some hint when he promised his apostles administrative positions in the world to come. That is made very plain in Matthew 19:

> Then Peter said in reply, 'See, we have left everything and followed you. What then will we have?' Jesus said to them, 'Truly, I say to you, in the regeneration, when the Son of Man will sit on his glorious throne, you who have followed me will also sit on twelve thrones, judging the twelve tribes of Israel. And everyone who has left houses or brothers or sisters or father or mother or children or lands, for my name's sake, will receive a hundredfold and will inherit eternal life. But many who are first will be last, and the last first.'
> (Matt. 19.27–30)

The fact that Jesus is speaking of the world to come is evident from the use of the word 'regeneration' (implying resurrection from the dead) and the time indicator: 'when the Son of Man will sit on his glorious throne'. It is easy to forget that resurrection has a physical dimension – the word means 'standing up again'. There will be resurrection bodies (1 Cor. 15) and there will be new heavens and a new earth (Rev. 22).

The word 'regeneration' has two meanings in the New Testament. It is used not only for the resurrection of the dead at Christ's return as above, but also for the new birth by God's Holy Spirit through faith in Christ that Jesus famously discussed with Nicodemus in John 3. It is this new birth that guarantees our future inheritance, as Peter explains:

> Blessed be the God and Father of our Lord Jesus Christ! According to his great mercy, he has caused us to be born again to a living hope through the resurrection of Jesus Christ from the dead, to an inheritance that is imperishable, undefiled, and unfading, kept in heaven for you, who by God's power are being guarded through faith for a salvation ready to be revealed in the last time. In this you

rejoice, though now for a little while, if necessary, you have been grieved by various trials, so that the tested genuineness of your faith – more precious than gold that perishes though it is tested by fire – may be found to result in praise and glory and honour at the revelation of Jesus Christ.
(1 Pet. 1.3–7)

Our inheritance is reserved for us in heaven, guaranteed by the resurrection of Jesus. But we are not there yet. Peter warns that trials will come. Faith will be tested. Jesus said that if the world hated him it would hate us too. So did Paul: 'All who desire to live a godly life in Christ Jesus will be persecuted' (2 Tim. 3.12). Just as the Jews have been and still are persecuted, the persecution of Christians around the world is causing increasing alarm at the present time. Now, as never before, we need to hold on to the promises of God – including the one he made to Abram.

Yet the inheritance will come. One day Christ will return at a time when the wickedness of the rulers of this world has reached a zenith far in excess of that of the Amorites whom Joshua dispossessed. The judgement of God will fall and the earth will finally be taken out of the hands of evil governments and put into the hands of the saints under the rule of Christ himself.

## The new covenant of Christ

We now address a question raised but left hanging in the previous section: why is there any need for a new covenant if the covenant with Abraham is the fundamental one? The answer to that lies in pursuing another question: how could God accept Abraham simply because he trusted God? After all, we have seen plenty of evidence that Abraham was far from perfect. He was a sinner like the rest of us. So on what basis could God accept him? How can the simple act of trust in God deal with sin? How could that possibly be righteous? Does sin not need to be atoned for? And yet Scripture says that Abraham's faith was accounted to him as righteousness.

This was a very practical issue for the recipients of the letter to the Hebrews. One can imagine many of its readers, when they heard of the vast superiority of the new covenant over the old, asking about their parents, grandparents and relatives who died without ever hearing about the new covenant. Yet they had believed God: they had done as instructed by Moses and brought animal sacrifices to atone for their sins. What about them? Did they really get forgiven or not?

The answer to that question lies in the fact that although, as we have seen, animal sacrifices could never take away sin, they foreshadowed the way God eventually did deal with sin through the sacrifice of Christ.

We live two millennia after Jesus died, and the good news at the heart of the Christian message is that when he died he bore our sins on the cross. Clearly, our sins were in the future when he died. That sequence in time perhaps enables us to understand our own salvation long after the crucifixion somewhat easier than the teaching of the New Testament that we must now consider – that the sacrifice of Christ also works backwards in time as well as forwards in time in order that God could righteously deal with the sins of believers who lived before Jesus died. The main passage that teaches this truth is found in Romans 3:

> But now the righteousness of God has been manifested apart from the law, although the Law and the Prophets bear witness to it – the righteousness of God through faith in Jesus Christ for all who believe. For there is no distinction: for all have sinned and fall short of the glory of God, and are justified by his grace as a gift, through the redemption that is in Christ Jesus, whom God put forward as a propitiation by his blood, to be received by faith. This was to show God's righteousness, because in his divine forbearance he had passed over former sins. It was to show his righteousness at the present time, so that he might be just and the justifier of the one who has faith in Jesus.
> (Rom. 3.21–26)

Sin is universal. It has infected all of us with the result that we have all sinned and fall short of the glory of God. On what basis, then, can we be justified? Only through redemption by the death of Christ. The animal sacrifices were used to teach Israel that 'without the shedding of blood there is no forgiveness of sins' (Heb. 9.22; Lev. 17.1). Those sacrifices could never take away sin, as we have seen, but they pointed the way forward to Jesus' death on the cross as the fulfilment of all that they stood for. He really effected redemption and we receive forgiveness because of it when we trust him.

Paul is very careful to explain that this shows God's righteousness in 'passing over former sins'. That is, the sins that Abraham, Moses and so on had committed in former times. God counted their faith in him as righteousness in the light of the fact that one day Jesus would come and die for those sins.

How much did Abraham know about that? One wonders in light of what Jesus himself said about him: "'Your father Abraham rejoiced that he would see my day. He saw it and was glad." So the Jews said to him, "You are not yet fifty years old, and have you seen Abraham?" Jesus said to them, "Truly, truly, I say to you, before Abraham was, I am"' (John 8.56–58).

'Before Abraham was, I am.' There is profound mystery here.

A question remains: does it, then, not make any difference at all whether one lives before the death and resurrection of Jesus or afterwards? The answer is that it does. In order to explain, we need to go back to the tabernacle that Moses set up in the desert, or the Temple that Solomon built in Jerusalem.

Each of these structures had two compartments divided off from one another by a veil. The first compartment after the entrance was called the holy place, the second was the holy of holies, or the most holy. It contained the ark of the covenant, with the tablets of the law, and was a symbol of the presence of God among his people.

The priests in Israel were daily ministering in the first compartment, but access to the second was strictly controlled. Only once a year on Yom Kippur, the Day of Atonement, was one man, the high priest, allowed to go behind the veil for a short time and stand in the presence of God. He had to sprinkle the blood of a sacrifice on the solid gold lid of the ark and on the ground before it and, standing in a cloud of incense, he represented the people before God and prayed for them.

The letter to the Hebrews explains to us the implications of this human access to God.

These preparations having thus been made, the priests go regularly into the first section, performing their ritual duties, but into the second only the high priest goes, and he but once a year, and not without taking blood, which he offers for himself and for the unintentional sins of the people. *By this the Holy Spirit indicates that the way into the holy places is not yet opened as long as the first section is still standing (which is symbolic for the present age).* According to this arrangement, gifts and sacrifices are offered that cannot perfect the conscience of the worshipper, but deal only with food and drink and various washings, regulations for the body imposed until the time of reformation.

(Heb. 9.6–10, emphasis mine)

The italicised key statement tells us that so long as the two-compartment arrangement was standing, the way into the direct presence of God was not open. Why? Because in both tabernacle and temple, the sacrifices were not capable of dealing with human guilt and so had no power to cleanse the conscience of the worshipper from guilt. That was true of Moses, it was true of David and, of course, of Abraham.

The time of reformation came with Jesus Christ:

But when Christ appeared as a high priest of the good things that have come, then through the greater and more perfect tent (not made with hands, that is, not of this creation) he entered once for all into the holy places, not by means of the blood of goats and calves but by means of his own blood, thus securing an eternal redemption. For if the blood of goats and bulls, and the sprinkling of defiled persons with the ashes of a heifer, sanctify for the purification of the flesh, how much more will the blood of Christ, who through the eternal Spirit offered himself without blemish to God, purify our conscience from dead works to serve the living God.

Therefore he is the mediator of a new covenant, so that those who are called may receive the promised eternal inheritance, since a death has occurred that redeems them from the transgressions committed under the first covenant.

(Heb 9.11–15)

Christ's offering of himself through the eternal Spirit does what the animal sacrifices could not do – purify the conscience. On that basis, he is the mediator of a new covenant that has application to all whom God called, including those who lived *before* the time of Christ.

The upshot of this long train of reasoning, whose importance can be judged by the space the letter to the Hebrews gives to it, is that not only were people in New Testament times and later, who put their faith in God through Jesus, justly accounted righteous by God on the basis of the death of Christ for their sins that took place in the past, the same is also true of people in Old Testament times who put their faith in God. Although they knew little about the coming Messiah, they also were accounted righteous because of his death long after their time.

It all makes coherent sense, even if it also stretches our minds, but reality tends to do that. Think of Einstein's theories and Quantum Mechanics. A real car is much more complex than a toy one!

## The new covenant for Christians

During the week in which he was crucified, the Lord Jesus celebrated the Passover festival in a borrowed room in Jerusalem. He had entered Jerusalem triumphantly some days before, but the euphoria had turned sour as the religious authorities realised they were threatened by his claim to be the King Messiah. Yet there were some who were loyal to him and they met at his invitation, to celebrate a last Passover together. Luke takes up the account:

And when the hour came, he reclined at table, and the apostles with him. And he said to them, 'I have earnestly desired to eat this Passover with you before I suffer. For I tell you I will not eat it until it is fulfilled in the kingdom of God.' And he took a cup, and when he had given thanks he said, 'Take this, and divide it among yourselves. For I tell you that from now on I will not drink of the fruit of the vine until the kingdom of God comes.' And he took bread, and when he had given thanks, he broke it and gave it to them, saying, 'This is my body, which is given for you. Do this in remembrance of me.' And likewise the cup after they had eaten, saying, 'This cup that is poured out for you is the new covenant in my blood . . .

'You are those who have stayed with me in my trials, and I assign [= make a covenant with] to you, as my Father assigned to me, a kingdom, that you may eat and drink at my table in my kingdom and sit on thrones judging the twelve tribes of Israel.'
(Luke 22.14–20; 28–30)

After they had had the meal something very dramatic occurred, for the King sat at that table with his subjects and offered them a cup that he said was the cup of a new covenant. He explained that, by this simple act, he was covenanting them a kingdom, which would mean that one day they would occupy thrones as rulers in Israel.

That was surely not easy to take in, for those who ruled Israel at the time were baying for his blood, and they were hostage to the occupying power of Rome. It would have been inconceivable for them to think that three centuries later the Roman emperor (Constantine) would acknowledge Jesus as his king – not that that was what Jesus meant. There were far greater things to come. Indeed, as we saw earlier, Jesus told Peter and the other disciples that they would not sit on those thrones until the resurrection of the dead (Matt. 19.28).

Later Paul authoritatively stated that the new covenant applied to all believers in Christ:

For I received from the Lord what I also delivered to you, that the Lord Jesus on the night when he was betrayed took bread, and when he had given thanks, he broke it, and said, 'This is my body which is for you. Do this in remembrance of me.' In the same way also he took the cup, after supper, saying, 'This cup is the new covenant in my blood. Do this, as often as you drink it, in remembrance of me.' For as often as you eat this bread and drink the cup, you proclaim the Lord's death until he comes.
(1 Cor. 11.23–26)

Throughout his life Abraham must have often reflected on the night he was justified by faith – when he looked up at the stars and believed the voice that told him he would have a son against all appearance to the contrary. He must also have thought again and again about all that had happened on the later night when God made the covenant with him in the darkness. On that occasion Abraham saw the lamp of the presence of God move between the sacrifices and heard that same voice promising him not only offspring but the inheritance of the land for them.

Those of us who have been justified by faith in the Lord Jesus should likewise take every opportunity to reflect on the wonder of our justification. Since the beginning of the Christian Church Christians have joined together on the first day of the week to do so as they celebrate the covenant Jesus made with his disciples by taking what we have come to know as the Lord's Supper. The bread and wine are no magic potion; taking them does not convey salvation. Rather, we take it because we have received salvation and wish to express our gratitude to him as our Saviour and our commitment to him as Lord.

The symbols point to the basis of the covenant – bread and wine, two elements on a table, representing the body and blood of our Lord separated in death and thereby expressing the heart of the gospel – he died for our sins.

When we take the cup of the new covenant we are confessing that Jesus died for us personally. We are also saying something else. A covenant is an instrument of government and rule. That is why the bread and the wine are often referred to as sacraments – from the Latin *sacramentum*, meaning 'an oath of allegiance'. Taking the cup, therefore, means we are consciously pledging ourselves to accept Jesus as Lord of our lives according to the terms of that covenant.

And what are those terms? They are recorded in Jeremiah 31.31–34 and repeated in Hebrews 8.8–13. For this new covenant is not something dreamed up by the early Christians in New Testament times, but something announced with all the authority of the prophets long before that in Old Testament times.

First, as we saw in the preceding chapter, there is a declaration of God's intention:

'Behold the days are coming, declares the Lord,
when I will establish a new covenant with the house of Israel

and with the house of Judah,
not like the covenant that I made with their fathers
on the day when I took them by the hand to bring them out
    of the land of Egypt.
For they did not continue in my covenant,
and so I showed no concern for them, declares the Lord.'
(Heb. 8.8–9)

Two important things are stated here:

1 The new covenant replaces not the covenant made with Abraham in
Genesis 15, but the much later covenant made with Israel after they
had left Egypt; that is, the Sinai covenant based on the law.
2 The new covenant was necessary, because the nation broke the
conditions of that Sinai covenant and, because it was a two-party
covenant, their infringement of it broke their relationship with God.

Now Hebrews sets out the terms of the new covenant, once again
continuing to cite the prophet Jeremiah in the Old Testament:

'For this is the covenant that I will make with the house of Israel
    after those days, declares the Lord:
I will put my laws into their minds,
    and write them on their hearts,
and I will be their God,
    and they shall be my people.
And they shall not teach, each one his neighbour
    and each one his brother, saying, 'Know the Lord',
for they shall all know me,
    from the least of them to the greatest.
For I will be merciful towards their iniquities,
    and I will remember their sins no more.'
(Heb. 8.10–12)

We see at once that the new covenant does not disregard the moral law
of God. On the contrary, instead of that law being written on tablets of

stone external to the people, God commits himself to writing them in the hearts and consciences of believers to get them into our spiritual and moral bloodstream, so that they become an integral part of who we are.

We have said before that God is righteous and he wants us to be righteous, not only in the sense of being right with God through faith in Christ, but also in the sense of living righteous, morally upright lives. We need to understand clearly that his method of achieving these goals is not to get us to try in our own strength to fulfil his moral laws – which can only lead to failure and despair – but to invite us to trust him to justify us by faith and thereafter to supply the power through his Spirit to enable us to live according to his standards – not, be it unapologetically emphasised once more, as a means of achieving salvation, but as a means of expressing a salvation that we have already received as a free gift.

Therefore, when we as Christian believers take the cup of the new covenant, as Jesus commanded us to do, we are effectively asking God to go on writing those laws on our hearts, minds and consciences, and give us the power to live lives pleasing to him.

Sometimes people react to this when they hear these ideas for the first time by saying: 'When the laws were outside me, written in the Bible or on a wall at church, I found that was enough to prick my conscience, and it was very difficult, indeed impossible, to live up to them since I just didn't have the power. I can understand why God gave Israel up when they broke the Sinai covenant.' They then ask: 'Won't it be far worse if God starts putting them in my heart? Will I not then be even more conscious of my sin and failure, so that God is more likely to give me up?'

Well, you certainly will be more conscious of your sinfulness and failure.

But now comes the wonderful part. The new covenant at this point is utterly different from the old. Far from saying that God will reject you, it says to you that if you repent of your sins, God will remember[2] them no more – that is, he will never bring them against you in penal judgment.

Why? Because they are covered in their entirety by Christ's death.

In this way the Lord's Supper is designed as an instrument to help us to grasp the glory of this good news and to understand God's provision for our growth in character and integrity.

Because this is real and not play acting, there are inevitable negative implications for us if we do not take it seriously. Paul says so explicitly:

> Whoever, therefore, eats the bread or drinks the cup of the Lord in an unworthy manner will be guilty concerning the body and blood of the Lord. Let a person examine himself, then, and so eat of the bread and drink of the cup. For anyone who eats and drinks without discerning the body eats and drinks judgement on himself. That is why many of you are weak and ill, and some have died. But if we judged ourselves truly, we would not be judged. But when we are judged by the Lord, we are disciplined so that we may not be condemned along with the world.
> (1 Cor. 11.27–32)

Precisely because taking the cup expresses a desire for Christ to rule in our lives, we should examine ourselves before we do so in order to see if there is unconfessed sin in our lives and repent of it. The Greek word for 'repent' is *metanoia*. It does not simply mean being superficially sorry for our actions, but is a radical concept meaning a fundamental change of mind about our sin, repudiating and turning away from it with God's help.

Some people when they hear this react by saying that if this is what the Lord's Supper involves it would then be better never to take it – or only very rarely – since we are not good enough to do so.

That option is not open to us. Paul does not say: 'Let a person examine themselves and then stay away from communion...' No. We are to examine ourselves and then participate, because the bread and wine remind us of the only basis on which we can be forgiven: Jesus' death for our sins.

Putting it another way, the command to remember the Lord in the communion service forces on us the regular discipline of:

- examining ourselves;
- repenting before God, if necessary;
- acknowledging Jesus' death on the cross as the only source of forgiveness and restoration;
- accepting that forgiveness with gratitude.

149

This aspect of the new covenant reminds us about another dimension to the concept of covenant as such: it is an instrument of government. The new covenant enshrines the principles on which the Lord governs his redeemed people as King. It therefore reminds us of the various different ideas that have been proposed throughout history for governing peoples, particularly the concept of a social contract. Two influential yet contrasting versions of that concept were introduced by Thomas Hobbes, a seventeenth-century English political philosopher, in his book *Leviathan*, and by Jean Jacques Rousseau, an eighteenth-century Swiss political philosopher, in his book *The Social Contract*. Hobbes took the view that a strong central human authority was needed to control people because of their predisposition to evil, whereas Rousseau thought that social harmony could be achieved because people were basically good.

Although Hobbes was more realistic about human sin, what both of their philosophies lacked was a transcendent dimension that infused ultimate meaning from outside the world. It is precisely that feature that the biblical covenantal world view supplies. The biblical idea of God writing his laws on human hearts is uniquely effective.

# Part 3

# GENESIS 16.1—19.38

THE LIFE OF ABRAHAM: STAGE 2
SUMMARY
I
A.  Hagar the surrogate
Infertile Sarai persuades Abram to take Egyptian Hagar as surrogate.
Hagar conceives, and despises Sarai, who dismisses her and she flees.
An angel of the Lord appears to her, tells her to return and promises
    her a vast offspring.
Ishmael is born.

B.  The covenant of circumcision
God appears to Abram, changes his name to Abraham, reaffirms the
    promise and establishes the covenant of circumcision.
God changes Sarai's name to Sarah and promises that Abraham will
    have a son with her, whom he is to call Isaac.
All males in the entourage are circumcised.

C.  The tent: Abraham entertains the angels
Abraham asks Sarah to make a meal for three angelic visitors. The
    visitors ask to see her and she listens at the door as they tell
    Abraham that she will give birth within a year. Sarah laughs at the
    prospect, but denies it.

II

A. The judgement of Sodom

Abram pleads with God for Sodom: 'Will you destroy the righteous with the wicked?' Abraham haggles and eventually God agrees to spare the city if ten righteous people are found in it.

B. Lot 'entertains' the angels

The angels meet Lot in the town square of Sodom and he offers them hospitality. They enter his home for a meal, but the sex-mad townspeople demand that Lot give up the visitors. In a gesture of utter compromise and disregard for the sanctity of sex and the family, Lot offers the crowd his daughters instead.

The angels blind the townspeople and beg Lot and his relatives to flee. His relatives mock him, and the angels forcibly take Lot and his wife out of the city to the small town of Zoar.

God destroys Sodom by raining fire from the sky. Lot's wife looks back and is turned into a salt pillar. Abraham sees the smoke from afar. We are told that God has delivered Lot because of Abraham.

C. The cave: Lot's daughters and their children

Lot and his two daughters move to a cave in the hills. They resort to incest with their drunk father in their desperation to have children – Moab and Ammon.

**PERVASIVE THEMES**

Stage 2 falls into two major parts, I and II. They both deal with aspects of the same topic, which Paul would describe as 'the works of the flesh'. The first aspect we might think of as 'religious' flesh – that is, the attempt to please God in our own strength, using our own resources and ideas. Abram and Sarai try to solve their own childlessness by using pious-sounding arguments to resort to having a surrogate mother, rather than trusting in God's promise and waiting. The second part has to do with the flesh in its seamy, overtly immoral side, with Lot as a sad case of living after the flesh, even though in the New Testament he is called a righteous man. Two more major themes are the sanctity of hospitality and the sanctity of sex.

The roots of the battle against the flesh are to be found in Stage 1. There, Abraham learns the principle of justification by faith in trusting God's promise. Nevertheless he finds that trust difficult to maintain faced with what might happen to Sarai in Egypt. He tries to solve the problem by his own subterfuge. He may have misjudged Pharaoh's attitude to the sanctity of marriage, although the latter might have changed his mind after sensing the supernatural nature of the plagues on his house.

In Stage 2 these features are now carried forward and analysed in greater depth and subtlety.

## LITERARY STRUCTURE AND THOUGHT FLOW

This stage is structured in two parallel halves, as reflected in the way they are labelled. It begins with surrogacy brought about because Sarai despairs of having children. It ends with incest because Lot's daughters despair of having children. Two disastrous ways of trying to ensure the family line continues.

The parallels bring out the subtlety of the flesh as an enemy of living by faith in God. In IA Sarai calls upon the Lord to judge between her and Abram. In IIA Abraham pleads with the Judge of all the earth to spare Sodom.

In IB Abram is enjoined to walk before the Lord and be blameless, and the covenant of circumcision (a cut in the flesh of the organ of transmission of life) is established. This is picked up in the New Testament as a symbol of having no confidence in the flesh. In IIB God judges both Lot's confidence in the flesh and his consequent failure to walk before the Lord. God judges Sodom's horrific abandonment to fleshly desire by raining fire from heaven.

In IC and IIC there is a dramatic contrast between the lightness of Abram's tent and the gloom of Lot's cave. In IC Sarah laughs at the idea that she could have a child, since she is worn out and her husband is old. In IIC Lot's daughters complain that their father is old and there are no (younger) men to give them offspring. Thus IC and IIC present two problems in preserving a family line.

# 11

# A surrogate son

## Hagar the surrogate

In the first part (A) Sarai despairs of having her own children. There are many women today who have to cope with infertility, but in the culture of the ancient world it could be harder to bear as it was often regarded as a mark of failure.

> Now Sarai, Abram's wife, had borne him no children. She had a female Egyptian servant whose name was Hagar. And Sarai said to Abram, 'Behold now, the LORD has prevented me from bearing children. Go in to my servant; it may be that I shall obtain children by her.' And Abram listened to the voice of Sarai.
> (Gen. 16.1–2)

This is the first time in the narrative that we hear Sarai speaking to her husband. In Egypt Abram had asked Sarai to compromise the meaning of 'wife' by denying their full relationship. This time it is Sarai who asks Abram to compromise the meaning of 'child' in a conversation full of the tension of infertility and childlessness – a topic that has been simmering in the background and no doubt breaking through to the surface every time God renewed his promise to them of children. 'The Old Testament is a book about infertility.' With these words Dr Ros Clarke opens her Lent reflection on Sarai in her much-recommended book *Forty Women*.[1] She goes on to say: 'Mothers are ten a penny in the Old Testament. But the women we know, the women we remember, the women whose stories matter, those women are, all too often, barren.'

Dr Peter Saunders, CEO of the International Christian Medical and Dental Association, writes:

The desire to have children is one of the strongest human instincts, and when it is thwarted the emotional pain can be intense and prolonged. Infertility treatments offer hope; but at what cost? As a Christian doctor, I am asked more questions about the ethics of this area than any other. With over two million infertile couples in the UK (one in eight), if we are not infertile ourselves, virtually all of us will know someone who is, so we need to have thought through the issues in a way that is consistent with God's plans and purposes.[2]

The advent of new medical procedures like IVF means that this is a major topic and we shall have to content ourselves here with thinking about the basic issues raised in the particular case of Abram and Sarai. It is recommended that readers wanting to know more refer to the CMF (Christian Medical Foundation) website[3] and to the book *Just the Two of Us?* by Eleanor Margesson and Sue McGowan.[4]

Sarai told Abram that the Lord was responsible for her infertility. There are different ways of understanding that view but hers clearly did not include the obvious step of joining her husband and taking the matter to God in prayer, as many couples have done throughout history, some of them recorded in the Bible. Sad to say, there is no suggestion that they did, although God had promised that the pain of her childlessness would one day be lifted. We have already been told that Abram believed God about the matter, yet Genesis is silent as to how much he used his faith convictions to comfort Sarai while she waited.

Waiting for the Lord's timing is one of the great themes of Scripture. For instance, Psalm 37.34 says: 'Wait for the LORD and keep his way, and he will exalt you to inherit the land; you will look on when the wicked are cut off.' And Isaiah 40.31: 'But they who wait for the LORD shall renew their strength; they shall mount up with wings like eagles; they shall run and not be weary; they shall walk and not faint.'

These verses are easy to read but may be very difficult to put into practice. We are in a hurry. We think we have some idea of what God intends to do. But nothing is happening so we start to wonder if we should be doing something. Such was the case for Sarai. In her desperation for a child she suggested to Abram that he take her maidservant Hagar as concubine/wife so that she could perform the duty of a surrogate mother, a practice not uncommon among the customs of the time, and increasingly common today. Professor of Old Testament R. K. Harrison writes that what Sarai did was 'in full accord with the prevailing local customs in northern Mesopotamia'.[5]

Alan Millard, Rankin Professor Emeritus of Hebrew and Ancient Semitic Languages at the University of Liverpool, explains:

Inheritance was a very important part of life; having a son to continue the family line was a prime concern for every man and ancient legal deeds make arrangements for adoption where a couple was childless, or provide other ways of supplying a child if a wife was barren. A deed from the Assyrian merchant colony at Kanesh, about 1850 BC, states 'The man, Laqipum, has married the woman Hatala, Enishru's daughter. Laqipum may not marry another woman, but in the City (Ashur) he may marry a "nun"[6]. But if within two years Hatala, the wife, does not provide him with offspring, she herself will purchase a slave woman, and later on, after she will have produced a child by him, she may then sell her wherever she pleases.'[7] Then, slightly later, in the Babylonian Laws of Hammurabi there is a provision: 'If a man marries a "nun" and she gives a slave woman to her husband and the slave woman bears him children, then afterwards that slave woman tries to assume equality with her mistress: because she has borne children her mistress shall not sell her for money; she shall put the slave-mark on her and reckon her among the slave women' (§146).[8]

There is a strange irony in the account of Hagar and Sarai. We are told that Hagar was an Egyptian, which immediately connects this episode with what happened to Abram and Sarai in that country. Perhaps Hagar was part of the provision that Pharaoh had made for Sarai when they were in Egypt?

The stories show a remarkable anti-symmetry. In Egypt, Abram pressured Sarai to deny her true relationship with him. She fell in with his desire and was taken into Pharaoh's harem. This time, Sarai is prepared to deny her true relationship as Abram's wife and she pressures him to take another partner, the servant girl Hagar. Now it is Abram who obliges Sarai. In Egypt he was motivated by fear and the desire for wealth. Here, Sarai is motivated by feelings of shame at her infertility, and her driving ambition to circumvent it at any cost. In neither episode do Abram and Sarai show any real interest in the implications of what they are doing for their own relationship, for Sarai's plan would mean that Abram's child had an Egyptian mother, whereas in Egypt the danger was that Sarai's child would have an Egyptian father.

Nor does Abram seem to have sensed any potential difficulty with this arrangement any more than he did with the previous one. So then, not for the first time in Genesis, we are told that a man listened to the voice of his wife without either of them consulting the Lord – or each other. Adam had done the same. He had listened to Eve even though he knew the ultimate source of the temptation. The resulting Fall brought with it massive consequences that we all have to endure – sometimes very painfully.

It is easy to be wise after the event!

The strong resonances between the narrative here and that of the Fall in Genesis 3 are worth pursuing a little further. In Genesis 3, Eve took something – the forbidden fruit – and offered it to her husband. To refuse the fruit would have been to refuse her. He obeyed her voice and took it. Here, Sarai took something – Hagar her slave girl – and offered her to Abram. To refuse her would have been to reject Sarai. He decided to obey Sarai and took Hagar. Both incidents happened without consulting God.

In a real sense Sarai and Abram re-enacted the Fall, as a number of commentators have noted.[9] One consequence of the entry of sin into the world was that childbearing became problematic and painful in more ways than one. It was so for Abram and Sarai. What they did also led to a certain kind of 'knowledge of good and evil' that both of them lived to regret.

It is worth paying attention to the exact wording of Sarai's request to Abram: 'And Sarai said to Abram, "Behold now, the LORD has prevented me from bearing children. Go in to my servant; it may be that I shall obtain children by her"' (Gen. 16.2). The word 'obtain' here translates the Hebrew *baneh*, which means 'build'. It is used in Genesis 11 for building the Tower of Babel and, just as in Hebrews 11, it contrasts the Babel Project with the Seed Project. It also shows that Sarai, like many women, regarded having children as immensely important. She desired – and it was a God-given desire – to build a family and therefore herself be built in terms of significance. It would be her way of 'making a name'.

Unfortunately, her surrogacy stratagem backfired. When Hagar became pregnant (in spite of Abram's age!) she began to despise Sarai, possibly because it was by now obvious that Sarai's infertility had not been Abram's fault but hers.

There follows the first recorded two-way discussion between a wife and husband in the Bible. And it was an argument! The atmosphere was tense and fractured. Sarai had miscalculated. She had expected servile co-operation, but discovered instead that Hagar was a real human being who had feelings and ambitions of her own. Surrogacy then and now is often fraught with ethical and psychological problems.

Sarai felt threatened, blamed Abram and even tried to play the religious card by calling upon the Lord to judge between them. That issue will fill the stage later in the story when Abraham is called upon to judge the situation in Sodom.

Once again Abram didn't respond to Sarai's accusations by looking to the Lord for guidance, and nor did she. He simply decided, as has been and is alas the case with many men, to wash his hands of the whole business, abdicating all responsibility by telling Sarai to do with Hagar what she liked – and use Hagar as a mere means to her ends.

It was a tragic dereliction of his role as husband and father. It revealed that Hagar's only use to him had been as a means of child production. Abram and Sarai were going to have to face bitter lessons about what can go wrong when you treat others merely as instruments to further your own ends rather than as people with significance in their own right.

One lesson was that their attempt at surrogacy gave rise to deep psychological and moral issues and was not compatible with God's design for the generation of offspring. Abram's tactic failed to calm Sarai's fury. She overreacted and dealt harshly with Hagar, who understandably fled. It was a multiple tragedy. Hagar had lost her home, Sarai her maid, Abram a wife/concubine and the child she was carrying. Ros Clarke memorably sums it up: 'Infertility makes Sarai desperate and destructive.

She jeopardises her marriage, forces another woman into having sex with her husband and then drives her, vulnerable and alone, out of the household and into the wilderness.'[10]

Harshness and injustice are no way to deal with the consequences of our own wrongdoing, but they are very tempting when nerves are raw. Sarai would have to discover that she could not get away with that kind of behaviour if ever she was to be mother of the promised seed.

Hagar did not get far before she and her meagre supplies were exhausted and she found herself by a spring in the desert. What should she do? Perhaps she was already having thoughts of returning and hoping for Abram's protection. After all, she knew how Abram felt about his unborn child.

God cared and heaven intervened. An angel was sent to Hagar and, addressing her by name, asked: 'Where have you come from and where are you going?' (Gen. 16.8). Hagar learned something about God that is beautifully captured in Psalm 139.2: 'You know when I sit down and when I rise up.' Sarai had called on the Lord to judge and God did judge, but not as Sarai would have wished. The angel told Hagar to return and submit to her mistress.

Returning was hard enough, submitting much harder. What would it all lead to? The angel went on to say what would happen to Hagar and her offspring:

'Behold, you are pregnant
  and shall bear a son.
You shall call his name Ishmael,
  because the LORD has listened to your affliction. [11]
He shall be a wild donkey of a man,
  his hand against everyone
  and everyone's hand against him,
and he shall dwell over against all his kinsmen.'
(Gen. 16.11–12)

It was not the most promising of announcements and yet it told Hagar that God had observed her plight, had heard her cry – so she was to call her son Ishmael (God hears). He had promised to care for her and would protect her and her offspring. She was also told to return and submit to Sarai – a very hard thing for her to do.

To her credit she took the encounter as a genuine experience of God and memorialised it by calling the name of the well *Beer-lahai-roi* ('the well of the living one who sees me'). What had happened had convinced her that God was a living God – a great step forward for anyone. And, above all, that he saw her. That gave her significance. Ros Clarke calls Hagar an invisible woman:

> No one asks Hagar whether she wants to sleep with Abram. None asks whether she wants to have his baby. No one asks whether she's fine with handing that baby over to another woman. Hagar doesn't matter. It's only her body, her baby, her life after all . . . God sees Hagar. She isn't invisible to him.[12]

Hagar was the first woman, indeed the only person we read of in Scripture, who ascribed a name to God, *El Ro'i* ('God who sees me').[13] It is striking that Sarai never did anything like this: there is no record even of God ever having spoken to her directly. We need to factor this into our understanding of God's sovereign choice of Isaac rather than Ishmael to carry the Seed Project.

## God hears and God sees

The meanings of the names Ishmael and El Roi reverberate down the centuries into our contemporary world, where there is a great deal of distasteful and hurtful objectivization and abuse of women by men, which has given rise to the #MeToo movement for social justice for marginalised women. If such men believed that there was a living God who saw these women, they would hesitate before mistreating them.[14] Indeed, a conviction that God sees each of us would have a salutary effect on regulating our behaviour. The fact is that God does see us at home, at work, on the internet and when we are alone in a hotel.

He also sees us when we are bullied at school, disliked on Facebook, rejected by our friends. There are no secrets from God. We may deceive others all too easily – as a rash of scandals in the contemporary Christian world has demonstrated. We cannot deceive him. God sees. God records and will one day judge our secrets (Rom. 2.16). We must not forget that his eyes, like a flame of fire, will one day be turned towards every one of us and reveal us as we really are (Rev. 1.1; 2.18; 19.12).

Even unbelievers have been known to appreciate the value of an all-seeing God. Lord May, a former president of the Royal Society, speaking in the context of the need to take steps to prevent global warming, said: 'Given that punishment is a useful mechanism, how much more effective it would be if you invested that power not in an individual but in an all-seeing, all-powerful deity that controls the world.' He felt that this would be 'immensely stabilising in individual human cultures and societies' and that 'a supernatural punisher may be part of the solution'.[15]

Hagar, like many women, found herself in a very unpleasant and difficult place through no fault of her own. It wasn't her fault that she had been born in Egypt, that she had been given by Pharaoh to Sarai and had had to travel with her into an alien land. Yet she discovered that God was no respecter of persons – that he was really concerned, not only about the Abrams and Sarais of this world, but about her plight and that of her unborn child. God was going to ensure that she would herself be the progenitor of a great nation. God named her child before he was born, as he later did with Isaac. God is more interested in the despised and rejected than we sometimes think. Perhaps it was Hagar's conviction that God saw her that gave her the courage to do the hard thing the angel commanded – to return and submit to her mistress?

Eventually, she had a son and called him Ishmael to celebrate the fact that God had seen her plight. The text states three times in two sentences that Hagar was his mother – a reminder perhaps that, once more, Abram had (unwisely) gone down to Egypt for help. But that had not been Hagar's fault, as she was already there.

A deeper analysis is given in the New Testament. There, Paul says of Ishmael that he was born 'according to the flesh'. 'The flesh' is a vivid term with Paul that refers to what humans are like when they make their decisions, expend their energy and try to live independently of God. It is doing things relying only on your own strength rather than trusting God. It represents the exact opposite of life energised by faith in God.

Hence, saying that Ishmael was born after the flesh is *not* a criticism of Hagar. It is a criticism of Abram and Sarai, who had lived 'after the flesh', however piously they tried to dress it up. Sarai could not bring herself to trust God to carry out his promise. Or, if she did believe what God had promised, she managed to convince herself that God helps those who help themselves. God clearly needed her help, she thought, so she persuaded Abram to agree to using her Egyptian maid as a surrogate. They both, Sarai and Abram, had given in to what Paul calls 'the mind governed by the flesh' – which, he says, 'is death' (Rom. 8.6).

Another way of thinking about the flesh in this sense is as the gravitational pull of our sinful nature that tries to pressurise us into compromising our moral integrity – as many of us know all too well.

It is important to notice *when* this happened to Abram. It was not *before* he was justified by faith but *afterwards*. The same was true of Paul. What he had to say about his own struggles with the flesh can help us understand Abram and Sarai's tensions, and ours as well. We all have to learn what Paul ruefully describes in the following passage from Romans:

> For I do not understand my own actions. For I do not do what I want, but I do the very thing I hate. Now if I do what I do not want, I agree with the law, that it is good. So now it is no longer I who do it, but sin that dwells within me. For I know that nothing good dwells in me, that is, in my flesh. For I have the desire to do what is right, but not the ability to carry it out. For I do not do the good I want, but the evil I do not want is what I keep on doing. Now if I do what I do not want, it is no longer I who do it, but sin that dwells within me.
>
> So I find it to be a law that when I want to do right, evil lies close at hand. For I delight in the law of God, in my inner being, but I see in my members another law waging war against the law of my mind and making me captive to the law of sin that dwells in my members. Wretched man that I am! Who will deliver me from this body of death? Thanks be to God through Jesus Christ our Lord! So then, I myself serve the law of God with my mind, but with my flesh I serve the law of sin.
>
> (Rom. 7.15–25)

Paul wanted to follow the law of God, so he tried hard to harness his will, his emotions and his intellect in order to perform its demands, only to find it just was not enough. He discovered another principle working in his members. 'Wretched man that I am!' he says. He writes these words at this point in Romans, not so much to unbelievers, but to believers, men and women who have been justified by faith and now find that they have to struggle with their 'flesh' in the ongoing process of sanctification.

It is just here that we too can easily get discouraged. We may have been believers for years and yet we still find that the pull of our old fleshly nature is stubbornly strong, even when we want so much to please the Lord. We feel that we have not made the progress we should have done. Indeed, in a sense, we re-run the Fall many times, yielding to temptation with monotonous regularity. We forget that as believers our flesh is no more acceptable to God than it was when we were unregenerate.

It may well be that the disillusionment and frustration we experience is because our attitude to the flesh is not radical enough. In the passage just quoted, Paul's bleak assessment is given: 'For I know that nothing good dwells in me, that is, in my flesh. For I have the desire to do what is right, but not the ability to carry it out.' We all have to learn the painful lesson that Abram and Sarai learned: the flesh is weak and cannot fulfil the promises of God. That negative lesson took a depressingly long time for them to learn – which could even be an encouragement to us, if we are beginning to feel like giving up.

Living by faith in God means that, as believers, we need to learn to depend on God's Spirit actively and consciously. We are involved in a battle between flesh and Spirit. Paul writes: 'For the desires of the flesh are against the Spirit, and the desires of the Spirit are against the flesh, for these are opposed to each other, to keep you from doing the things you want to do' (Gal. 5.17).

It was a steep learning curve for Abram, and later for Paul, and it will be for us as we try to keep in step with the Spirit: 'So then, brothers, we are debtors, not to the flesh, to live according to the flesh. For if you live according to the flesh you will die, but if by the Spirit you put to death the deeds of the body, you will live' (Rom. 8.12–13). This is a deliberate action that must constantly be repeated, calling on God to supply the strength we need and ceasing to rely on our own resources. It can be tough going and may well involve discovering more about 'the flesh' and its sinfulness after conversion than we did before.

Abram was now 86 years old and having to cope with a child in his family. The mind boggles at what that must have meant, even in these days when 70 is no longer considered old. Then 13 years passed between the end of Genesis 16 and the beginning of chapter 17, during which time Abram and Sarai had to live with the turbulent consequences of their actions 'in the flesh'. The irony is that their behaviour may well have served to delay the birth of Isaac, as they had to face lessons that might not have been necessary if they had behaved differently. In later centuries, much of the wandering of Israel and delay in entering the promised land was caused by their disobedience to the Lord – living 'after the flesh' once more.

As well it might, the text draws a veil over their family life as Ishmael grew up into his teenage years. Some things are best passed over in silence. To say the least, a boy of whom it was prophesied before his birth that his hand would be against every man must have been quite a handful to cope with. We can only speculate. Many of us know just how hard dealing with youthful truculence and obstinacy can sometimes be. It must have been very difficult trying to cope with a 'wild donkey' in the home. Certainly a vivid reminder of the battle with untameable human nature that we humans have to face. Remember what Paul says in Romans 8.7: 'For the mind that is set on the flesh is hostile to God, for it does not submit to God's law; indeed, it cannot.'

'Lord, please give us patience and understanding . . .'

As far as we know from the narrative, God was silent for more than a dozen years. His is a severe mercy.

To sum up, Genesis relates some of what happened in Abram's family, but it does not attempt to reflect on it, analyse it or apply it in any detail for future generations, including ours. Is that a defect?

As a parent, I suspect not. Experience of family life shows that no two situations are the same. Of course we can see the mistakes that we and others make with our children, but it is very easy to compound the difficulty by imagining that, because we can see what went wrong, we will automatically know how to put it right. Not so. We may well find that what helped in one situation doesn't help in a similar situation, even in the same family.

Though we might wish it, more detail of Abraham and Sarah's family life than what God has decided to give us would not necessarily help us any further. Life is horrendously complex and, in each generation, parenting demands a humble dependence on the mercy, grace, power and presence of God. We all start as amateur parents – and often don't rise much above that.

# Coping with infertility

This whole incident raises the question of childlessness and surrogacy in general – a topic of intense concern for many people, not least Christian believers, since one in seven couples struggle to conceive.

The Bible draws our attention to the distress caused by infertility, not only in the case of Sarai and Abram, but of Rebekah and Isaac, Rachel and Jacob, and Hannah and Elkanah in the Old Testament, and Elizabeth and Zechariah in the New. As for surrogacy, Rachel gave her maidservant Bilhah to Jacob: 'Here is Bilhah, my servant. Sleep with her so that she can bear children for me and I too can build a family through her' (Gen. 30.3, NIV). Similarly Leah gave Jacob her maid Zilpah.

Even though these decisions were permitted by ancient customs, their outcome was jealousy, rivalry, favouritism and inevitable discord within the family. These women, and some of the men, knew what it meant to weep, experience deep sorrow, face the bitter, insensitive jibes of other women who had children, and pray in despair to God. The desire for children is a powerful, created instinct, so our response to infertility must in the first instance be understanding and compassion at the brokenness of our world.

It will, rightly, be said that in each of the cases just cited, God himself intervened and children were eventually born. However, there is clearly no guarantee, even for believers, that there will be supernatural intervention and many devoted Christian couples have remained childless.

What, then, about medical intervention? Advanced medicine is one of God's great gifts to humanity and it will be argued by some that if a certain technology helps produce children, we should therefore use it.

Yet others will say that just because we have the technology or the means to do something does not necessarily mean that it is always morally right to use them – Sarai and Abram being a case in point.

I should explain that in my own concern to defend the Christian faith publicly, there have been two overarching questions about creation: the first is the status of the universe – was it created or not? The second is the status of human beings – were they created in the image of God or not? It was this second question that motivated me some years ago to take a degree in bioethics, which helped me realise in particular just how sensitive beginning-of-life and end-of-life scenarios are. Understandably so, since human life made in the image of God is a very precious thing. I am aware that every case is unique and that Christians may and do come to different conclusions. It is, nevertheless, a healthy thing to try to evaluate them from a biblical perspective and to do what Abram and Sarai did not do – talk to God about it.[16]

Philippa Taylor, who was Head of Public Policy for the Christian Medical Fellowship and currently heads up the Care Leadership Programme, stresses the centrality of the fact that all humans bear the image of God:

> As human beings made in God's image, everyone is a unique and precious creation. The dignity of our humanity comes from God, whose image we bear. Surrogate motherhood is a clear violation of human dignity – of the child, of the rearing mother and of the gestational mother – because persons made in God's image are not fundamentally things, or commodities, that can be objectified, purchased or used for a price. Wyatt challenges us that: 'to abuse, manipulate or ill-treat another human being is to show contempt for God . . . to treat the divine image with contempt.' . . .
>
> Superficially, surrogacy may appear to be a reasonable response to the pain of a childless couple or the financial needs of a surrogate woman, and acceptable as the autonomous choice of the adults involved. As the scenarios illustrate, there are few legal and practical limits to the freedom to have a child 'when I want' and 'how I want'. Yet these choices take no regard of the basic presumption that a child's best interest is to be born into a natural family structure in

which the family relationships have not been intentionally confused. The child and the surrogate, the most vulnerable ones and the ones most likely to be harmfully affected, receive little, or no, protection.

The problems are deeper than this though. Professor of Ethics and author Gilbert Meilander writes perceptively about our eagerness to be masterful and independent. He, like C. S. Lewis, warned of the effect that such so-called freedom will ultimately lead to: 'What we call Man's power over Nature turns out to be a power exercised by some men over other men with Nature as its instrument . . . Man's conquest of Nature turns out, in the moment of its consummation, to be Nature's conquest of Man.'[17]

How clearly this is illustrated by 21st Century surrogacy! A moral vision, shaped by a Christian understanding of the person and family, has to be prepared to say 'no' to some exercises of human freedom and to turn away from technology that is possible but unwise. It will be hard to state in advance the precise boundaries that ought to limit our freedoms but we must be prepared to look for them. We must be prepared to acknowledge that there may be suffering we are free to end, but ought not to, that there are children who might be produced through artificial means, but ought not to be.

In a Google world that allows (indeed encourages) individuals almost complete freedom to pursue any number of different reproductive options, with little consideration of its effects on others, it will seem almost radical to suggest that Christians struggling with infertility reject this and pursue alternative ways of fulfilling their deep and God-given desire for parenthood. In a world where there are many sad, abused, abandoned and disabled children, surely adoption or fostering, caring for the unwanted and rejected is a better and more godly way. At the same time, the Christian community should learn to recognise, honour and support the painful sacrifices that such couples make.[18]

There is much more to be said and the reader who wishes to explore this important issue further can find useful resources from the Christian Medical Fellowship.[19]

# 12

# The covenant of circumcision

God appeared yet again:

> When Abram was ninety-nine years old the LORD appeared to
> Abram and said to him, 'I am God Almighty; walk before me, and
> be blameless, that I may make my covenant between me and you,
> and may multiply you greatly.' Then Abram fell on his face. And
> God said to him, 'Behold, my covenant is with you, and you shall
> be the father of a multitude of nations. No longer shall your name
> be called Abram, but your name shall be Abraham, for I have made
> you the father of a multitude of nations. I will make you exceedingly
> fruitful, and I will make you into nations, and kings shall come from
> you. And I will establish my covenant between me and you and your
> offspring after you throughout their generations for an everlasting
> covenant, to be God to you and to your offspring after you. And
> I will give to you and to your offspring after you the land of your
> sojournings, all the land of Canaan, for an everlasting possession,
> and I will be their God.'
> (Gen. 17.1–8)

As a preamble to the making of the covenant, God solemnly changes
Abram's name (meaning something like 'exalted father') to Abraham
(meaning something like 'father of many nations'). Thus God repeated
the promise he had made to Abram in Genesis 15 of an abundance of
offspring (the many nations) and his commitment to give Abraham and
his seed the land for an everlasting possession.

This is the first time we read of God giving a person a new name in the
Bible and it is clearly of immense import, as it was designed to reinforce
the promise. It would only make sense if Abraham actually became a

father of many nations – something not fulfilled in his lifetime, even though God speaks here as if it has already been accomplished – another evidence that God's promises are so sure that once made they are as good as done: 'I have made you the father of a multitude of nations' (Gen. 17.5).

As a mathematician I like Christopher Watkin's topological metaphor of 'folding time': 'promise and fulfilment stretch and squeeze time, folding distant points so that they sit adjacent to each other, like a baker kneading a batch of dough, such that . . . Christ can say, "Your father Abraham rejoiced at the thought of seeing my day; he saw it and was glad."'[1]

Does the term 'a multitude of nations' contain a hint that not only the descendants of Isaac but those of Ishmael would regard Abraham as their progenitor – as would the multitude from every nation on earth who would regard him as their spiritual father?

It does not take a great deal of imagination to think of Abraham, now a powerful tribal leader in the region, being asked by his neighbours and acquaintances what the significance of his new name was. Since there was yet no evidence of its being fulfilled, confessing its meaning would be a mark of his faith and a witness to the God who promised.

Similarly, in the New Testament, Jesus renamed Simon as Peter. Again, that encapsulated Jesus' intention to build his Church out of 'living stones' like him.[2] It is interesting to speculate on how Peter might have explained the meaning of his name in the time before Pentecost!

Likewise, through the centuries, in many cultures, upon conversion people have been given a Christian name that expresses the hope that it will turn out to be an apt characterization of the person receiving the name.

God now institutes a further covenant with Abraham. It is called the covenant of circumcision, because the minor surgical act of circumcision was its emblem:

And God said to Abraham, 'As for you, you shall keep my covenant, you and your offspring after you throughout their generations. This is my covenant, which you shall keep, between me and you and your offspring after you: Every male among you shall be circumcised.

170

You shall be circumcised in the flesh of your foreskins, and it shall be a sign of the covenant between me and you. He who is eight days old among you shall be circumcised. Every male throughout your generations, whether born in your house or bought with your money from any foreigner who is not of your offspring, both he who is born in your house and he who is bought with your money, shall surely be circumcised. So shall my covenant be in your flesh an everlasting covenant. Any uncircumcised male who is not circumcised in the flesh of his foreskin shall be cut off from his people; he has broken my covenant.'
(Gen. 17.9–14)

The fact that this covenant is a two-party covenant between God and Abraham immediately raises the question of its relationship with the one-party covenant of Genesis 15. That will become evident as we explore its meaning. However, before we do that, we need to pay close attention to what is being set up here. Certain factors are prominent.

Circumcision is for infant males only – apart, of course, from the first generation to receive it, like Abraham and his family. It was normally to be performed by fathers on their newborn male infants at eight days old. It is an operation to remove a small piece of skin from the male organ of procreation. It carries with it a solemn commitment to perpetuate the covenant it represents under severe penalty of being cut off from the people.

The heavy emphasis on the male aspect indicates a strong push to make fathers take their responsibility. This is of direct relevance to the contemporary world, where many of the woes in our social fabric stem from the irresponsibility and dereliction of duty of fathers who leave women with the burden of rearing the family, and giving it a sense of direction and meaning. The moral, spiritual and financial cost of broken families, particularly in Western cultures, is incalculable.

The challenge to Abraham and those who came after him was to take both husbandhood and fatherhood seriously and to engage in the process of integrating their children into the great narrative of God's purposes for the nation. Paternal commitment was to be regarded as essential to the transmission of the covenant from generation to generation. It was calculated to impress on fathers (and mothers) the fact that they were involved in something far bigger than themselves, something that had a divine spiritual and moral dimension in which they were called to play a substantial and vital role.

That in itself could be an effective antidote to the selfishness that often reigns when a man – yes, even a professing believer – tires of his wife and gets involved with a younger woman without any thought of the damage this will cause to himself, his wife and children and other families affected. May I be permitted to say that if you find yourself in that situation, please, please stop and think of the consequences of the path you are tempted to follow. Don't imagine you can't help it because you 'love' her. Your emotions are distorting your vision and blurring all negative consequences. It is hard for you to think it, but you will probably live to regret what you are doing when it is too late to do anything much about it. You made a marriage commitment, you brought children into the world. These facts are not altered by your raging emotions. By repenting and seeking restoration with the Lord's help, you will save yourself and others from the mainly unforeseen consequences of what can only be described as your madness. Stand before the Lord and make your commitments and their concomitant responsibilities your central focus.

In keeping with all of this we find throughout the biblical narrative an unwavering emphasis on the importance of teaching children from an early age. It was important for parents to answer their children's questions, especially at the great Jewish festivals. For instance, the institution of Passover had in it the following clause: 'And when your children say to you, "What do you mean by this service?" you shall say, "It is the sacrifice of the LORD's Passover, for he passed over the houses of the people of Israel in Egypt, when he struck the Egyptians but spared our houses"' (Exod. 12.26–27). Later, in Proverbs, a fundamental principle was laid down: 'Train up a child in the way he should go; even when he is old he will not depart from it' (Prov. 22.6).

We recall that all of this is set against the background of a promise to bring blessing through Abraham to the whole world. It is self-evident that increased taking of parental responsibility as mandated here in Genesis would utterly transform global society for good. Studies have shown that children need both parents – father and mother.[3] The tragedy is that those people who ought to know better tend to shy away from admitting this in order to avoid criticism and disapprobation. Political correctness may negate common sense.

In the Christian context, parents often have a service of dedication for their new child, in which they appear as a family publicly before their church congregation and formally take on responsibility to bring their child up according to the word of God, asking for the congregation's support and prayer.[4]

How grateful my wife and I are for our own parents who, like all parents, were not perfect, but nevertheless took time to fill our young minds with the riches of Scripture and in this way laid down a foundation for life that has stood the test of time magnificently.

Allow me to ask the parents among my readers: what have you committed yourselves to do for your children in this respect and how are you implementing your commitments?

Let us now have a more detailed look at the meaning of:

# Circumcision in the Old and New Testament

Circumcision was, first, a physical mark applied to all Abraham's physical posterity. Over the centuries the practice fell into disuse at times so that, for instance, after the years of wandering in the desert when Israel entered the promised land under Joshua, he circumcised all the people who had been born on the journey, as they had not been circumcised by their parents.

It should be noted, however, that circumcision did not in every case mean recognition of a person as a member of the special nation that was later called Israel – for example, Ishmael, though circumcised, was not permitted to remain in the clan.

## A physical mark with a deeper meaning

The outward physical removal of a piece of flesh was a pretty blunt but very graphic and understandable way of teaching Abraham and his offspring not to put their trust in the flesh at the moral and spiritual level. Using biblical language, one might say that the flesh, in more senses than one, needed to be cut off, not trusted.

This implied that circumcision was designed to be more than a merely physical ritual. It was a symbol to represent an underlying moral and spiritual reality. The relationship of symbol to reality has always been a contested issue in religious contexts. The danger is that the symbol could be confused with the reality. A wedding ring is a symbol of marriage, but wearing one does not make you married. It is meaningless unless you are already married. Similarly, baptism, as I understand it, is a symbol of being a Christian, but the ritual of baptism does not in itself convey eternal life and make you a Christian if you have not already become one through putting your faith in Christ.

## Circumcision of the heart

That circumcision was always intended to convey something deeper than the physical is clear in the Old Testament. In Deuteronomy we find the command: 'Circumcise therefore the foreskin of your heart, and be no longer stubborn' (10.16). Again, in the same book, we have: 'And the LORD your God will circumcise your heart and the heart of your offspring, so that you will love the LORD your God with all your heart and with all your soul, that you may live' (30.6).

This idea is repeated by the prophet Jeremiah: 'Behold, the days are coming, declares the LORD, when I will punish all those who are circumcised merely in the flesh' (Jer. 9.25). The key idea here is that all of us need to cut bad stuff out of our hearts – the works of the flesh. Here is a biblical list of them: 'Now the works of the flesh are evident: sexual immorality, impurity, sensuality, idolatry, sorcery, enmity, strife, jealousy, fits of anger, rivalries, dissensions, divisions, envy, drunkenness, orgies, and things like these' (Gal. 5.19–21).

I said we need to cut them out, but we find in practice that we don't have the strength to do so. We need to allow the Lord to perform the initial basic cut in order for our hearts to be free of all that gets in the way of our loving God with purity and integrity. We shall consider that process, called the 'circumcision of Christ', below.

The first Christian martyr, Stephen, accused the crowd of Jews in Jerusalem of failing to distinguish between symbol and reality, in that they were proud of the first but ignored the second: 'You stiff-necked people, uncircumcised in heart and ears, you always resist the Holy Spirit. As your fathers did, so do you' (Acts 7.51).

Similarly, Paul explained to the church in Rome that true Jewishness means not only being circumcised but having the inner spiritual convictions that are in accordance with the law of God:

> For circumcision indeed is of value if you obey the law, but if you break the law, your circumcision becomes uncircumcision. So, if a man who is uncircumcised keeps the precepts of the law, will not his uncircumcision be regarded as circumcision? Then he who is physically uncircumcised but keeps the law will condemn you who have the written code and circumcision but break the law. For no one is a Jew who is merely one outwardly, nor is circumcision outward and physical. But a Jew is one inwardly, and circumcision is a matter of the heart, by the Spirit, not by the letter. His praise is not from man but from God.
> (Rom. 2.25–29)

This means that physical circumcision did not make people spiritual children of Abraham. Paul makes this point again in Romans 9.6–7: 'But it is not as though the word of God has failed. For not all who are descended from Israel belong to Israel, and not all are children of Abraham because they are his offspring, but "Through Isaac shall your offspring be named."'

## Circumcision and salvation

Circumcision performed another important role that was very rapidly lost sight of. In a key passage Paul explains to the church at Rome, whose members were from both Jewish and Gentile backgrounds, that circumcision was a seal of the righteousness of faith that Abraham had while still uncircumcised:

> We say that faith was counted to Abraham as righteousness. How then was it counted to him? Was it before or after he had been circumcised? It was not after, but before he was circumcised. He received the sign of circumcision as a seal of the righteousness that he had by faith while he was still uncircumcised. The purpose was to

make him the father of all who believe without being circumcised, so that righteousness would be counted to them as well, and to make him the father of the circumcised who are not merely circumcised but who also walk in the footsteps of the faith that our father Abraham had before he was circumcised.
(Rom. 4.9–12)

The precise order of events in the life of Abraham is crucial for our understanding of biblical teaching. The principal fact is that Abraham was first justified and then circumcised 13 years later, which means that his *justification had absolutely nothing to do with the rite of circumcision.* The rite of circumcision was an outward physical sign to indicate that Abraham had been justified. Performance of the rite was not the *means* of justification.

It is very important to grasp this, since the idea that a rite or ritual can convey salvation has been endemic for centuries and has led to much confusion. That has particularly been the case with the rite of Christian baptism, which was instituted to celebrate publicly that the person being baptised had already become a Christian through personal faith in Christ – hence the New Testament order: believe and be baptised (Mark 16.16; Acts 2.41).

Paul goes on to explain that the same argument applies to the law of Moses that was introduced much later even than circumcision – the law of Moses is not a means of justification either.

For the promise to Abraham and his offspring that he would be heir of the world did not come through the law but through the righteousness of faith. For if it is the adherents of the law who are to be the heirs, faith is null and the promise is void. For the law brings wrath, but where there is no law there is no transgression.

That is why it depends on faith, in order that the promise may rest on grace and be guaranteed to all his offspring – not only to the adherent of the law but also to the one who shares the faith of Abraham, who is the father of us all, as it is written, 'I have made you the father of many nations.'
(Rom. 4.13–17)

In spite of this, human nature is such that many people came to regard circumcision and the keeping of the law of Moses as the means of salvation, just as many people have come to regard baptism and holy communion as the means of salvation.

## The true circumcision

However, the New Testament picks up the notion of circumcision and applies it to Christian believers, not at the physical level of a physical rite but at the spiritual level of a transformative experience. Paul writes to the church at Philippi:

> For *we are the circumcision*, who worship by the Spirit of God and glory in Christ Jesus and put no confidence in the flesh – though I myself have reason for confidence in the flesh also. If anyone else thinks he has reason for confidence in the flesh, I have more: circumcised on the eighth day, of the people of Israel, of the tribe of Benjamin, a Hebrew of Hebrews; as to the law, a Pharisee; as to zeal, a persecutor of the church; as to righteousness under the law, blameless. But whatever gain I had, I counted as loss for the sake of Christ. Indeed, I count everything as loss because of the surpassing worth of knowing Christ Jesus my Lord. For his sake I have suffered the loss of all things and count them as rubbish, in order that I may gain Christ and be found in him, not having a righteousness of my own that comes from the law, but that which comes through faith in Christ, the righteousness from God that depends on faith . . .
> (Phil. 3.3–9, emphasis mine)

Paul here explains that he did not resent or reject the fact that he was a physical descendant of Abraham and had been circumcised to express this. Yet he clearly understood that, as far as salvation was concerned, neither his physical descent, nor his appropriation of the rite of circumcision, nor his concerted efforts to keep the law was of any avail whatsoever. Where salvation was concerned, sharing the faith of Abraham and acting accordingly was all that mattered.

Paul applies this principle to all believers:

Look: I, Paul, say to you that if you accept circumcision, Christ will be of no advantage to you. I testify again to every man who accepts circumcision that he is obligated to keep the whole law. You are severed from Christ, you who would be justified by the law; you have fallen away from grace. For through the Spirit, by faith, we ourselves eagerly wait for the hope of righteousness. For in Christ Jesus neither circumcision nor uncircumcision counts for anything, but only faith working through love.

(Gal. 5.2–6)

Thus believers in Christ, whether physically circumcised or not, should put no confidence in the flesh, renouncing all trust in their own effort, observance of the law, ritual and ceremony.

The deepest of all New Testament applications of the concept of circumcision has to do with the fact that the unregenerate heart cannot make itself love God, as Paul and most Christians have discovered. If ever we are to be able to love God we must be cut loose from the flesh and be planted in the Spirit. As we mentioned earlier, only the Lord can wield the knife to do that and in a vivid metaphor Paul says how:

Therefore, as you received Christ Jesus the Lord, so walk in him, rooted and built up in him and established in the faith, just as you were taught, abounding in thanksgiving . . . In him also you were circumcised with a circumcision made without hands, by putting off the body of the flesh, by the *circumcision of Christ*, having been buried with him in baptism, in which you were also raised with him through faith in the powerful working of God, who raised him from the dead.

(Col. 2.6–7, 11–12, emphasis mine)

Paul elsewhere uses the phrase 'in the flesh' to denote the unregenerate state: 'Those who are in the flesh cannot please God. You, however, are not in the flesh but in the Spirit, if in fact the Spirit of God dwells in you. Anyone who does not have the Spirit of Christ does not belong to him' (Rom. 8.8–9). Regeneration (conversion) involves being transplanted from being in the flesh to being in the Spirit. Notice the

178

tense in the verse cited in the previous paragraph: 'In him also you *were* circumcised . . .' It was performed by the Lord at our conversion and is called the circumcision of Christ. We should notice, however, that this circumcision is not made with hands – that is, it is not a physical ritual or ceremony, but rather a spiritual reality. It follows, in particular, that what corresponds in the New Testament to circumcision in the Old Testament is certainly not water baptism, which is very obviously 'made with hands'.

What this means is that when we repent and trust Christ we are justified by faith. Furthermore, we are simultaneously cut by the Lord from being in the flesh and transplanted into the Spirit. There is a change to the very roots of our being. We are no longer in the flesh but in the Spirit. In that sense we have been circumcised by Christ.

We now need to grasp that this has happened and so we should believe it and reckon with it in daily life. For simply because we have become believers in Christ does not mean the flesh is no longer around to trouble us, as we have already seen well illustrated in the life of Abraham. It is sadly possible for us (like Abraham) to live 'after the flesh'. But, and here is the key point: *we do not now have to give in to the flesh.*

It may not feel as if this is true and if we are wobbly we may fall into temptation. However, it is as surely true as God's word is true. If we are believers, the roots of the flesh that held us down have already been cut by the Lord himself. This means that we, in spite of niggling feelings to the contrary, are now actually free not to have to follow the dictates of the flesh. In direct, conscious dependence on God we can find the strength to live and walk in the Spirit. Laying hold on the energy God has released through raising Jesus from the dead, we will experience the transformation of our characters into his image.

I am not suggesting that this is easy. Indeed it is a profound challenge to those of us who are Christians to believe what God has said about this at the deepest level as we begin to walk in Christ and in the Spirit. Those ideas resonate directly with God's command to Abram in Genesis 17: 'Walk before me, and be blameless' (v. 1). The New Testament version of it is in Paul's letter to the Galatians:

But I say, walk by the Spirit, and you will not gratify the desires of the flesh. For the desires of the flesh are against the Spirit, and the desires of the Spirit are against the flesh, for these are opposed to each other, to keep you from doing the things you want to do . . . If we live by the Spirit, let us also keep in step with the Spirit. (Gal. 5.16–17, 25)

In the days that followed, Abraham and his wife had to learn many of the lessons we have just discussed in connection with circumcision.

God's next action was to change Sarai's name to Sarah, moving from an older dialect Hebrew form to a newer, both forms meaning the same: 'princess'. She is the only woman in the Bible whose name was changed by God. God promised her the honour of being a mother of nations and kings.

God informed them that Sarah would bear a son to Abraham from whom nations and kings would come. 'Then Abraham fell on his face and laughed[5] and said to himself, "Shall a child be born to a man who is a hundred years old? Shall Sarah, who is ninety years old, bear a child?"' (Gen. 17.17).

If, as suggested earlier, we put this into a contemporary context by halving the ages here, Abraham would have been 50 and Sarah 45. These days menopause usually sets in around the late 40s and most women over 45 cannot conceive naturally,[6] so there is a reasonable fit.

This incident reminds us of Luke's account of Zachariah and Elizabeth. God sent an angel to tell Zachariah that he would have a son, and he protested: 'How shall I know this? For I am an old man, and my wife is advanced in years' (1.18). Like Abraham, Zachariah found it impossible to believe in a supernatural overcoming of the inevitable effects of old age. Zachariah was struck dumb for his unbelief – after all, he was a priest, he believed in God and prayer, and it was an angel speaking with him! Surely it was not all that big a step to go from there to believing in the supernatural power of God to grant him a child? The dumbness was apposite judgement for his inconsistency. He had nothing to say.

I cannot help pointing out that if those today who claim to be priests do not believe in the supernatural, then they will have nothing to say either.

However, Abraham was not struck dumb on this occasion. He said: 'Oh that Ishmael might live before you' (Gen. 17.18). It would seem that over the intervening years Abraham had accepted Ishmael as the promised son. His statement demonstrated his affection for the boy. Was he implying: 'Surely Ishmael can fulfil the promise? Maybe it is not ideal, his mother is not Sarah, but don't we have all the essentials here? Ishmael is my son and full of potential. Why deprive me of the joy of this relationship to wait even longer for the fulfilment of a promise that now seems even more remote and improbable than ever before? I am content – why can't you be?'?

Whatever Abraham thought, God insisted that Sarah would be the one to bear his son and heir. The son of promise had to have both Abraham and Sarah as parents in order to qualify as a worthy transmitter of the covenants. God also insisted that the child should be called Isaac – recording Abraham's laughter. God would appear to have a sense of humour – not surprisingly, since he created us with that delightful human capacity. Abraham would never be allowed to forget that particular bout of spontaneous hilarity.

However, none of this meant that Ishmael would be forgotten by God. God said:

'As for Ishmael, I have heard[7] you; behold, I have blessed him and will make him fruitful and multiply him greatly. He shall father twelve princes, and I will make him into a great nation. But I will establish my covenant with Isaac, whom Sarah shall bear to you at this time next year.'
(Gen. 17.20–21)

Now, at long last, the time was set: there was only one more year to wait for their very own child. His birth was soon to be further confirmed by a rather strange visitation.

## Abraham entertains the angels

And the LORD appeared to him by the oaks of Mamre, as he sat at the door of his tent in the heat of the day. He lifted up his eyes and looked, and behold, three men were standing in front of him. When he saw them, he ran from the tent door to meet them and bowed

himself to the earth and said, 'O Lord, if I have found favour in your sight, do not pass by your servant. Let a little water be brought, and wash your feet, and rest yourselves under the tree, while I bring a morsel of bread, that you may refresh yourselves, and after that you may pass on – since you have come to your servant.'
(Gen. 18.1–5)

Abraham saw three 'men' before him, yet the incident is described as an appearance of the Lord. Who were these three? Were they merely humans? Or angels? Or were two of them angels and the third the Lord? Mysterious.

There is a certain ambiguity, perhaps intentional, in the way this incident is related – especially in light of what is usually understood to be a comment on it in Hebrews: 'Let brotherly love continue. Do not neglect to show hospitality to strangers, for thereby some have entertained angels unawares' (Heb. 13.1–2).

There clearly came a point where Abraham became aware that this was a supernatural visitation by God, who appeared in the guise of angels and men. Was this a faint foreshadowing of the time when God would become man in his Son the Lord Jesus, the promised Seed of Abraham?

In an elaborate display of Middle Eastern hospitality Abraham modestly offered 'a morsel of bread' and yet got Sarah to make bread while he ordered a whole calf to be prepared – a massive overkill to feed three visitors!

Such generous hospitality is beautifully expressed in a nineteenth-century poem by James Russell Lowell (1819–91):

'This tent is mine,' said Yussouf, 'but no more
Than it is God's; come in and be at peace;
Freely shalt thou partake of all my store,
As I of his who buildeth over these
Our tents his glorious roof of night and day
And at whose door none ever yet heard Nay.'

The incident also shows the importance of giving hospitality, not only to members of our own culture, clan or clique but to strangers – a further indicator that Abraham was to convey blessings to the whole world. We never know just who we might encounter or be entertaining. It would seem that, even now, we are not completely shut off from what is usually unseen.

Scripture in general stresses the importance of hospitality. Much of the activity of the Lord himself, and the disciples, took place in homes and, particularly in the early days of Christianity, the believers broke bread from house to house. There was a real sense of home-based interdependence and fellowship.

Abraham did not join the three visitors to eat, but stood under a tree and watched them. The dialogue that followed highlights the supernatural dimension to this encounter.

> They said to him, 'Where is Sarah your wife?' [How did they know about Sarah?] And he said, 'She is in the tent.' The LORD said, 'I will surely return to you about this time next year, and Sarah your wife shall have a son.' ['The LORD said' presumably meant one of the three?] And Sarah was listening at the tent door behind him . . . So Sarah laughed to herself, saying, 'After I am worn out, and my lord is old, shall I have pleasure?' The LORD said to Abraham, 'Why did Sarah laugh and say, "Shall I indeed bear a child, now that I am old?" Is anything too hard for the LORD? At the appointed time I will return to you, about this time next year, and Sarah shall have a son.' But Sarah denied it, saying, 'I did not laugh', for she was afraid. He said, 'No, but you did laugh.'
> (Gen. 18.9–15)

Sarah covered her fear and embarrassment by telling a lie and was gently corrected for it. This is only the second time in the Bible that God is said to address a woman directly. The first time was when he spoke to Eve, and the topic was the same – childbirth and believing a lie.

'Is anything too hard for the LORD?' This is one of the great rhetorical questions of Scripture. It is easy to get cynical about the promises of the Lord to the extent that they appear to us as unrealisable in a practical sense, as they did to Sarah. Sometimes those who really trust the Lord with quiet confidence in such circumstances are looked on patronisingly and incredulously: 'So you really take it that seriously, do you? Come on!' The question 'Is anything too hard for the LORD?' is a challenge to us to trust him more confidently.

Paul takes a deeper look at what was involved in Abraham's faith in God at this point in the narrative:

> In hope he believed against hope, that he should become the father of many nations, as he had been told, 'So shall your offspring be.' He did not weaken in faith when he considered his own body, which was as good as dead (since he was about a hundred years old), or when he considered the barrenness of Sarah's womb. No distrust made him waver concerning the promise of God, but he grew strong in his faith as he gave glory to God, fully convinced that God was able to do what he had promised. That is why his faith was 'counted to him as righteousness'. But the words 'it was counted to him' were not written for his sake alone, but for ours also. It will be counted to us who believe in him who raised from the dead Jesus our Lord, who was delivered up for our trespasses and raised for our justification.
> (Rom. 4.18–25)

Abraham was no fool. He realised that, at the age of 100, from the perspective of genetic procreation his body was as good as dead. The issue for him, then, was whether God could create new life out of such deadness. Notice, however, that it was not Abram's faith that eventually created new life in his body. No, God did that in response to Abraham's faith.

Similarly, we are called upon to believe that God raised Jesus bodily from the dead. Again, it is not our faith that raised him – that would be nonsensical. It was the power of God that raised him. We are to place our faith in something God did and, if we do, it will be accounted to us for righteousness, just as Abraham's faith was accounted to him.

Also, even though Sarah initially laughed, she eventually also came to trust God's promise. Hebrews informs us: 'By faith Sarah herself received power to conceive, even when she was past the age, since she considered him faithful who had promised' (11.11).

# 13

# The judgement of Sodom

After the fashion of Hebrew storytelling, the narrative now leaves us in suspense awaiting the birth of Isaac, while appearing to divert to a completely different topic – the fate of Lot in Sodom.

However, it is not such a different topic, as what happens displays another aspect of 'the flesh'. This time it is not what we might call the 'religious' flesh, but rather the seamy, deviant side of the flesh, as exemplified in the city where Lot lived, whose name has given us an ugly word for a particular kind of sexual perversion. This topic is flagged up by the narrator saying that, as the three strange persons turned to leave Abraham's tent, they looked down towards Sodom, thus indicating their next destination. No doubt Abraham, as he led them to the door, noticed the direction of their glances and thought uncomfortably of his nephew Lot. God had more to say to him on that account.

The dialogue that follows has no real parallel elsewhere in the Bible. It is an unprecedented discussion between a man and God.

The LORD said, 'Shall I hide from Abraham what I am about to do, seeing that Abraham shall surely become a great and mighty nation, and all the nations of the earth shall be blessed in him? For I have chosen him, that he may command his children and his household after him to keep the way of the LORD by doing righteousness and justice, so that the LORD may bring to Abraham what he has promised him.' Then the LORD said, 'Because the outcry against Sodom and Gomorrah is great and their sin is very grave, I will go down to see whether they have done altogether according to the outcry that has come to me. And if not, I will know.'
(Gen. 18.17–21)

God first informs Abraham why he chose him. This is the only place in the Bible where he does so. The late Chief Rabbi, Lord Jonathan Sacks, comments:

> This tells us three things about what it is to be an heir of Abraham. First, it means that we are to be guardians of our children's future. We must ensure that they have a world to inherit . . . Second, education – directing our children and our household after us – is a sacred task . . . Third, how do you keep the way of the Lord? By doing what is right and just.[1]

It would be impossible to overstate the importance of these principles in a world where children so often bear the brunt of neglect, abuse and suffering.

God then tells Abraham about his intention to judge the evil of Sodom, but asks the man's opinion about the justice of such judgement – an intriguing example of 'and God said to them' (Gen. 1.28). It would be hard to read this passage without thinking of a prior instance of judgement in Genesis – the Flood. In a single passage in Luke Jesus used both the Flood in the days of Noah and the fiery judgement of Sodom in the days of Abraham as a thought model to illustrate his future return in judgement:

> Just as it was in the days of Noah, so will it be in the days of the Son of Man. They were eating and drinking and marrying and being given in marriage, until the day when Noah entered the ark, and the flood came and destroyed them all. Likewise, just as it was in the days of Lot – they were eating and drinking, buying and selling, planting and building, but on the day when Lot went out from Sodom, fire and sulphur rained from heaven and destroyed them all – so will it be on the day when the Son of Man is revealed. (Luke 17.26–30)

The two incidents of judgement have many things in common. The background to the Flood highlights a contrast between the evil on the earth and the righteousness of Noah:

The LORD saw that the wickedness of man was great in the earth, and that every intention of the thoughts of his heart was only evil continually. And the LORD was sorry that he had made man on the earth, and it grieved him to his heart. So the LORD said, 'I will blot out man whom I have created from the face of the land, man and animals and creeping things and birds of the heavens, for I am sorry that I have made them.' But Noah found favour in the eyes of the LORD.

(Gen. 6.5–8)

The background to the fiery judgement of Sodom is the contrast between the evil of that city and the righteousness of Abraham.

The narrative of the dialogue between God and Abraham begins with a unique insight into what the Lord thought of the man and it shows just how outstanding he was. God had chosen him with the express purpose of commanding 'his children and his household after him to keep the way of the LORD by doing righteousness and justice' (Gen. 18.19). The word translated 'chosen' here is the Hebrew *yadar*, which means 'know' and conveys the idea of friendship.[2] God's idea of friendship is self-disclosure – 'shall I hide . . .' – an attribute repeated by Jesus to his disciples in his final discourse: 'No longer do I call you servants, for the servant does not know what his master is doing; but I have called you friends, for all that I have heard from my Father I have made known to you' (John 15.15). Three times over in Scripture Abraham is called the friend of God (2 Chron. 20.7; Isa. 41.8; Jas 2.23).

God informed Noah about his decision to judge the earth by flooding it with water. He told him why he was doing so, but did not discuss the morality of it with him. God instructed him to build an ark that would save him and his family.

By contrast, God was about to discuss the case of Sodom and Gomorrah with Abraham. That was something unprecedented. And yet it is of the essence of friendship to focus on a common interest. C. S. Lewis writes:

Friendship arises out of mere Companionship when two or more of the companions discover that they have in common some insight or interest or even taste which the others do not share and which, till that moment, each believed to be his own unique treasure (or burden). The typical expression of opening Friendship would be something like, 'What? You too? I thought I was the only one.'

. . . It is when two such persons discover one another, when, whether with immense difficulties and semi-articulate fumblings or with what would seem to us amazing and elliptical speed, they share their vision – it is then that Friendship is born. And instantly they stand together in an immense solitude.[3]

And in this incident Abraham and God stand together in a unique solitude as they contemplate side by side one of the hardest issues imaginable. It was to be highly instructive for Abraham – the remarkable thing is that it is regarded as an expression of friendship.

If we are going to teach others what moral behaviour means, we need first to learn what it is ourselves. So it was with Abraham. In order to fulfil God's command to teach his children how to behave, Abraham himself needed to learn what righteousness and justice were. He had already started the process, in that his faith in God had been accounted to him as righteousness, but the learning curve was about to become very much steeper as God had this remarkable discussion with him about doing righteousness and justice not simply at a personal level, but governing and making judgements at the more political level of a city community.

Abraham and his descendants after him would have to learn to take their place and stand for righteousness among the nations of the world. In order to train him, God informed Abraham that he, God, was about to assess and deal with the evils being perpetrated in the city of Sodom.

The 'men' (presumably just two of them) left for Sodom, and Abraham remained standing before the Lord. He knew what was at stake. The Lord intended to judge Sodom, but Abraham's nephew Lot and his family were there. Would the judgement be indiscriminate, or was there hope that Lot and his family might be saved? Abraham had intervened earlier to rescue Lot by force. Not only that, but he had also rescued the king of Sodom and restored them their possessions and their city – a city that God was about to destroy?

One can imagine Abraham wondering why God had allowed him to restore the fortunes of Sodom when he was about to destroy it. What now? Might he have to rescue Lot once more – this time from Sodom itself? What could or should he say to God? Could he persuade God to preserve Lot whatever happened? And if so, what reasoning could he use? It is one thing to assess individuals and try to do them justice, but what about a community in which there is a whole spectrum of moral behaviour – a sprinkling of decent and a great number of utterly perverse people? How can you measure one against the other and come up with a fair decision as to what to do? These days we often hear about the risk of 'collateral damage' in armed response to the evils of terrorism. Abraham clearly did not wish Lot to end up as such.

The conversation between God and Abraham about justice brilliantly illustrates what the friendship between God and man can mean. What a difference there is between the conversation God had with Adam and Eve regarding the moral disaster of their transgression and the alienation it caused, and this conversation about the moral disaster of Sodom with Abraham, the friend of God. Yet God showed grace both to Adam and to Abraham. No doubt emboldened by the Lord's invitation for him to participate, Abraham asked the Lord a series of questions, as one friend might do to another:

> Then Abraham drew near and said, 'Will you indeed sweep away the righteous with the wicked? Suppose there are fifty righteous within the city. Will you then sweep away the place and not spare it for the fifty righteous who are in it? Far be it from you to do such a thing, to put the righteous to death with the wicked, so that the righteous fare as the wicked! Far be that from you! Shall not the Judge of all the earth do what is just?' And the LORD said, 'If I find at Sodom fifty righteous in the city, I will spare the whole place for their sake.'
> (Gen. 18.23–26)

The issue is clear. Would God's judgement be indiscriminate? Abraham's appeal to God was based on his conviction that God was the Judge of all the earth. He would surely do what was just and right, wouldn't he?

Having secured the city from judgement if 50 righteous people were found in it, Abraham, protesting his humility in oriental fashion, argued the number down by increments until he reached an agreement at ten. At that point the Lord ended the conversation and left.

It is noticeable that Abraham did not directly discuss whether or not the city deserved judgement. He seemed to be concerned only with the righteous people who might be found there. What sort of moral calculus lay behind his reasoning anyway? Was it good moral judgement to let all the wicked escape, which Abraham's proposal implied? Surely that amounted to him essentially defending injustice? Bias so easily clouds judgement, especially where the defence of relatives is involved.

The basic principle to be held on to, then and now, is certainly the confidence Abraham had that the Judge of all the earth would do right. The New Testament repeats this assessment. Peter writes of Jesus: 'When he was reviled, he did not revile in return; when he suffered, he did not threaten, but continued entrusting himself to him who judges justly' (1 Pet. 2.23).

Human moral behaviour is infinitely complex and beyond our capacity to sort out, even in our own case. Our understanding is limited, so we need to learn to have confidence in the Lord's righteous justice as he tries to educate our moral judgement.

What happened to Sodom and Lot is not immediately given to Abraham to know. We next read of Abraham when he sees the smoke rising from the destruction of Sodom and Gomorrah, which may initially have led him to the erroneous conclusion that Lot had perished with the city. Abraham may have lived with this uncertainty for some time – how long, we do not know.

What did not occur to Abraham in his discussion with the Lord is that there was an alternative to his proposal of pitting the salvation of the entire city against a specific number of righteous inhabitants who might be found there. The alternative was what actually happened: the destruction of the wicked city accompanied by the salvation of the righteous inhabitants, by the Lord providing a way of escape for them. For there was another principle at work that is elucidated in the New Testament in explicit connection with Lot: 'the Lord knows how to rescue the godly from trials' (2 Pet. 2.9).

One thing is striking by its absence – Abraham was not told by God to take his army and rescue Lot, as he had done earlier. God would deal with it on his own. What does that imply? Should Abraham have left it to God the previous time? Did he even discuss that rescue plan with God?

## Lot 'entertains' the angels

The two angels arrived in Sodom and found Abraham's nephew sitting in the gate of the city, the place where the governing body met.[4] Lot seems to have become something like a city magistrate. He did not at first realise who these men were. Commendably, his first instinct was to offer hospitality to wayfaring strangers in his home, as Abraham had done. We note that he was no longer camping near Sodom – he now had a dwelling in the city, a solid house with walls and doors.

When the men hesitated, Lot pressed them to come home with him. They accepted and he organised a simple meal of flat bread (matzot) for them – nothing like the banquet Abraham and Sarah had prepared. Nevertheless it shows that Lot had retained some sense of the hospitality that was central to the oriental way of life. There is, however, no mention of Lot's wife at this point.

After the meal there was uproar at the door of Lot's dwelling. A mob consisting, apparently, of every last man of the city was outside the house. Hospitality to strangers was not sacred to them. Nor was sex. Not bound by anything as old-fashioned as the normal code of hospitality, they insisted that Lot bring out his visitors so they could be subjected to a horrific abuse of hospitality – homosexual rape. Their own bodies were not sacred to the men of Sodom, nor were the bodies of the visitors. Their evil was blatant and led to the proverbial 'they proclaim their sin like Sodom' (Isa. 3.9).

Lot's seat in the administration of Sodom had given him no leverage with this mob. Were these the men of Sodom whom Abraham had rescued with Lot? Hard to believe. The New Testament tells us that Lot himself was a profoundly unhappy and tormented man. Peter says that he was 'greatly distressed by the sensual conduct of the wicked (for as that righteous man lived among them day after day, he was tormenting his righteous soul over their lawless deeds that he saw and heard)' (2 Pet. 2.7–8).

He had become immersed in a society so profoundly immoral that it had almost completely eroded his moral compass. His conscience was still functioning, but only just, in that he seemed to have some vague awareness that something was seriously wrong. So in a desperate attempt to defend the men to whom he had given hospitality, he stepped outside, shut the door behind him and faced the howling crowd. No doubt he despised the men of Sodom as much as he despised himself. It must have been heartbreaking to look back to his conversations with Abraham in earlier times, now to realise all that he had lost by making the fateful choice to barter his soul for Sodom.

He knew that homosexual rape was horrific, and in an attempt to avoid it he abdicated every last vestige of fatherly responsibility and suggested to the sex-mad men at his door that they violate his virgin daughters instead of his visitors. He had lost all concept of the sanctity of their sexuality and, incredibly, placed hospitality to his visitors above it, pleading with the mob:

'Only do nothing to these men, for they have come under the shelter of my roof.' But they said, 'Stand back!' And they said, 'This fellow came to sojourn, and he has become the judge! Now we will deal worse with you than with them.' Then they pressed hard against the man Lot, and drew near to break the door down. But the men reached out their hands and brought Lot into the house with them and shut the door. And they struck with blindness the men who were at the entrance of the house, both small and great, so that they wore themselves out groping for the door.
(Gen. 19.8–11)

The mob mocked Lot's claim to be a judge and threatened to attack his visitors. Lot then discovered he had been entertaining angels unawares. The angels of God's judgement pulled him into the house, shut the door, and supernaturally blinded the raging crowd so that they couldn't even find the door. The angels' action reminds us of the very different situation where God shut the door of the ark after Noah, his family and the animals had entered.

Lot's house was no ark, however. No one was safe in it. It would burn with the rest of Sodom. The visitors told him to hurry and assemble any relatives and friends he had in the city, as they were about to destroy it because of its sin. However, Lot had totally lost his credibility. His feeble attempts at warning made no sense to his prospective sons-in-law. They took his entreaties for a joke and laughed at the idea of God's supernatural judgement, just as Abraham and Sarah had laughed at the supernatural promise of a child and just as the people of Noah's day had mocked the idea of coming judgement.

Mocking the supernatural is fashionable with a certain kind of atheist today who thinks they are representing scientific enlightenment. It will turn out to have been a dangerously unwise strategy, in addition to being 'profoundly unscientific', to quote Richard Dawkins' snide remark in one of our debates[5] about my commitment to the supernatural nature of Christ's miracles and resurrection.

In spite of Sodom's scepticism about God, its day of judgement had come. The angels pleaded with Lot to take his wife and daughters immediately and get out. Even then the man vacillated and had to be forcibly dragged out. Lot just didn't get it. The angels told him to escape as far away and as fast as he could, yet incredibly he once more hesitated and pleaded with them not to take him too far out of Sodom and allow him to stay in the little city of Zoar (see Gen. 19.17–20).

It was the land that had originally appeared attractive to Lot (Gen. 13.10) and it was, among others, the king of Zoar (also called Bela) whom Abraham had defeated in order to rescue Lot in the first place. In fact, Zoar appears to be the only one of the five cities mentioned in Genesis 14 that was spared the conflagration. Yet here Lot was, pleading to go there, when one might have thought he would have wanted to get as far away as possible from Sodom. Yet that is just the problem with moral desensitization. It left Lot with no sense of shame or conviction that there was much if anything wrong with his behaviour. He was living in the illusory world of denial that is all too common in such situations.

The angels granted his request and spared the little city. Presumably they did so knowing he would have to learn the hard way that neither Zoar nor any other city could offer real security.

The mercy shown to Lot as he was dragged out of Sodom is reminiscent of a statement in the book of Jude: 'And have mercy on those who doubt; save others by snatching them out of the fire; to others show mercy with fear, hating even the garment stained by the flesh' (Jude 22–23).

There is a vivid contrast between Lot pleading for Zoar, which was spared, and Abraham pleading for Sodom, which was not. Lot's argument had to do with the size of the city – the name 'Zoar' means 'little' or 'insignificant', as the text indicates. Abraham's argument was not to do with the size of the city per se, but with the number of righteous people in it.

The punishment of Sodom fitted the crime. Supernatural judgement fell as a firestorm, possibly volcanic in origin and no doubt accelerated by the deposits of bitumen and petroleum in the region. Fire engulfed those cities whose evil men had been inflamed by the inner fires of lust.

God sterilised the entire region.

Lot escaped by the skin of his teeth. Lot's wife nearly did, yet she ended in tragedy: 'But Lot's wife, behind him, looked back, and she became a pillar of salt' (Gen. 19.26). The word translated 'looked' here may connote a looking with consideration or intention, as in the English expression 'take a good look'.[6] Lot's wife's look was no fleeting glance. It showed where her heart was. She was, presumably, a Sodomite by birth.

The explanation in the *Shalvi/Hyman Encyclopaedia of Jewish Women* represents a traditional Jewish view that Lot's wife was called Idit and her sin had to do with salt:

Lot wanted the members of his household to participate in the meritorious act of hospitality, as had Abraham, and he asked his wife to bring them salt. She responded: 'Do you even wish to learn this bad habit from Abraham?' (Genesis Rabbah 50.4) She finally complied with her husband's request, but she acted cunningly in order to remove the guests from her house. She went to her women neighbours to borrow salt. They asked her: 'Why do you need salt, why didn't you prepare enough beforehand?' She answered, 'I took enough for our own needs, but guests came to us and it is for them that I need salt.' In this manner all the people of Sodom knew that Lot was harbouring guests. They stormed his house and demanded that he hand them over to the townspeople (*Midrash Aggadah* [ed. Buber], Genesis 19.6). Because she sinned through salt, Lot's wife was punished by being turned into a pillar of the same material (Genesis Rabbah 50.6).

In the New Testament Peter uses God's judgement on these ancient cities to illustrate what will one day happen to ungodly people in general: '. . . if by turning the cities of Sodom and Gomorrah to ashes he condemned them to extinction, making them an example of what is going to happen to the ungodly . . .' (2 Pet. 2.6).

In this context, Peter issues a solemn warning of the danger of false and immoral teachers laying waste the Church. He describes them as:

waterless springs and mists driven by a storm. For them the gloom of utter darkness has been reserved. For, speaking loud boasts of folly, they entice by sensual passions of the flesh those who are barely escaping from those who live in error. They promise them freedom, but they themselves are slaves of corruption. For whatever overcomes a person, to that he is enslaved. For if, after they have escaped the defilements of the world through the knowledge of our Lord and Saviour Jesus Christ, they are again entangled in them and overcome, the last state has become worse for them than the first. For it would have been better for them never to have known the way of righteousness than after knowing it to turn back from the holy commandment delivered to them. What the true proverb says has happened to them: 'The dog returns to its own vomit, and the sow, after washing herself, returns to wallow in the mire.' (2 Pet. 2.17–22)

Peter is referring here to people who have had contact with Christianity and gained some knowledge of Christ that has helped them to get temporarily clear of the defiling influence of the world. Unfortunately, they have got caught up once more and overwhelmed by the corruption in which they were previously involved.

To get the point across, Peter relates a popular and vivid ancient metaphor about dogs returning to their vomit or pigs going back to wallow in the mire. The nature of the dog is not changed by vomiting, nor is the nature of a pig changed by washing. Likewise, these people, no matter how much they professed Christianity, were never genuinely regenerate. In the parables of Jesus, genuine believers are often called sheep, never dogs or pigs. Peter is using his imagery carefully. He is not talking about true believers who, like himself, got caught out under pressure, temporarily denying the Lord, but then repenting and receiving the Lord's forgiveness. No, Peter is referring to people like Lot's wife, whose backward look showed what had been in her heart all the time. You could take her out of Sodom, but you could not take Sodom out of her. It still dominated her affections.

The Lord himself used Lot's wife as a warning when he drew attention to the destruction of Sodom and Gomorrah as a prototype of what would happen at his cataclysmic return in judgement:

'Likewise, just as it was in the days of Lot – they were eating and drinking, buying and selling, planting and building, but on the day when Lot went out from Sodom, fire and sulphur rained from heaven and destroyed them all – so will it be on the day when the Son of Man is revealed. On that day, let the one who is on the housetop, with his goods in the house, not come down to take them away, and likewise let the one who is in the field not turn back. *Remember Lot's wife.* Whoever seeks to preserve his life will lose it, but whoever loses his life will keep it. I tell you, in that night there will be two in one bed. One will be taken and the other left. There will be two women grinding together. One will be taken and the other left.' And they said to him, 'Where, Lord?' He said to them, 'Where the corpse is, there the vultures will gather.'
(Luke 17.28–37, emphasis mine)

Turning back from the journey of discipleship with the Lord is a very serious thing. Jesus said so explicitly to a would-be follower: 'Yet another said, "I will follow you, Lord, but let me first say farewell to those at my home." Jesus said to him, "No one who puts his hand to the plough and looks back is fit for the kingdom of God"' (Luke 9.61–62).

Salt is a preservative. It makes things last longer. The grim figure of Lot's wife crystallised into a pillar of salt serves as a solemn warning that if we wish to be the true salt of the earth we need to look to 'Jesus, the founder and perfecter of our faith' (Heb. 12.2) – and never look back with longing to the world we have left behind.

# The cave: Lot's daughters and their children

And Abraham went early in the morning to the place where he had stood before the LORD. And he looked down towards Sodom and Gomorrah and towards all the land of the valley, and he looked and, behold, the smoke of the land went up like the smoke of a furnace.

So it was that, when God destroyed the cities of the valley, God remembered Abraham and sent Lot out of the midst of the overthrow when he overthrew the cities in which Lot had lived. (Gen. 19.27–29)

One wonders what Abraham thought as he saw the billowing smoke from the raging furnace of the cities' destruction. As we suggested earlier, he may well have imagined that the Lord had not even found ten righteous people in Sodom, and that Lot must therefore have died in the fire. Did Abraham feel guilty that it was his sorry adventure in Egypt that produced the wealth leading to the tension between him and Lot in the first place?

We also may feel guilty for having given bad advice that led to someone losing their way – perhaps even someone we love, in our own family, or a friend . . .

Yet God remembered Abraham and rescued Lot. Is this a reference to the earlier conversation? Abraham was concerned with rescuing the righteous – and God had done precisely that in response to Abraham's pleading. Discussing and pleading with God is what we call prayer, about which we recall the statement of the apostle James: 'The prayer of a righteous person has great power as it is working' (Jas. 5.16).

The New Testament tells us that Lot's deliverance from the judgement on Sodom illustrates an important principle of God's justice. Peter writes:

And if he [God] rescued righteous Lot, greatly distressed by the sensual conduct of the wicked (for as that righteous man lived

197

among them day after day, he was tormenting his righteous soul over their lawless deeds that he saw and heard); then the Lord knows how to rescue the godly from trials, and to keep the unrighteous under punishment until the day of judgement, and especially those who indulge in the lust of defiling passion and despise authority. (2 Pet. 2.7–10)

Although it is hard to believe – indeed, perhaps only God could see it – Scripture tells us that deep down Lot was a righteous man in the positional sense that he had been justified by faith. However, his behaviour was far from righteous. Therefore, God rescued him, but he suffered permanent loss.

Paul explains precisely what is involved in God's final assessment of the behaviour of believers:

According to the grace of God given to me, like a skilled master builder I laid a foundation, and someone else is building upon it. Let each one take care how he builds upon it. For no one can lay a foundation other than that which is laid, which is Jesus Christ. Now if anyone builds on the foundation with gold, silver, precious stones, wood, hay, straw – each one's work will become manifest, for the Day will disclose it, because it will be revealed by fire, and the fire will test what sort of work each one has done. If the work that anyone has built on the foundation survives, he will receive a reward. If anyone's work is burned up, he will suffer loss, though he himself will be saved, but only as through fire. (1 Cor. 3.10–15)

Lot is a tragic example of what this means. He was literally saved through fire. He lost everything: wife, family, home, career, reputation, dignity and wealth. It matters what we believers do with our lives. Yes, God can rescue us if we mess up, but that does not mean he removes the consequences of our behaviour – and those consequences may be eternal.

If I as a believer drive negligently and cause an accident that leaves both me and the person I collided with permanently disabled, it may be that upon repentance I receive God's forgiveness and even their forgiveness, but it does not mean God removes the consequences and heals the disabilities. You cannot forgive a disability.

A classic biblical example of this is when God sent Nathan the prophet to rebuke David for his adultery with Bathsheba and murder of her husband Uriah. Nathan told the repentant David that God had forgiven him, but he also told him of the dire consequences his sin would have.

> "'Now therefore the sword shall never depart from your house, because you have despised me and have taken the wife of Uriah the Hittite to be your wife." Thus says the Lord, "Behold, I will raise up evil against you out of your own house. And I will take your wives before your eyes and give them to your neighbour, and he shall lie with your wives in the sight of this sun. For you did it secretly, but I will do this thing before all Israel and before the sun."' David said to Nathan, 'I have sinned against the Lord.' And Nathan said to David, 'The Lord also has put away your sin; you shall not die. Nevertheless, because by this deed you have utterly scorned the Lord, the child who is born to you shall die.' Then Nathan went to his house.
>
> (2 Sam. 12.10–15)

Sin always has consequences. God's forgiveness does not always remove them, as Lot had to learn.

The last we read of him is that he became afraid of living in Zoar, the little city near Sodom where he had begged the angels to let him go to in order to avoid having to go to the hills as they had told him. Insecurity now drove him to those hills and he was reduced to living in a cave alone with his two daughters.

Noah, his wife and his sons with their wives survived the Flood and were able to start repopulating the earth. Not so Lot – only he survived and his two unmarried daughters. In their now-empty, sterile world they saw no chance of marriage and children and so, in the moral vacuum created by their background culture and in their abject desperation, they plied their father with wine and, when he was drunk, committed incest with him.[7] Perhaps all final remnants of their respect for him as a father had evaporated when Lot offered them to the Sodomite mob to take their virginity? How awful now that he was the one to take their virginity, as they used him as a surrogate husband, a genetic means to an end. In a sense, children and therefore inheritance meant more to them than to their father.[8]

Two babies were born, Moab and Ammon,[9] who in turn fathered nations that eventually became some of the most evil in all of biblical history. At one stage during their desert wanderings the Israelites committed immorality with the women of Moab who invited them to join in the worship of their pagan gods, in particular the god Baal of Peor (Num. 25). The tribe of Ammon became infamous for the hideous practice of sacrificing their children to the god Molech.[10] Sad to say, their influence on the Israelites went so deep that Moses had to warn them against doing the same thing: 'You shall not give any of your children to offer them to Molech, and so profane the name of your God' (Lev. 18.21).

Isaiah prophesied God's judgement on Moab and, in an interesting throwback to the days of Lot, indicated that the inhabitants of Moab would flee to Zoar (Isa. 15.5) – old habits die hard!

Stepping back from this whole episode in Abraham's story we can see that its two constituent parts, which we labelled A and B, give insight into the dangers of 'the flesh' from two perspectives.

On the one hand there is what we might call the 'religious' side of the flesh. Abram, though he believed in the promises of God, instead of trusting God he accepted Sarai's attribution of her infertility to God and attempted to realise the promises in the energy of the flesh by using Hagar as a surrogate wife. In so doing they heaped up endless trouble for themselves and their posterity, some (more) of which we are about to see.

Also, Saul of Tarsus, before his conversion, was a religious man, fanatically so. He was proud that he was circumcised and, so he thought, had kept all the laws and rituals of his Jewish faith. He discovered to his horror that it was possible to be like that and yet be fighting against God. He was doing it all in the flesh; that is, in his own strength. He needed, as we also do, to learn the true meaning of circumcision – a reminder not to put our confidence in the flesh.

On the other hand, the account of Lot shows us the insidious dangers, not of the religious 'flesh' but of the sensual, seamy side of the flesh – the self-destructive narcissism that characterised the city of Sodom.

Sadly believers, though not 'in the flesh', can tragically live 'after the flesh' in either of these two senses, often with disastrous consequences. Only walking in the Spirit and, like Abraham in the central part of this section, having fellowship with the Lord in trusting him alone will help us to avoid these pernicious extremes.

Like Abraham, we too are called upon to judge the situation in Sodom, which is an increasingly difficult thing to do in our politically correct hypersensitive cancel culture. It will take courage, and that not of ourselves.

Another very important lesson to be drawn from this section is that we must show hospitality to strangers. As we mentioned earlier, the injunction 'Do not neglect to show hospitality to strangers, for thereby some have entertained angels unawares' (Heb. 13.2) refers to Abraham's mysterious visitors. Kass says:

> Paradoxically, because of the city's quest for self-sufficiency, city dwellers are more likely to forget about human vulnerability and man's dependence on powers not under human control... For all these reasons, men in every city will commit injustice toward strangers – eventually also toward neighbors – unless the city is informed by teachings of hospitality, teachings that in turn are informed by fear-awe-reverence for God and the ability to discern the divine image present in all human beings.[11]

It is a strange paradox that the advanced technologies in our smart cities, with their wired-world and internet of things that connects us all together, are actually fostering isolation and loneliness. Hospitality generally involves food, whether little or much, and it is a tragic irony of our age when a table in a home or a restaurant can be devoid of conversation or even eye contact between the diners as they all have their eyes (and even ears) fixed on tablets and smart phones.

It would be sad, would it not, to sit silent in the presence of an angel while we restlessly consulted our mobile phones? But then we would never become aware of who it had been and so never know what we had missed.

# Part 4

# GENESIS 20.1—22.19

**THE LIFE OF ABRAHAM: STAGE 3**
**SUMMARY**
A. Abraham denies Sarah among Philistines (20.1–18)
Abimelech takes Sarah. God warns him in a dream.
'I know that you have done this in the integrity of your heart.'
    Abimelech rewards Abraham, who prays for healing of closed
    wombs.


B. The birth of Isaac and the expulsion of Ishmael (21.1–21)
The birth of the promised seed: Isaac. Sarah laughs.
Ishmael laughs. God's promise for Isaac and Ishmael.
The expulsion of Hagar and her son.
Abraham rises early in the morning . . . takes bread and water . . .
Hagar fears the death of her son. An angel of the Lord calls from
    heaven: 'Lift up the boy and hold him fast with your hand.' The
    provision – a well. God's promise


C. Abraham swears an oath to Abimelech (21.22–34)
A problem of the ownership of wells.
Abraham's covenant with Abimelech at Beersheba.

D.  Akedah: the binding of Isaac (22.1–19)

God tests Abraham – he asks him to give him Isaac.

Abraham rises early in the morning . . . takes wood . . .

The binding of Isaac. An angel of the Lord calls from heaven: 'Do not lay your hand on the boy for now I know that you fear God.' The provision – a lamb. Justification by works. God swears oath to Abraham. Abraham dwells in Beersheba – Seven wells.

## PERVASIVE THEMES

In this stage both Abraham and Abimelech are concerned with security – for themselves and their children. Abraham's denial of his true relationship with Sarah in section A runs the risk of imperilling the identity of her child. In B, Abraham seeks to secure Isaac by removing any potential threat from Ishmael and his mother Hagar. In C, Abimelech and Abraham swear an oath for security. In D, the matter of security reaches a climax when God tests Abraham as to whether his security really rests in God or in Isaac. When Abraham passes the test, God himself swears an oath to Abraham to give him maximum security.

## LITERARY STRUCTURE AND THOUGHT FLOW

The overall structure of the stage is parallel, XYXY, in that the first pair of sections correspond to the second pair as follows:

A and C each has to do with Abraham and Abimelech and their attempts to create mutual security.

B and D have in common the theme of sacrificing sons in two different senses and God's provision to save them.

In B, Abraham rises early in the morning and provides Hagar with bread and water. As Hagar despairs, an angel makes an announcement from heaven and points to a well that saves his son Ishmael's life. In D, Abraham rises early in the morning and provides wood for the offering that he gets his son Isaac to carry for him. As Abraham is about to slay his son, an angel makes an announcement from heaven and points to a ram for the burnt offering that takes the place of Abraham's son Isaac and saves his life.

There is also evidence of a chiastic structure, XYYX, in that the beginning and end sections correspond, as do the two middle sections as follows:

In both A and D God says: 'I know . . .' In A, God speaks to Abimelech about his character and says: 'I know that in the integrity of your heart you did this.' In D, God speaks to Abraham and says: 'Now I know that you fear me.' In A, God speaks to reassure Abimelech of his innocence. In D, God speaks to Abraham to tell him that his faith in God has been proved genuine by his willingness to offer Isaac – in theological terms, Abraham has been justified before God by his works. The thought flows from the limited assurances humans can offer one another to the certainty that only God can deliver and the conditions on which it can be obtained.

# 14

# Sarah and Hagar

## Abraham denies Sarah as his wife

Abraham took up his nomadic life once more and steered yet again towards the south (Negev) until he reached the small town of Gerar in the south-eastern corner of Canaan, where he settled. And he got nervous, as he had been the last time he was in that area, fearing for his own security. Once again he tried to protect himself in Gerar by repeating the half-truth that Sarah was his sister. It is almost incredible that at this late stage, when the promise of a son was about to be fulfilled, Abraham would yet again take the risk of imperilling the identity of his child, with which his wife was probably already pregnant.

Abraham had forgotten God's explicit promise in Genesis 15, that he would be Abraham's shield. This assurance was not a living reality to him and he crumpled morally. Cowardice took over. The inevitable then happened. Just as Pharaoh had done earlier, the local leader Abimelech,[1] king of Gerar, sent for and took Sarah. This time, God's intervention to shield her was immediate and direct:

> God came to Abimelech in a dream by night and said to him, 'Behold, you are a dead man because of the woman whom you have taken, for she is a man's wife.' Now Abimelech had not approached her. So he said, 'Lord, will you kill an innocent people?'
> (Gen. 20.3–4)

His conversation with God about justice and innocence resonates strongly with the previous discussion that Abraham had had with the Lord regarding Sodom. The issue was the same: would God slay the innocent? Abimelech's question is essentially the same as Abraham's: 'Will not the Judge of all the earth do right?'

It is now clear that, just as Abram had misjudged Pharaoh, the older Abraham misjudged Abimelech even more. The latter, aggrieved, told the Lord that not only did Abraham say that Sarah was his sister, but Sarah had corroborated the fact. God exonerated Abraham in his reply, saying that he knew Abimelech was guiltless and for that reason had kept Abimelech from sinning.

Abimelech decided to have it out with Abraham in what turned out to be a rather embarrassing conversation for the latter: 'What did you see, that you did this thing?' (Gen. 20.10). The question is precise: not simply 'Why did you do it?' but 'What actual evidence led to your action?' Abimelech wanted to know what Abraham's reasoning was and why he risked allowing Abimelech to commit 'a great sin'.

Abraham confessed that he did it because he had concluded there was no fear of God in the place and he had thought he would be killed. Abraham then made a feeble attempt to justify his stance. Derek Kidner points out that Abraham erred on facts (v. 11) in thinking that there was no fear of God among Abimelech's servants; then he erred on values (v. 12), in that he tried to rationalise his denial of his true relationship with Sarai by telling a half-truth that she was his sister; and he also erred on his motives (v. 13), in that he asked Sarai to be complicit with him in passing him off as her brother. He also compromised his calling to witness to the one true God, Creator of heaven and earth. For the literal translation of verse 13 is 'when the gods (*Elohim*) caused me to wander', which 'is the language and wry attitude of the pagan; one man of the world might be speaking to another'.[2]

This passage makes me wonder just how much Abimelech understood about God, as I see in it a powerful message to us that we need to be extremely careful not to underestimate others who may not share our knowledge.

Some scholars are sceptical that such a denial could really have happened a second time and suggest that we have two accounts of something that only happened once. However, Abraham confessed to Abimelech that he had adopted the 'wife as sister' ploy as an ongoing policy 'in every place to which we come', thus suggesting that it had happened before.

In any case, it does not take much insight into human nature to see that we humans are boringly repetitive and predictable, especially when it comes to our sinful propensities. The hard things to cope with in our personalities are repeated sins and failures. Think of Peter's streak of fear that paralysed him from time to time. On this occasion, Abraham must have been deeply embarrassed. Yet God in his mercy and grace didn't discard the man but offered him forgiveness and a fresh start. Indeed, Abraham prayed for the healing of Abimelech and his wives, and presumably Abimelech learned of this. What Sarah thought of the whole business is passed over in silence, perhaps mercifully so! What is astonishing, though, is that not long afterwards Abraham's son Isaac tried the same ploy and pretended to (another?) Abimelech that his wife Rebekah was his sister!

There is an important general lesson here. It is very easy to make embarrassing and unnecessary mistakes in judging the ethics of others, especially non-believers. Like Pharaoh before him, Abimelech turned out to be more honourable than Abraham initially thought. Not all kings in the region were as dissolute and evil as the king of Sodom – indeed Abimelech appears to have been God-fearing to some extent. God told him: 'I know that you have done this in the integrity of your heart.' Abraham's fears were ill-proportioned to the facts. We need to be very careful in assessing what we see. The reader will not have missed the frequent emphasis on the verb 'to see' throughout the Abraham narrative – God sees, Abraham sees, Hagar sees, Lot sees. Clearly the idea is not only visual experience but perception and comprehension.

The first chapter of Genesis tells us that all men and women, Pharaoh and Abimelech included, are made in the image of God. One aspect of this is that humans are moral beings, as shown in Genesis 3. All of us have a conscience that instructs us about good and evil. That is why there are so many common elements in the moral codes of peoples around the world, as C. S. Lewis noted long ago in the appendix to his book *The Abolition of Man*. In particular, Lewis found that versions of the so-called Golden Rule – 'Do unto others as you would have them do unto you' – is to be found all over the world in virtually every religion and philosophy, including Roman pagan religion and contemporary humanism.

These facts constitute hard evidence in favour of the view that we have been created as moral beings. We are hard-wired for morality, even though our consciences may and do become distorted and even seared when we ignore them or go against them for a long time.

On a personal level, I have found that it is much easier to discuss differences between religions regarding how a person relates to God if you have first shown appreciation for the moral standards of the people with whom you are having the conversation. No one appreciates being talked down to from an assumed moral high ground.

In the event, Abimelech turned out to be a man of considerable honour and integrity. He not only returned Sarah to Abraham, but he gave Abraham cattle and sheep plus a thousand pieces of silver. Once again, it is astonishing how Abraham increases his wealth at every wrong turn.

## The birth of Isaac and the expulsion of Ishmael

God had closed the wombs of the women in Abimelech's household and Abraham had prayed for this circumstance to be reversed. Now God opened Sarah's womb. Against all gynaecological odds, Sarah eventually gave birth to a child.[3] God's original promise had finally come to fruition. This wonderful fulfilment is mentioned no fewer than three times in the first two verses of Genesis 21. The emphasis conveys the important message that God delivers on his promises. His word is to be taken seriously. His faithfulness needs constant emphasis to give us stability in the midst of all the uncertainties of life.

A delighted Abraham named his son Isaac ('he laughs') and their home was doubtless filled with laughter as they rehearsed all that had happened. 'And Sarah said, "God has made laughter for me; everyone who hears will laugh over me." And she said, "Who would have said to Abraham that Sarah would nurse children? Yet I have borne him a son in his old age"' (Gen. 21.6–7). To use the apt phrase of C. S. Lewis, Sarah was very much 'surprised by joy' and was probably also amused by the absurdity of her situation as an aged mother. Their laughter was very different from the boy Ishmael's mocking laughter (a related word) at Isaac, or the mockery that Lot's prospective sons-in-law imagined his warning of impending doom to be. Laughing at claims to supernatural interventions of God is not without precedent (Jude 18; 2 Pet. 3.3–4).

210

Sarah's name is frequently repeated in this birth announcement. She, the wife of Abraham, is now the mother of his child. Only she could fulfil that role as far as the promised seed was concerned.

When the baby was weaned (at the age of two or even three in that culture then) there was a great feast of celebration. Possibly there had been nothing like it since Melchizedek entertained Abram years before. No doubt there was a great deal of joy and laughter as well.

However, not all of the laughter pleased Sarah. She heard the teenage Ishmael, perhaps 15 at that time, laughing in mockery. The celebration turned sour for Sarah. In a fit of maternal jealousy she reacted with fury and ordered Abraham to throw the slave woman and her son out of the house. She was not prepared to tolerate the idea of Ishmael being an heir with Isaac. She used the term 'slave woman' twice, instead of the name Hagar, in order to put her in her place in front of Abraham. It was spiteful, vindictive and unworthy behaviour, as Sarah herself was responsible for the situation in which they found themselves. Winston Churchill's words might have helped, had they been available: 'By swallowing evil words unsaid, no one has ever harmed his stomach.'

Abraham, who loved Ishmael, was deeply displeased, indeed angry. He had thrown Hagar out once before on Sarah's say so, but God had sent her back and Abraham had learned to love Ishmael. Yet this time God intervened to tell Abraham to do as his wife Sarah requested. It was an extremely fraught situation. How could God support Sarah's appalling high-handedness and thereby expect Abraham to sacrifice his son Ishmael?

R. K. Harrison makes the interesting comment that

it is important in this connection to notice that Sarah's action could have been defended according to the ancient Sumerian code of Lipit-Ishtar (ca. 1850 BC), one of the sources underlying the legislation of Hammurabi, which stated that the freedom received by the dispossessed slave was to be considered adequate compensation for the act of expulsion.[4]

Abraham did what God said, maybe thinking that the situation was mitigated by God's promise that Ishmael would also father a great nation.

The Roman historian Josephus regarded Ishmael as the father of the Arabs.[5] Also, Ishmael is regarded by Muslims, who call him Ismail (and Hagar, Hajar), as the ancestor of several northern prominent Arab tribes and the forefather of Adnan, an ancestor of Muhammad.

Abraham could clearly have afforded to settle a proportion of his possessions, servants, transport and food on Hagar and send her off to a safe place, setting her up for life. After all, Ishmael was his son and therefore a potential heir. Yet Abraham seems to have made no attempt to do so. He simply got up early in the morning, gave Hagar some bread and water, and sent her away, apparently accompanied only by her son. It must have been a grim and emotional experience. What can Abraham have been thinking? Did he give her so ridiculously little by way of supplies because he secretly hoped she would be forced to return later that day? Did he even think at all? He was losing the teenage son he had come to love. Sarah, on the other hand, was delighted to get rid of Hagar and her child. She had no regrets whatsoever.

As far as Abraham and Sarah were concerned this was the end of their involvement with Hagar and Ishmael. Mother and son walked out of the family life of Abraham and were gone.

# New Testament insights

We have noted all the way through, from the announcement of the covenant in Genesis 15, that major events in this narrative are taken up by Paul in the New Testament and applied to Christian believers as spiritual offspring of Abraham.

First, it is clear from the New Testament that a major factor in all of this was that Isaac had been chosen by God to carry the Seed Project forward and Ishmael had not. Paul writes:

But it is not as though the word of God has failed. For not all who are descended from Israel belong to Israel, and not all are children of Abraham because they are his offspring, but 'Through Isaac shall your offspring be named.' This means that it is not the children of the flesh who are the children of God, but the children of the promise are counted as offspring. For this is what the

promise said: 'About this time next year I will return, and Sarah shall have a son.'
(Rom. 9.6–9)

Isaac was chosen, Ishmael was not chosen, so Ishmael had to leave. Paul writes about it in his letter to the Galatians:

Now you, brothers, like Isaac, are children of promise. But just as at that time he who was born according to the flesh persecuted him who was born according to the Spirit, so also it is now. But what does the Scripture say? 'Cast out the slave woman and her son, for the son of the slave woman shall not inherit with the son of the free woman.' So, brothers, we are not children of the slave but of the free woman.
(Gal. 4.28–31)

When Paul says that Ishmael was born according to the flesh, and Isaac according to the Spirit, he is not, of course, denying that both were actual physical births. Nor, as we said earlier, is the first statement a criticism either of Hagar or of the genuineness of her personal spiritual experience of God. It is a criticism of Abraham and Sarah, who resorted to their own ingenuity and effort to produce a child – that is, they placed their confidence in the flesh. Isaac was the child for whom they had to trust God and so was born 'according to the Spirit'.

In Paul's time there was tension in some churches regarding how a person could be justified before God. One group held that it was by keeping the law and its rituals, like circumcision, the other that it was by faith in God through Christ alone – and perhaps there were some who believed it was both.

Paul's response was uncompromising:

Look: I, Paul, say to you that if you accept circumcision, Christ will be of no advantage to you. I testify again to every man who accepts circumcision that he is obligated to keep the whole law. You are severed from Christ, you who would be justified by the law; you have fallen away from grace. For through the Spirit, by faith, we

ourselves eagerly wait for the hope of righteousness. For in Christ
Jesus neither circumcision nor uncircumcision counts for anything,
but only faith working through love.
(Gal. 5.2–6)

As always, Paul maintains that salvation comes through faith in Christ
alone. It does not come from efforts to keep the law, but the wonder of
it is that it produces the quality of character and behaviour of which the
law approves.

He makes these distinctions abundantly clear in the following passage,
which will repay close attention:

> For you were called to freedom, brothers. Only do not use your
> freedom as an opportunity for the flesh, but through love serve one
> another. For the whole law is fulfilled in one word: 'You shall love
> your neighbour as yourself.' But if you bite and devour one another,
> watch out that you are not consumed by one another.
>
> But I say, walk by the Spirit, and you will not gratify the desires of
> the flesh. For the desires of the flesh are against the Spirit, and the
> desires of the Spirit are against the flesh, for these are opposed to
> each other, to keep you from doing the things you want to do. But if
> you are led by the Spirit, you are not under the law. Now the works of
> the flesh are evident: sexual immorality, impurity, sensuality, idolatry,
> sorcery, enmity, strife, jealousy, fits of anger, rivalries, dissensions,
> divisions, envy, drunkenness, orgies, and things like these. I warn you,
> as I warned you before, that those who do such things will not inherit
> the kingdom of God. But the fruit of the Spirit is love, joy, peace,
> patience, kindness, goodness, faithfulness, gentleness, self-control;
> against such things there is no law. And those who belong to Christ
> Jesus have crucified the flesh with its passions and desires.
>
> If we live by the Spirit, let us also walk by the Spirit. Let us not
> become conceited, provoking one another, envying one another.
> (Gal. 5.13–26)

Genuine salvation produces the fruit of the Spirit. If there is no fruit,
then the claim to be genuine is spurious.

# God rescues Hagar and Ishmael

Paul also uses the story of Hagar and Ishmael to *illustrate* the difference between living according to the flesh and living according to the Spirit, but that does not carry any necessary implication regarding their own actual *experience* of God. Nor does the fact that Isaac was chosen to carry the Seed Project and Ishmael was not. They had different roles, but the role a person plays and their experience of God are two different things.[6]

For God cared for Hagar and Ishmael. When they were ejected from Abraham and Sarah's home, Hagar's meagre supplies ran out very quickly as she wandered aimlessly in the desert. Finally, exhausted, she left the boy lying under a bush and sat down some distance away, not wishing to watch him starve to death in the heat. She wept as only a mother would when forced to part with her child. Yet it appears that Ishmael had been praying, crying to God for help. Maybe he recalled why he had been named Ishmael in the first place – 'God hears'. In any case we are told that God heard the boy (not Hagar, though presumably he heard her also). An angel called to her and told her not to fear – God would make of Ishmael a great nation. Looking up she saw a well full of life-giving water. Her fears began to lift . . .

God's attitude to Hagar and Ishmael was very different from Sarah's.

The last we read of Hagar and her son in Genesis is this: 'And God was with the boy, and he grew up. He lived in the wilderness and became an expert with the bow. He lived in the wilderness of Paran, and his mother took a wife for him from the land of Egypt' (Gen. 21.20–21). Ishmael was a wiry and resourceful character – a real survivor. We read that God was with the boy – both boys, in fact! God forgets no one.

# Sarah and Hagar in the New Testament

Paul has more to say about Sarah and Hagar in Galatians that can help us go deeper into the message of Abraham. However, the reader may prefer to get the overall picture first and skip directly to p. 227, coming back here later.

Paul writes:

> But the son of the slave was born according to the flesh, while the son of the free woman was born through promise. Now this may be interpreted allegorically: these women are two covenants. One is from Mount Sinai, bearing children for slavery; she is Hagar. Now Hagar is Mount Sinai in Arabia; she corresponds to the present Jerusalem, for she is in slavery with her children. But the Jerusalem above is free, and she is our mother.
> (Gal. 4.23–26)

A question for many interpreters of Scripture is: what does Paul mean by saying that the Sarah–Hagar account can be interpreted 'allegorically'? Is it not the case, when the author of Genesis talks about Hagar, he means the actual Egyptian woman of that name and not the covenant at Sinai for, if he did, he would have said so? If we may understand a text in ways that the original author never intended, then we could make any text mean anything we liked and be left with no way of assessing whether or not the interpretation was true or false. This is a serious point and it deserves a thorough answer.

By far the best explanation I have found is that given in chapter 15 of David Gooding's book, *The Riches of Divine Wisdom*. This book is a superb introduction to the ways in which the New Testament uses the Old, and the interested reader is strongly advised to read it. Gooding's reasoning is in particular highly instructive in the way it pulls much of the Abraham narrative together.

First, Paul, here in Galatians (and elsewhere), treats the Abraham narrative altogether as history: 'The whole force of his legal argument [Gal. 3.17] regarding God's covenant with Abraham and his descendants, depends on its historicity and dating.'[7] Paul is speaking as a historian and a lawyer.

Moreover, when he goes on to claim that the seed to whom the inheritance was promised was Christ (Gal 3.16) he is not indulging in unhistorical allegorizing: 'For Paul, Christ was not an allegorical descendant of Abraham's (whatever that might mean), nor merely a spiritual descendant of his; Christ was literally and physically descended from him.'

And when Paul subsequently says that Ishmael was born 'according to the flesh' and Isaac was born 'through promise' and 'according to the Spirit', how absurd it would be to think Paul meant that Isaac's birth was an allegorical and not a physical birth. The birth was a miracle of God's grace and power performed in accordance with God's original promise; but in Paul's thinking it was no less a literal, physical, historical event for all that.

It is therefore clear that whatever Paul meant by using the term 'allegory' he did not mean that the story of Abraham, Sarah and Hagar and their sons was intended by its author as a non-historical allegory. It was intended as a historical record. What Paul is saying is that it, like many other Old Testament stories, carries additional significance as a prototype of something on a much larger scale – just as Stephen, the first Christian martyr, pointed out in his speech before the Sanhedrin that the way in which Joseph was rejected by his brothers, thought of as dead yet eventually becoming their saviour, is a prototype of the way in which Jesus was rejected and crucified by his nation and yet eventually became their Saviour.

For instance, when Ishmael was born of the slave girl Hagar, she tried to run away, but the angel of the Lord sent her back and she had to live in Abraham's house until the promised seed, Isaac, was born. Ishmael and Hagar were then at once cast out.

This, according to Paul, is a prototype of the fact that the nation descended from Abraham was originally without the law, but when God gave them the covenant of the law at Sinai it led to religious slavery in certain senses, yet God had given it as a temporary measure until the advent of the Promised Seed, Jesus Christ our Lord. That changed everything, as Paul explains:

> Now before faith came, we were held captive under the law, imprisoned until the coming faith would be revealed. So then, the law was our guardian until Christ came, in order that we might be justified by faith. But now that faith has come, we are no longer under a guardian, for in Christ Jesus you are all sons of God, through faith. (Gal. 3.23–26)

That transition is symbolised by the casting out of Hagar.

In light of this, let us consider Paul's key statement, as translated by Gooding: 'For these women are [i.e. represent] two covenants, one [covenant, which was given] from mount Sinai, bearing children unto slavery, [and] which as such [Greek: ἥτις, *hētis*, not the simple relative pronoun, ἥ, *hē*] is [i.e. corresponds to] Hagar (Gal 4:24).'

According to Paul, the basis of the analogy between Hagar and the covenant from Sinai is the fact that the covenant from Sinai brings forth children unto slavery. That means the Sinai covenant is well represented by Hagar since she was a slave.

Gooding continues:

Of course, Paul's statement that the Sinai covenant 'brings forth children unto slavery' is couched in highly metaphorical, though typically Semitic, language. Hagar's son was a literal child; the Sinai covenant's 'children' were metaphorical children; that is, people whose attitudes, characters, and quality of life are formed by their attempt to live according to that covenant's principles.

But the point Paul is making about the Sinai covenant is no less real and historical because it is expressed in metaphorical language. As explained in Chapter 1, metaphor is used to stand for something real. Even genuine Jewish believers, says Paul, who all down the centuries until the Son of God came lived under the terms and conditions of the Sinai covenant, were like children in a wealthy family: heirs of their father, but during their childhood nothing different from slaves. 'We were held in bondage', he says, 'to the elementary rules of the world' (see Gal. 4.1–7).

Moreover, and this is a key historical observation, very many Jews in Paul's day lived in a kind of religious slavery, just as multitudes of people from different religious backgrounds still do today.

We could put it this way: Abraham used Hagar in his misguided attempt to achieve God's promise of new life in the form of a child, and many people in Paul's time and today misuse the law. Their mistake was and is to think that God gave the law at Sinai so that by their efforts to keep it they might merit justification and eternal life.

Yet in Galatians 3 Paul is at pains to explain that this was not the purpose of the Sinai covenant. Its basic principle was 'You shall therefore keep my statutes and my rules; if a person does them, he shall live by them: I am the LORD' (Lev. 18.5).

The biblical law of God has underpinned life in Europe and the West for centuries. That it contains excellent advice on how to live, which we ignore at our peril, has been amply documented by Tom Holland's recent magisterial book *Dominion: The making of the Western mind*.[8] Even leading atheists concur with this view. For instance, German atheist intellectual Jürgen Habermas has given clear warning of the dangers of a shift in our moral base from a Judeo-Christian one to the postmodern:

Universalistic egalitarianism, from which sprang the ideals of freedom and a collective life in solidarity, the autonomous conduct of life and emancipation, the individual morality of conscience, human rights and democracy, is the direct legacy of the Judaic ethic of justice and the Christian ethic of love. This legacy, substantially unchanged, has been the object of continual critical appropriation and reinterpretation. To this day, there is no alternative to it. And in light of the current challenges of a post-national constellation, we continue to draw on the substance of this heritage. Everything else is just idle postmodern talk.[9]

However, and this is what many find very hard to grasp, attempts to keep that law, though they may be well intentioned, cannot give us eternal life and God's acceptance. Paul puts it bluntly:

For all who rely on works of the law are under a curse; for it is written, 'Cursed be everyone who does not abide by all things written in the Book of the Law, and do them' [see Deut. 27.26]. Now it is evident that no one is justified before God by the law, for 'The righteous shall live by faith.' But the law is not of faith, rather 'The one who does them shall live by them.' Christ redeemed us from the curse of the law by becoming a curse for us – for it is written, 'Cursed is everyone who is hanged on a tree' – so that in Christ Jesus the blessing of Abraham might come to the Gentiles, so that we might receive the promised Spirit through faith.
(Gal. 3.10–14)

If we take that law seriously, we find it convicts us of sin, and, because we have not kept it fully, it curses us. That is very strong language, to which many react, saying something like: 'But that is unfair. I am doing my best to keep God's moral law. Like everyone else I am not perfect and it would be arrogant to claim I was. Yet I am told here that if I don't keep *all* of the law, it curses me. Surely that is utterly unreasonable and unfair?'

However, strange though it may seem, *keeping the whole law was the basis of the covenant at Sinai to which all the people agreed.* Recall its institution:

> Moses came and told the people all the words of the LORD and all the rules. And all the people answered with one voice and said, 'All the words that the LORD has spoken we will do.' . . . And Moses took half of the blood and put it in basins, and half of the blood he threw against the altar. Then he took the Book of the Covenant and read it in the hearing of the people. And they said, '*All that the LORD has spoken we will do, and we will be obedient.*' And Moses took the blood and threw it on the people and said, 'Behold the blood of the covenant that the LORD has made with you in accordance with all these words.'
>
> (Exod. 24.3, 6–8, emphasis mine)

We have already seen that the all-important thing about a covenant is its precise terms as a legal document. We need to think carefully here. The covenant at Sinai was not the law. The covenant was a two-party covenant agreement between God and the people based on the law. If the people broke the law, the relationship was broken.

The point at issue here is the apparent severity of the conditions. Surely, one might argue, it would be sufficient to keep most of the law as best one could. After all, if a person gets 70 per cent in their final exams at university, they will get a first class honours – no one worries about the fact that they fell short by 30 per cent of the possible total.

The answer to that is that God's law is not like a university examination. Paul stresses here that God's standard is 100 per cent. The apostle James says exactly the same in a passage condemning believers for showing partiality:

If you really fulfil the royal law according to the Scripture, 'You shall love your neighbour as yourself', you are doing well. But if you show partiality, you are committing sin and are convicted by the law as transgressors. *For whoever keeps the whole law but fails in one point has become accountable for all of it.* For he who said, 'Do not commit adultery', also said, 'Do not murder.' If you do not commit adultery but do murder, you have become a transgressor of the law. (Jas. 2.8–11, emphasis mine)

Why is it like that?

Let us first note that certain relationships are like that in the nature of things. Suppose an anchor is connected to a ship by a chain with a hundred links. If one link breaks, the ship is cast adrift and we would never think of saying that this is unfair, since one link is only one per cent of the whole.

We are talking about relationship with a holy God who cannot tolerate any level of transgression. So if we wish to base our relationship with him on keeping all his commandments we shall have to do so 100 per cent without fail.

You say, 'But no one could!' Quite true – but Israel thought they could and they needed to find out by long and hard experience that it was impossible. Sin was a more serious business than they imagined.

As a result, when they did fail in Old Testament times, God provided a temporary solution by instituting a system of sacrifices to teach them that sin needed to be atoned for. But that system did not deal with the real problem. That is why the Old Testament said that there would have to be a new covenant. Hebrews explains the situation by citing Jeremiah:

But as it is, Christ has obtained a ministry that is as much more excellent than the old as the covenant he mediates is better, since it is enacted on better promises. For if that first covenant had been faultless, there would have been no occasion to look for a second. For he finds fault with them when he says:

'Behold, the days are coming, declares the Lord,
when I will establish a new covenant with the house of Israel

221

and with the house of Judah,
not like the covenant that I made with their fathers
on the day when I took them by the hand to bring them out
    of the land of Egypt.
For they did not continue in my covenant,
and so I showed no concern for them, declares the Lord.'
(Heb. 8.6–9, citing Jer. 31.31–34)

The last verse in this passage shows the seriousness of breaking the conditions of the covenant. It also shows us why Christ had to die and be made a curse for us: in order to redeem us from the curse of the broken law (Gal. 3.13). As we have just seen, Paul spelled it out in Galatians 3.10–14, which begins 'For all who rely on works of the law . . .'. Note once more the emphasis on 'all'. There was nothing wrong with the laws. They were, and remain, good counsel. Think of the laws brought in during the pandemic – laws about handwashing, wearing masks and social distancing. All of them good and necessary, but they could not cure Covid-19; they could not bring the dead back to life. They could only contain the disease, if followed. Similarly, says Paul, 'if a law had been given that could give life, then righteousness would indeed be by the law' (Gal. 3.21).

In a parallel passage in Romans Paul explains what the law does:

Now we know that whatever the law says it speaks to those who are under the law, so that every mouth may be stopped, and the whole world may be held accountable to God. For by works of the law no human being will be justified in his sight, since through the law comes knowledge of sin.
(Rom. 3.19–20)

Suppose I visit the doctor because I am experiencing breathlessness. I might be given some tests on a treadmill that show my heart is struggling to cope. It is now clear that there is a problem with my heart and I require treatment. The tests reveal my condition, but cannot cure it. Similarly, a thermometer can show I have a fever, but it cannot cure it.

Going back to Galatians Paul goes on to say that what happened was that the Scripture imprisoned everything under sin, so that the promise by faith in Jesus Christ might be given to those who believe.

Now before faith came, we were held captive under the law, imprisoned until the coming faith would be revealed. So then, the law was our guardian until Christ came, in order that we might be justified by faith. But now that faith has come, we are no longer under a guardian, for in Christ Jesus you are all sons of God, through faith.

(Gal. 3.22–26)

The tragedy was that many of Paul's fellow Jews would not have it and, rejecting his message of salvation through trusting Christ, insisted on trusting their efforts at keeping the law. Many religious people around the world today, sadly even professing Christians, do exactly the same even though they find it to be a form of slavery. The casting out of Hagar reminds us that the two ways of approaching salvation can no more co-exist than Isaac and Hagar could co-exist in the same home.

We move on now to a further example of Paul's exposition of this Old Testament prototype.

## Mount Sinai and Jerusalem as metaphorical mothers

Gooding translates Galatians 4.25 as follows: 'the Mount Sinai is in Arabia and is in line with [Greek: συστοιχεῖ, *systoichei*] the present Jerusalem, for she is in slavery along with her children'[10]. When Paul refers to the present Jerusalem and her *children* he is not, of course, speaking allegorically. He is referring to the literal city in his time. When he refers to her as a mother and her citizens as children he is using a timeless metaphor familiar to all of us.

Jesus addressed Jerusalem city as a mother, and her citizens as her children (Luke 13.34). So Russians speak of their country as Mother Russia. So students in many countries will speak of their university as their *alma mater*. No one would think of these examples as allegorical!

Hence, Paul says that because the covenant given at Mount Sinai brings forth children unto slavery, it corresponds to a slave woman, Hagar, who gave birth to Abraham's son into slavery. For that reason Paul then argues that Mount Sinai corresponds to the contemporary city of Jerusalem that is also in slavery, along with her children.

Importantly, Paul is not deducing this from the details of the story of Abraham and Hagar says Gooding:

He is stating it as a fact of contemporary history that he knew only too well – he had himself lived a part of his life in that self-same religious slavery, and for the same reason, namely a mistaken idea of the purpose of the law from Mount Sinai.

And that was sad, not only because of the inevitable resultant slavery, but for another historical and geographical reason. When God made the original covenant with Abraham and his seed, Abraham was already in Canaan. Hence in the preamble to the covenant God said to Abraham, 'I am the Lord that brought you out of Ur of the Chaldeans, *to give you this land* to inherit it' (Gen 15:7). And when Abraham enquired how he could be sure he would inherit it, God replied by making an unconditional covenant guaranteeing to give it to Abraham and his seed (Gen 15:8–21).

But Mount Sinai, Paul points out, was in Arabia. Now Arabia was the part of the world that Hagar's son, Ishmael, and his descendants eventually regarded as their home (see Gen 21:21; Ps 83:6). But much more significantly, at the level of its prototypical meaning, Mount Sinai was not in Canaan, and Arabia was not part of the promised inheritance. When Israel received the covenant from Mount Sinai they were not in the promised land, but only on their way toward it. That covenant certainly showed them the behaviour that God expected of them both while they were in the wilderness and after they entered Canaan. But the basis of Israel's legal entitlement to their inheritance was the unconditional covenant God made with Abraham and his seed, not the law from Sinai. And, as Paul had earlier pointed out (Gal 3:16), the seed mentioned in the Abrahamic covenant was primarily Christ . . . All who put their faith in him, and not in their own efforts to keep the Sinai law, will most certainly inherit the inheritance promised to Abraham and his seed (3:29).

Unfortunately the Jerusalem of Paul's day, the religious capital and mother city of worldwide Judaism, rejected Christ as the key to the eventual possession of the promised inheritance, and instead based her hope of inheritance on her own effort to keep the law from Sinai. Official Judaism and much of Christendom does so still.

At verse 24 Paul told us that these women (i.e. Hagar and Sarah) represented two covenants. He then explained that Hagar represented the covenant from Sinai but did not tell us which covenant Sarah represented. But now this detail becomes clear: Sarah represents the unconditional covenant which God made with Abraham (Gen 15). It was according to the God-given promise of that covenant that she, the free woman, gave birth to the free-born son Isaac.[11]

In this way, Hagar corresponds to the Sinai covenant that in turn corresponds to the Jerusalem that is now, and Sarah corresponds to the Abrahamic covenant that in turn corresponds to the Jerusalem that is above. That Jerusalem, as we saw earlier, is composed of the vast community of Jews and Gentiles who are the spiritual children of Abraham and Sarah because like them (and like Paul) they have learned to base their hope of eternal life, not on their efforts to keep the law of Moses, but solely on God's unconditional promise given to those who put their faith in Christ.

Isaiah too uses the Hagar–Sarah story as a prototype:

'Sing, O barren one, who did not bear;
   break forth into singing and cry aloud,
   you who have not been in labour!
For the children of the desolate one will be more
than the children of her who is married,' says the LORD.
(Isa. 54.1)

Gooding explains:

Paul was not the only one to see that the story of Genesis 15–21 was both historical and a prototype. Isaiah had too, centuries before. At

Isaiah 51:1–2 he calls on his nation to 'Look unto Abraham your father, and unto Sarah that bare you; for when he was but one I called him, and I blessed him, and made him many'. Since then, however, as a result of the nation's trust in itself and in its idols instead of in the living God who was their maker and husband, Jerusalem had experienced alienation from God, desolation of the city, and the carrying away of her children into exile and slavery.

But now Isaiah, in God's name, promises Jerusalem restoration of her children, and cites Sarah's experience as a prototype. Sarah at first had been barren. Losing faith in God's promise, she had suggested, to her great eventual sorrow, that Abraham take Hagar. For now, while she herself was barren, Hagar had the husband, bore a child, despised Sarah, and flaunted her son in mockery of Sarah's infertility as a woman (Gen 16). Moreover Abraham came to dote on Hagar's son, if not on Hagar, and would have been content for Sarah to continue barren, provided that he could count Ishmael as his heir (Gen 17). Sarah's desolation must have seemed complete.

But in God's good time the tables were turned. Sarah, the one-time barren woman, had a child. And, though God blessed Hagar and her son and promised them numerous descendants (Gen 16:10; 21:18), God promised Abraham vastly more children, both physical and spiritual, through Sarah (Gen 17:16; Rom 4:16–18).

Since Pentecost, Isaiah's glowing prophecy has already been fulfilled to an extent far beyond, perhaps, what Abraham and Sarah could ever have imagined. And even greater fulfilments lie ahead (Rom 11:12–27). For just as we might say that Copernicus is the father of modern science, since he, by his example, showed to all subsequent scientists the principles which they should follow, so Abraham and Sarah, by their experience, have demonstrated to multi-millions since, what it means to believe God and to be justified by faith. In this sense these millions are their spiritual children.

Unhappily another detail of the prototype has been repeatedly fulfilled. 'As then he who was born after the flesh [namely Ishmael] kept on persecuting him who was born after the Spirit [namely

Isaac: see Gen 21:9], even so it is now', says Paul (Gal 4:29). The persecution of those born after the Spirit by those born after the flesh has continued all down the centuries. But it does but show the need to understand what justification by faith really means and then to stand unflinchingly for it. And here a precise understanding of the New Testament's interpretation of the Old Testament will be important.[12]

David Gooding has done us a great service in showing that a clear understanding of how the New Testament uses the Old greatly enriches our appreciation of the whole storyline of the Bible.

The idea of prototype imparts to the narrative a momentum that adds considerably to the credibility and depth of the Seed Project as we trace its historical trajectory, to which we must now return.

# Abraham swears an oath to Abimelech

As we know, Abimelech, the local king, and Abraham, who was now resident in his territory at Gerar, had already had dealings with one another – much to Abraham's embarrassment. Abimelech had recognised Abraham as someone of equal status to himself and therefore a force to be reckoned with. He therefore understandably approached Abraham with a request to make a non-aggression treaty between themselves and their descendants. Abimelech could see that Abraham's success had to do with the fact, as he put it, that the Lord was with Abraham and, whatever he did or did not understand as to who the Lord was, he asked Abraham to swear this treaty by God.

Understandably, Abimelech wanted to make provision for his own security, as did Abraham for his. Just as God had reassured Abraham by making a (one-party) covenant with him, so here these two men made a (two-party) covenant with each other in order to secure their mutual futures as best they could. That pact was soon to be tested in a dispute over water rights.

We have seen how the lives of Hagar and Ishmael were saved by the timely 'discovery' of a well. That reminds us of the vital importance of wells in that part of the world. No one can live without water and access to a well. Even more so, possession of one was greatly coveted, especially by herdsmen like Abraham and Abimelech.

Abimelech seemed now to be so concerned with security that he seized a well – or at least his servants did. Abimelech protested innocence of the deed when Abraham remonstrated with him. Abraham, embarrassed once more, brought a gift of animals for Abimelech and they made a covenant stipulating that Abraham had dug the well, so it was his. The place was named Beer-sheva ('Well of the Oath').[13] By this means he was trying to secure a water supply for his family and livestock in perpetuity. However, Genesis later informs us that the Philistines reneged on the oath and stopped up the well after Abraham's death, so Isaac had to dig it out again. His action led to strife and he eventually had to give up the well and dig another two before he was at peace. In addition more oaths were sworn (Gen. 26.18–22). One cannot live without water.

Abraham clearly had an anxious streak in his character. Sometimes he was fearful, almost paranoid, for his own security. That character defect had led him into deep trouble and stinging rebuke in connection with his wife twice over. Now that the promised child Isaac had arrived, Abraham inevitably paid great attention to securing the boy's future. After all, the fulfilment of God's promises to Abraham now depended on Isaac's survival and that of Isaac's offspring after him. Abraham wished to do everything in his power to safeguard Isaac. Securing the well was one important step in that direction.

As we look back thus far in Abraham's life we can trace just how much God had been faithful to his promise in Genesis 15 to shield the man. If Abraham had understood this better, he might not have been so nervous and jumpy about security.

And that is a good place to pause a while to think about our own human desire for security. This world can be a dangerous place, especially for believers. All of us have concerns about securing our future and that of our dependants. What is a balanced perspective on the matter? How much security do we need? Should we avoid risk completely? Should we fear antagonism, persecution or even death? How can we quell anxious fears? In what sense does God shield those who trust him?

The first thing is to recognise that fear and anxiety are very real. It was real to Abraham and it is all too real for many Christian believers, Peter not least among them. God recognises this and speaks to us about it in Scripture, where we frequently meet the injunction 'Do not fear'. The first person we meet in Scripture who was afraid was Adam. Abraham was the first person to be told directly by God not to fear (Gen. 15.1). There is no need to tell someone not to fear if they are not fearful. God knew his man and spoke to his heart with grace and understanding.

The opposite of fear and uncertainty is confidence in the love and care of God.

Jesus dedicated part of the Sermon on the Mount to the question of security. He first laid down a basic principle regarding getting wealth accumulation into proportion – a matter that played a considerable role in Abraham's thinking. Jesus said:

'Do not lay up for yourselves treasures on earth, where moth and rust destroy and where thieves break in and steal, but lay up for yourselves treasures in heaven, where neither moth nor rust destroys and where thieves do not break in and steal. For where your treasure is, there your heart will be also.' (Matt. 6.19–21)

Treasure, by definition, consists of (material) possessions that go beyond normal daily needs, and Jesus' warning addresses itself to that common human desire for more. Investment is a good idea – provided it is investment in the world to come. There are many examples of this in the New Testament. Luke tells us of a group of women, some of them quite well-to-do, who provided for Jesus and his disciples out of their own means (Luke 8.1–3). He also tells us of a businesswoman, Lydia, originally from Thyatira, who provided a base in her home in Philippi for Paul and his team to carry out the first evangelism in Europe. There are many examples of this kind of gospel patronage. Perhaps the most famous is the story of a brave and far-sighted Christian cloth merchant and trader, Humphrey Monmouth, who in 1523 partnered with William Tyndale and became his patron, funding Tyndale's mission to translate the Scriptures into English, thus making them available to the common man. Monmouth took great risks to smuggle Tyndale's Bibles into England in his ships. He was incarcerated in the Tower of London for a whole year because of his support for Tyndale and Luther. When we think of the untold numbers of people who came to faith in Christ through Tyndale's translation, we see that what Humphrey Monmouth did was a massive investment in the world to come.[14]

Motivation for our work is the next point to which Jesus draws our attention: 'No one can serve two masters, for either he will hate the one and love the other, or he will be devoted to the one and despise the other. You cannot serve God and money' (Matt. 6.24).

Notice the term 'serve'. It is, of course, perfectly possible to *serve* God and *use* money, examples of which we have just considered. The danger is that we do the reverse – we *serve* money and *use* God when we are in trouble.

And it is serving God that Jesus tells us is the key to conquering fear. He says: '*Therefore* I tell you, do not be anxious about your life, what you will eat or what you will drink, nor about your body, what you will put on' (v. 25, my emphasis). In our discussion earlier about Abram and Melchizedek we saw that Jesus' answer to anxiety is to seek first God's rule in our lives – and all the other things will be added. That is exactly what Abraham and Sarah repeatedly failed to do. Most of their fears and concerns resulted from the fact that in so many situations they failed to consult God first, if at all.

The result was that Abraham's insecurity grew deeper and lasted longer than was really necessary. It propelled him to grasp wealth, make treaties, dig wells and in general do anything to make secure provision – especially for Isaac.

By contrast, Paul's trust in God was not dependent on the level of his worldly security. In fact he lost everything when he became a believer. Not only that, but he subsequently suffered severe persecution that left him more than once within an inch of death. In a letter to the church at Philippi, which, although poor, had been generous to him, he explained the secret of how he coped with life's ups and downs:

I rejoiced in the Lord greatly that now at length you have revived your concern for me. You were indeed concerned for me, but you

had no opportunity. Not that I am speaking of being in need, for I have learned in whatever situation I am to be content. I know how to be brought low, and I know how to abound. In any and every circumstance, I have learned the secret of facing plenty and hunger, abundance and need. I can do all things through him who strengthens me.
(Phil. 4.10–13)

That is a very sobering and challenging stance. How much of my own apparent confidence in the Lord is dependent on my being a recipient of his generosity? How much would that confidence diminish if those things were removed? It boils down to this: do I trust God the Giver, or is my trust much more in what he gives me?

The first disciples were taught a lesson on this by Jesus himself. He sent out a large group of them into the towns and villages, and they returned to report to him what had transpired:

The seventy-two returned with joy, saying, 'Lord, even the demons are subject to us in your name!' And he said to them, 'I saw Satan fall like lightning from heaven. Behold, I have given you authority to tread on serpents and scorpions, and over all the power of the enemy, and nothing shall hurt you. Nevertheless, do not rejoice in this, that the spirits are subject to you, but rejoice that your names are written in heaven.'
(Luke 10.17–20)

They were delighted in their success at using the special powers he had given them. But he saw an indication in their reaction that they were in danger of putting their confidence in those powers rather than in his word. So he said to them: 'Do not rejoice [i.e. place your confidence] in this . . . but rejoice that your names are written in heaven.' And how could they know that? They had to trust Jesus' word for it.

This tendency to trust the gift rather than the Giver has sadly characterised some churches, which have encouraged members to put their trust in the so-called 'supernatural' gifts[15] of healing, prophecy, tongues and so on rather than in the word of God. The problem with this is that, as Jesus himself taught in the Sermon on the Mount, his name is so powerful that people sometimes prophesy and do great things in his name without even being believers:

'Not everyone who says to me, "Lord, Lord", will enter the kingdom of heaven, but the one who does the will of my Father who is in heaven. On that day many will say to me, "Lord, Lord, did we not prophesy in your name, and cast out demons in your name, and do many mighty works in your name?" And then will I declare to them, "I never knew you; depart from me, you workers of lawlessness."' (Matt. 7.21–23)

It is a sobering thought that relying on a 'gift' you think you have for your assurance of God's acceptance is to build your house on sand and could lead to disaster.

With this as background we must now return to Abraham, who was about to face the hardest test that anyone could ever be called upon to face. His coming through it makes him a unique hero of faith in God.

# 15

# God tests Abraham

## Akedah: the binding of Isaac

It was hard for Abraham to let Ishmael go. After all, Ishmael was his first son. He had come to love him and pin on him his hopes of a future nation (Gen. 17.15–22). Now that Isaac had arrived, all of that seems to have been quickly forgotten as Abraham concentrated on Isaac and his future. Isaac was a precious gift of God, the seed of promise, and Abraham and Sarah now bore the responsibility of training him to carry the weight of God's far-reaching Seed Project.

As Abraham saw it, all God's promises were concentrated in Isaac. Their fulfilment depended on his survival. Abraham, therefore, would use all of his resources to make sure he did survive. He was never going to let Isaac go.

And in that attitude is where the danger we have just been discussing lurked. Was the focus of his trust shifting, to be concentrated on Isaac the gift, rather than on the God who had given Isaac to him? Or was it a mixture of both? In any case, did it really matter?

The account that follows is one of the most famous of stories, unique in world literature. It begins with the narrator informing us what is about to happen: 'After these things God tested Abraham . . .' (Gen. 22.1). The object of testing is explained to us in Deuteronomy: 'And you shall remember the whole way that the LORD your God has led you these forty years in the wilderness, that he might humble you, testing you to know what was in your heart, whether you would keep his commandments or not' (Deut. 8.2). God put them through experiences that would prove the genuineness of their faith. The fact that it was a test is confirmed in Hebrews 11.17: 'By faith Abraham, when he was tested, offered up Isaac, and he who had received the promises was in the act of offering up his only son . . .'

We are not told that Abraham knew in advance it was to be a test. For if he had known, it might have altered its nature. Yet we, the readers of the account, are told in advance, and this should indicate to us that Abraham was expected to come through it.

God spoke to Abraham, using his new name for the first and only time in Genesis: "'Abraham!' And he said, "Here am I." He said, "Take your son, your only son Isaac, whom you love, and go to the land of Moriah, and offer him there as a burnt offering on one of the mountains of which I shall tell you'" (Gen. 22.1–2).

Moriah was a mountain range in Israel upon which Solomon was later said to have built the Temple (2 Chron. 3.1). It was the place where the city of Jerusalem was eventually situated and, therefore, would eventually become a place of great biblical significance, although Abraham knew nothing of that at the time.

At God's command, Abraham had already 'sacrificed' one son, Ishmael, by sending him away. That was bad enough. To hear God now command him to kill Isaac, the son whom the same God had promised, shook Abraham to the core of his being. It shocks almost everyone when they hear it, triggering all kinds of reactions and raising all kinds of questions. First, there is the knee-jerk response that this is morally outrageous. We all know how we react to a murderer who claims, 'God told me to do it.' Surely it is unthinkable that God could, let alone would, command a human sacrifice? For this utterly abhorrent practice, carried out by adherents of the Ammonite god Molech, is roundly condemned elsewhere in the Bible itself (Lev. 20.1–5). That gives urgency to the question: how, then, can it be countenanced here in Genesis?

Famous thinkers have wrestled with this story. Franz Kafka wrote that the Akedah was 'an old story not worth discussing any longer'[1] and he produced three alternative renderings of the story as playful fables. Kafka was in part responding to the work of Danish philosopher Søren Kierkegaard, who devoted an entire book to trying to understand the Akedah. His *Fear and Trembling* (1843) is regarded by scholars as the most difficult of all his works. Kierkegaard wrote the book under the pseudonym Johannes de Silentio, and in it Abraham's silence towards his loved ones about what he was intending with Isaac is one of Kierkegaard's enigmas as he wrestles with the ethical problems raised by

234

Abraham's response to God's command. It is interesting that philosopher C. Stephen Evans, co-editor with Daniel Conway of *Kierkegaard: Fear and Trembling,*[2] referenced just above, contrary to many biblical scholars, believes that Genesis 22 is historical, and he holds that it is possible for someone to have an authentic personal revelation from God.[3]

Trying to cope with the ethical problem, some scholars make the (not very convincing) suggestion that Abraham was familiar with pagan child sacrifice, so he went along with it at first only to learn the major lesson it was meant to teach: that God was utterly against human sacrifices. For Kierkegaard, however, Abraham was culpable of the attempted murder of his son. Yet he adds that this cannot be the whole story, as Abraham's actions reveal a superior dimension of responsibility – responsibility to God: 'the single individual as the single individual stands in an absolute relation to the absolute', and his responsibility consists in 'his relation to the absolute'. Abraham was, therefore, a 'true knight of faith'.

The story is complex and in order to tackle it we need first to think about what it actually says and how Scripture itself interprets it.

One thing, though, needs to be emphasised at the start: Abraham did not, in fact, sacrifice his son. That he thought he might have to do so is a different matter. We shall, therefore, try to explore the account carefully, keeping an open mind as much as possible before coming to a verdict, if indeed we can reach one.

God said three things to Abraham that showed him God recognised the depth of his fatherly devotion to Isaac: 'your son, your only son Isaac, whom you love'. Then came the gentle-sounding request, 'Take your son . . .', which prefaced a verbal missile that ripped into Abraham's soul, shredding it with unbearable psychological intensity: 'Go to the land of Moriah, and offer him there as a burnt offering.'[4]

The word translated 'go' here can also be rendered as 'go by yourself' (*lech lecha* in Hebrew) is striking because it is an exact repetition of what God said to him when he called him in Genesis 12. And how could Abraham forget the words he had heard all those years ago directly from the voice of God? Then, God had called him to sacrifice his past to travel to a land of great future promise. Now the same words were apparently being used to command him to sacrifice that future. How could that possibly be? Surely God did not intend to take back what he had given?

Not long before this pivotal event, God had told Abraham to obey his wife Sarah and send his son Ishmael and Ishmael's mother Hagar away. That was hard enough, as he had loved Ishmael. Now to be asked to take his son Isaac, his only son whom he loved, the promised son, the apple of his eye, his inheritance and sole hope for posterity, and offer him up as a sacrifice was utterly unthinkable! It made no sense. Surely it could not be? Was it not morally impossible?

Isaac's name derives from the Hebrew for 'laughter'. There was no laughing now as God asked Abraham to return the greatest gift he had ever given him. God was asking Abraham to choose between Giver and gift. Abraham was facing the hardest imaginable choice of that kind.

This trial of faith in God involved an entirely new dimension. When God had earlier commanded him to 'walk before me and be perfect', Abraham had been 100 years old and he was now older by the time of Isaac. There is considerable dispute as to how old Isaac was at this time but, as the subsequent narrative shows, he was old enough to take a gruelling three-day walk carrying wood. It would seem that he was more likely to have been a young man rather than a boy. Let's imagine he was 15 so that Abraham would have been 116.

Putting it into contemporary terms (of physical strength) we should imagine facing life's hardest choice at around 58 – in the prime of life.

Abraham's head was spinning. Isaac was the son for whom he had waited many years. All his hopes for the future were now bound up with him. Surely to fulfil God's request would inevitably spell the end of the whole Seed Project that depended crucially on Isaac's continued survival?

'Offer him as a burnt offering . . .' The sheer awfulness of it may have reminded Abraham of the dreadful darkness that had surrounded him during the making of the original covenant in Genesis 15. The idea of a (whole) burnt offering was of something given in its entirety to God. Moses was later to institute daily burnt offerings in Israel. Each morning and evening an entire animal was to be burnt as a symbol expressing the nation's commitment to offering itself completely to God.

A clear understanding of this is shown by the fourfold repetition of the word 'all' in the statement of the perceptive scribe who talked with Jesus about the greatest of the commandments:

'You are right, Teacher. You have truly said that he is one, and there is no other besides him. And to love him with *all* the heart and with *all* the understanding and with *all* the strength, and to love one's neighbour as oneself, is much more than *all* whole burnt offerings and sacrifices.'
(Mark 12.32–33, emphasis mine)

God was asking Abraham for his all – an all that God himself had given him. Abraham had asked God what he would receive from him. God had promised and delivered a son along with a guaranteed inheritance for his posterity. Now all of that was on the line. What would Abraham choose, if pushed to the limit: the gift, Isaac, or the Giver, God? How could he resolve the tension that was tearing him apart?

It is one thing to be prepared to make the ultimate sacrifice oneself, as many Christian martyrs have done and still are doing. It is entirely another to be faced, like Abraham, with making such a sacrifice involving someone else – especially one's own child. That circumstance added an obvious moral dimension to the situation since it seemed very much as if God's moral commandment forbidding murder was conflicting with God's personal commandment to Abraham. It was an almost unimaginable moral dilemma. Hebrew scholar Aryeh Amihay, from the University of California, Santa Barbara, comments:

Kierkegaard presents the paradox of faith as an arch that strains between the obligation of the believer to God, and the obligation to a moral conduct decreed by God, both defined by an absolute duty of obedience. For Kierkegaard it is imperative that God would prevent Abraham's ordeal from completion, because otherwise the paradox would have no longer been sustained: Abraham would have violated a moral code. The paradox is sustained only by Abraham's willingness to violate it for the sake of God, and yet never committing an immoral deed.

The introduction of a true paradox into the discussion emphasises how rare and remote the contradiction between obedience to God and moral duties is in any religious system. But the possibility nevertheless exists and defines the meaning of obligation, as it is tested under excruciating circumstances, when a believer is compelled to resolve a moral dilemma and determine the higher obligation.[5]

We do not read of any verbal response from Abraham made to God's command to him. There is no record of him either protesting or pleading for the life of Isaac as he had earlier pleaded for Sodom and Lot. He appears to have submitted and done what God requested, thereby demonstrating an awe-inspiring degree of faith in his higher obligation to obey God. Was this a further example of his trust that the Judge of all the earth would do right? That is, that all would eventually be morally in order?

Kierkegaard, in *Fear and Trembling*, thought that what Abraham was asked to sacrifice was reason itself, since there is a complete contradiction between God's promise to bless the world through Isaac and his request now to kill him. However, the New Testament indicates that something far deeper was at stake, and gives us information that is not to be found in the book of Genesis. That means we have to rely for its authenticity on the fact that the New Testament is the inspired word of God, so what it says about the working of Abraham's mind is to be taken as true and authoritative. This is in accordance with our Lord's statement to his apostles regarding the supernatural character of biblical revelation:

'I still have many things to say to you, but you cannot bear them now. When the Spirit of truth comes, he will guide you into all the truth, for he will not speak on his own authority, but whatever he hears he will speak, and he will declare to you the things that are to come. He will glorify me, for he will take what is mine and declare it to you. All that the Father has is mine; therefore I said that he will take what is mine and declare it to you.'
(John 16.12–15)

This is a clear reference to supernatural communication from the mind of God to the human contributors to Scripture. We need to take that seriously when it comes to what the letter to the Hebrews says about Abraham's thought processes: 'He considered that God was able even to raise him from the dead, from which, figuratively speaking, he did receive him back' (Heb. 11.19).

We have no record that Abraham discussed his inner thoughts with any other human – a silence that has led to much scholarly contemplation.[6] Only God knew them. We have already seen, in connection with Isaac's conception, that Abraham eventually and not without difficulty came to believe that God by his supernatural power could and would generate physical life through human bodies – his and Sarah's – bodies that, for the purpose of procreation, were as good as dead (Rom. 4.19).[7]

Regarding God's devastating request to offer up Isaac, it would appear from what we have just cited from Hebrews 11 that Abraham similarly reasoned that, since he had no hope of being a father again, if he really had to kill his son, then in order to fulfil the promise that Isaac would be Abraham's heir, God would have to raise him from the dead.

Under the circumstances, far from being a sacrifice of reason, this is a stunning example of the use of reason based on an unshakeable conviction that God would keep his word, even if it meant he had to use supernatural power to perform a spectacular miracle. We do not know exactly when Abraham reached this conclusion, but the fact that he did get to it in the end, even though mind and emotions were in utter turmoil, was a feat of staggering proportions, both intellectually and emotionally. Kierkegaard was completely wrong to suggest that Abraham sacrificed his reason.

Also, the power of God to raise the dead brings a new perspective to this incident. Criticism of God's command to Abraham to offer up his son tends to come from people whose world view is naturalistic. They deny any supernatural dimension to life. Once you are dead you are dead. Hence terminating life must be an unqualified evil? No – not quite, even on atheistic presuppositions. Doctors, for instance, whatever their world view, faced with the moral dilemma of whether or not to terminate a pregnancy where the embryo, though alive, is defective and threatening the life of the mother, will take the life of the embryo. They have made the choice for one death to avoid two. They have not violated the biblical command not to murder.

If that is true, then under atheistic presuppositions we need to be careful when we make judgements about a world with a supernatural dimension, especially since, in this instance, as we need to keep reminding ourselves, Abraham did not actually in the end kill Isaac.

We are told that, in order to do what God had commanded, Abraham got up early in the morning. Those words form a verbal echo reminding the reader that they were last used by the narrator when Abraham got up early in the morning to bid farewell to Ishmael and thus 'sacrifice' him in the sense of letting him go. That had been hard enough, for Abraham loved the lad, his firstborn, even though his mother was a servant. Yet he had to send Hagar and Ishmael away because God commanded him to do so.

But now something infinitely worse threatened Abraham: having to let go of Isaac by offering him up, and this, inexplicably, to be done in response to the command of God – the very God who had promised him descendants as numerous as the stars in the sky. Surely that promise was not meant in the end only to apply to Ishmael, of whom God had said that he would become a great nation?

Abraham took two 'lads' with him as well as his son Isaac. He saddled his donkey and seemed ready to go before he thought of 'splitting' wood for the fire that would have to be lit. Maybe this rather odd order of events is one of those touches of authenticity that indicates possible confusion in his mind caused by the sheer enormity of what God had asked him to do.

When earlier bidding farewell to Ishmael he had provided Hagar with some bread and water. Now he gave the wood to Isaac to carry, whereas he himself carried fire and a knife, instruments that Abraham knew would be the means of his losing Isaac.

It was three days' journey by foot to the region of Mount Moriah to the north. The days are, perhaps mercifully, passed over in silence. Calvin makes the pertinent comment that those three days made the ordeal for Abraham even worse: 'God does not require him to put his son immediately to death, but compels him to revolve this execution in his mind during three whole days, that in preparing to sacrifice his son, he may still more severely torture all his own senses.'[8] They were three days of acute, indescribable suffering. They constitute a convincing rebuttal of the superficial and dangerously false notion that people chosen by God for a special role will never have a rough time. Isaac's suffering would be compressed into a shorter timespan.

Abraham and Isaac eventually reached the place 'of which God had told him'. That piece of information tells us that God must have earlier communicated more detail to Abraham than appears in the narrative. Hebrew narrative minimalism once more.

Abraham instructed the two men with them to wait while 'he and the boy' went to worship. Calling his son 'the boy' may represent the beginning of detachment. In Abraham's mind, was the boy already as good as gone? Or do his next words, that they would 'come again to you' imply that both of them would return from the mountain? Did this represent an evasion, or an unconscious prophecy, or could it just be that it was at this time Abraham's faith in God had assured him God could raise the dead, and this convinced him he would return with Isaac? After all, we know he did come to that realisation at *some* point. Why not right then?

Father and son slowly ascended the mountain – 'they went both of them together' (from a Hebrew root meaning 'to be one'). Genesis Rabbah (the Jewish Midrash commentary) says, one might think almost presciently, that Isaac with the wood on his back was like a 'condemned man carrying his own cross'. Centuries later, one in whom the promise to Abraham found its full and final fulfilment did exactly that: 'he went out, bearing his own cross' (John 19.17). But this was a Son who had the choice – Isaac had none.

Isaac broke the silence: 'And Isaac said to his father Abraham, "My father!" And he said, "Here am I, my son."' Isaac calls him *Avi*, my father, speaking to him in the affectionate tones of a son to his dad. This is the very first conversation in the Bible between a father and a son. It is brief and poignant.

Isaac was clearly old enough to know what worship involving animal sacrifice was like. He asked the obvious question: 'Behold, the fire and the wood, but where is the lamb for a burnt offering?' Isaac didn't mention the knife, perhaps because there was more than a flutter of apprehension in his heart. 'Have you forgotten the lamb, Dad? Where is it?' How could Abraham now avoid telling Isaac the awful truth? 'Abraham said, "God will provide for [see for] himself the lamb for a burnt offering, my son."'

It must have taken supreme mastery of his emotions for Abraham to answer in this way. Was it a pious evasion or (much more likely) a deliberate, and prophetic, expression of a hitherto unprecedented trust in divine providence? And what was Isaac meant to think? This would scarcely have assuaged his rising fear, would it?

We don't know. We are on holy ground here and even attempting to understand what is going on has the feel of intruding on something so very sacred that we need to take great care to avoid violating it in any way.

It is interesting and important to see how Jews interpret this key event. To cite Rabbi Ari Kahn:

> Yitzchak's death was never a possibility – not as far as Avraham was concerned, and not as far as God was concerned. God's commandment to Avraham was very specific, and Avraham understood it very precisely: Yitzchak was to be 'raised up as an offering,' and God would use the opportunity to teach humankind, once and for all, that human sacrifice, child sacrifice, is not acceptable.
>
> This is precisely how the sages of the Talmud (Taanit 4a) understood Akeidat Yitzchak. Citing the Prophet Jeremiah's exhortation against child sacrifice (Chapter 19), they state unequivocally that such behavior 'never crossed God's mind' – referring specifically to the sacrificial slaughter of Yitzchak.[9]

However, even so, I am not myself convinced that Abraham knew in advance that Isaac would be delivered from being killed, for, as we have seen, Abraham believed that if Isaac died, then God could use his almighty power to raise him from the dead. Yet it may be that Abraham spoke more than he knew and there rose in his heart the thrilling thought that he might not need to kill Isaac. His words in the end turned out to be exactly right – God did provide a lamb.

'So they went both of them together.'

What was now going through Isaac's mind? His silence conveys a hint that he might have had some understanding of his father's words. It may have been beginning to dawn on him that he was the intended sacrifice. What that would have meant to a young person is hard to appreciate.

The story casts a mighty shadow over subsequent history: *Where is the lamb?* 'Behold, the Lamb of God, who takes away the sin of the world.'

*Where is the lamb?* 'He was . . . like a lamb that is led to the slaughter, and like a sheep that before its shearers is silent, so he opened not his mouth.' *Where is the lamb?* As father and son trudged slowly up the mountain it is hard not to see the footprints of a greater Son who utterly trusted his Father as he trudged painfully up what was probably the very same mountain to the hill at Calvary. *Where is the lamb?* 'I saw a Lamb standing, as though it had been slain...'

The steps stopped: 'When they came to the place of which God had told him, Abraham built the altar there and laid the wood in order and bound Isaac his son and laid him on the altar, on top of the wood.'

The Jewish name for this incident is the Hebrew word *Akedah* ('binding'). It occurs only here in the Old Testament. Binding surely implies some passive co-operation on Isaac's part. Many scholars assume that at this time Isaac was roughly the same age Ishmael had been when he and his mother left. A strong, outdoor-work-hardened teenager of around 15 could easily have outrun or overpowered an elderly man – let alone one over a hundred years old. Yet Isaac did not attempt to do so.

Was he terrified, or did he have a deep trust in the Lord as to the fulfilment of the promises his father must often have shared with him? Or did God meet him in his need and give him a supernatural sense of peace that virtually anaesthetised him to the reality of what was about to happen? Did Isaac in some sense deep down want to do his father's will? Did a conversation take place that is hidden from us, in which Abraham desperately tried to give some explanation of why he was threatening to destroy all their joint divinely communicated expectations by extinguishing his life? We do not know.

We can easily imagine anxiety giving rise to fear as Isaac allowed himself to be bound on the altar by his father. That fear would have turned into paralysing terror as it dawned on Isaac that he was the intended lamb and his soul, if not his voice, screamed within him: 'Dad, Dad, why have you forsaken me?', similar to what one day a greater Son of a greater Father would cry from a cross erected, according to tradition, in the very same place on Moriah.[10]

'Then Abraham reached out his hand and took the knife to slaughter his son.' (Gen. 22.10) The son lay helpless on the altar, with his eyes glued to the fearful knife in the hand of the father he loved. What was

Abraham thinking in that moment? Hebrews tells us that, at that precise moment, when Abraham 'was in the act of offering up his only son . . . He considered that God was able even to raise him from the dead . . .' Spectacular confidence in God! There would be a way.

It was a breathtaking moment, when the world must have seemed to stop as the very hosts of heaven waited to see the outcome. 'He spared not his own Son . . .'

The indescribable silence was suddenly broken by a voice from another world as 'the angel of the LORD called to him from heaven and said, "Abraham, Abraham!" And he said, "Here am I." He said, "Do not lay your hand on the boy or do anything to him, for now I know that you fear God, seeing you have not withheld your son, your only son, from me."' (Gen. 22.11–12)

That voice froze the motion of the upraised hand holding the sacrificial knife. Abraham was not permitted to slaughter his son. The supreme test of faith was over. He had passed it magnificently and, as Hebrews adds, figuratively speaking he received his son back from the dead (Heb. 11.19).

By climbing the Tower of Babel, no one reached heaven. By climbing Moriah, Abraham did. Heaven had heard the cry of his breaking heart. And, in the Mount of the Lord, heaven had provided: 'And Abraham lifted up his eyes and looked, and behold, behind him was a ram, caught in a thicket by his horns.' (Gen. 22.13)

A burnt offering was still necessary. Abraham's passing the test did not mean that the matter of sacrifice was instantly set aside as irrelevant and forgotten. Abraham, no doubt with heart overflowing in gratitude and indescribable relief at God's perfect timing, took the ram and offered it up as a burnt offering *instead of* his son. This has theological significance as an illuminating instance of the thoroughly biblical principle of substitutionary atonement. That principle reaches its full expression in the death of Christ in our place as he himself explained: 'For even the Son of Man came not to be served, but to serve, and to give his life as a ransom for many' (Mark 10.45).

We should note that this was the second time the call of an angel saved the life of one of Abraham's children. Hagar had left Ishmael under a bush to die when an angel called to her as she wept and showed her the well that saved their lives. On that occasion the angel said to her: 'Up! Lift up the boy, and hold him fast with your hand, for I will make him into a great nation' (Gen. 21.18). In complete contrast Abraham was told the exact opposite: 'Do not lay your hand on the boy...'. Their intentions were different: Abraham had lifted up his hand to kill his son; Hagar had set her son down and left him and now God told her to reach out her hand to save him. Yet on both occasions the angelic commands were directed at the same goal: the saving of life, Ishmael's and Isaac's. Abraham loved both of his boys – and so did God.

## Shadows of the cross

Isaac was a near sacrifice, and did not know what awaited him. Nor did Abraham, for that matter. And Isaac had no choice. Jesus did. Jesus endured Gethsemane: 'Father, if it is possible let this cup pass from me.' Jesus was a real sacrifice. Yet we never call the death of Jesus a 'human sacrifice'. Horrific practices like this are utterly condemned in Scripture. They were in fact one of the reasons why God commanded Joshua to invade Canaan to execute his judgement.

Jesus was fully human, but never only human. The New Testament unashamedly uses Old Testament sacrificial language to describe his death on the cross. Jesus is the Lamb of God that takes away the sin of the world; he is one who came to give his life a ransom for many; his body was given for us and his blood shed; he is the propitiation for our sins; he made peace by the blood of his cross; this he did once and for all by the sacrifice of himself. The story of Abraham and Isaac is deep, their psychological pain unimaginable. The story of the cross is immeasurably deeper. Who can fathom Jesus' cry: 'My God, my God, why have you forsaken me?'?

All that Jesus accomplished flowed from his love of his Father God. Of him Paul said: 'He who did not spare his own Son but gave him up for us all, how will he not also with him graciously give us all things?' (Rom. 8.32).

Never had Abraham's worship been more profound. In deep gratitude, he 'called the name of that place, "The LORD will provide"; as it is said to this day, "On the mount of the LORD it shall be provided."' The name Moriah and the word translated 'provided' are derived from the Hebrew *ra'ah* ('to see'). Compare the English expression 'see to it' as a synonym for 'provide'. Hagar had learned that God sees and provides at *Beer Lahai Roi* – 'the well of the God who sees'. Here Abraham learned the same truth. It is not hard to imagine that if Abraham had known it, he would have sung that beautifully expressive old hymn: 'Great is your faithfulness . . . All I have needed, your hand hath provided. Great is your faithfulness, God unto me.'

Perhaps it is not too much to say that as Abraham had trudged up the mountain with Isaac its very name was in some deep way resonating in his mind and shoring him up with hope?

## Justification by works

God said: 'Now I know that you fear God.' But did not the omniscient God know already? Could God not have foreseen that Abraham would offer his son, if asked to do so, and thus all the agony of letting him go through with it could have been dispensed with?

The answer to this may lie in the fact that there are different kinds of knowledge. For instance, I learned at school that Siberian winters are very cold. But when I visited that part of the world, I experienced the bitterness of the cold for myself. I now knew it in a different way, by direct acquaintance. There is a real difference between the two.

It would appear that, whatever the implications of God's foreknowledge and omniscience, he not only insists we gain knowledge by experience. He himself wishes to see in our actual real-time behaviour convincing evidence that our faith in him is genuine.

Abraham confirmed in God's sight the reality of his faith by his actions. He proved that his faith was genuine. He passed the test. The New Testament letter of James interprets this incident as illustrating the important principle of justification by works: 'Was not Abraham our father justified by works when he offered up his son Isaac on the altar?' (Jas. 2.21).

This immediately gives rise to the question of the relationship of justification by works to justification by faith. It is a common notion that we are justified before God by faith and before men and women by our works. But that cannot be the case, as there were no people around to see what happened, apart from the direct participants Abraham and Isaac.

The actual difference, as explained by the apostle James, is something else altogether. Speaking of Abraham, James says:

> You see that faith was active along with his works, and faith was completed by his works; and the Scripture was fulfilled that says, 'Abraham believed God, and it was counted to him as righteousness' – and he was called a friend of God. You see that a person is justified by works and not by faith alone.
> (Jas. 2.22–24)

James makes it clear that Abraham's works did not earn him salvation. No – James says that Abraham's faith was 'completed by his works'. That is, the works are evidence that the faith is real. They are the fruit, but not the grounds of justification. The works demonstrate that the person has already been justified by faith in God – so that, as James puts it, 'the Scripture was fulfilled that says, "Abraham believed God, and it was counted to him as righteousness."'

Another insight into justification by works is to be found in Luke's account of the conversion of Zacchaeus the tax collector. When the man received Jesus joyfully, invited him to his house and said that he would donate half his goods to the poor, as well as making generous reimbursement to those he had defrauded, Jesus said this: 'Today salvation has come to this house, since he also is a son of Abraham' (Luke 19.9). Zacchaeus's change in lifestyle was evidence that he was a son of Abraham in two senses: he had been justified by faith and that faith had been confirmed by his works.

We might think about the matter this way. Suppose God had put the following hypothetical question to Abraham: 'If I were to ask you to release your son and give him back to me, what would you say?' Even if he said yes, it would not be credible evidence of what he would do if really called upon to part with Isaac. That is why God insisted on reality, even though it was extremely painful.

God had not finished dealing with Abraham. The angel called a second time, not to repeat what had already been said, but to add a solemn oath to reinforce the original promise to Abraham. Because all that had happened on the mountain was geared to bringing Abraham to discover the secret of total security. Abraham had achieved some limited security for himself and Isaac when he and Abimelech swore a mutual protection oath at Beersheba – the Well of the Oath. But that security was as nothing compared with what was given to Abraham by the unique oath sworn by the Lord himself:

> 'By myself I have sworn, declares the LORD, because you have done this and have not withheld your son, your only son, I will surely bless you, and I will surely multiply your offspring as the stars of heaven and as the sand that is on the seashore. And your offspring shall possess the gate of his enemies, and in your offspring shall all the nations of the earth be blessed, because you have obeyed my voice.'
> (Gen. 22.16–18)

David Gooding puts it memorably:

> By God's own leading he stood an old man on top of a mountain, with his son in whom all the promises and all his hopes had been vested, now bound on the altar, and with the knife raised in his own hand, about – at God's demand – to slay his son, and be left, as far as he knew, with nothing, with no hope for the future, nothing but God and his promises and his faith in those promises.
>
> But in this changing world there is no greater security to be found than, bereft of all hope in all else, to be left with nothing but God and faith in him and his promises. That is eternal security.[11]

It was also the height of courage and powerfully illustrates C. S. Lewis's definition of that virtue:

> Courage is not simply one of the virtues but the form of every virtue at the testing point which means at the point of highest reality. A

chastity or honesty or mercy which yields to danger will be chaste or honest or merciful only on conditions. Pilate was merciful till it became risky.[12]

Abraham risked everything.

The oath God swore to Abraham endured through the centuries so that when we get to the New Testament we find both Mary, the mother of Jesus, and Zacharias, the father of John the Baptist, recalling it.

First, Mary:

'He has helped his servant Israel,
    in remembrance of his mercy,
as he spoke to our fathers,
    to Abraham and to his offspring for ever.'
(Luke 1.54–55)

Next, Zacharias:

'Blessed be the Lord God of Israel,
    for he has visited and redeemed his people
and has raised up a horn of salvation for us
    in the house of his servant David,
as he spoke by the mouth of his holy prophets from of old,
    that we should be saved from our enemies
    and from the hand of all who hate us;
to show the mercy promised to our fathers
    and to remember his holy covenant,
the oath that he swore to our father Abraham, to grant us
    that we, being delivered from the hand of our enemies,
might serve him without fear,
in holiness and righteousness before him all our days.'
(Luke 1.68–75)

For Mary, Zacharias and many others the most important clause in the oath was freedom for the people of God from their enemies so that they could serve him without fear. The cry of Exodus has expressed the longing of believers around the world for centuries: 'Let my people go that they may serve me!' (Exod. 8.1).

That same element of bringing certainty in the face of opposition and fear appears again in a further reference to the oath in the letter to the Hebrews:

> For when God made a promise to Abraham, since he had no one greater by whom to swear, he swore by himself, saying, 'Surely I will bless you and multiply you.' And thus Abraham, having patiently waited, obtained the promise. For people swear by something greater than themselves, and in all their disputes an oath is final for confirmation. So when God desired to show more convincingly to the heirs of the promise the unchangeable character of his purpose, he guaranteed it with an oath, so that by two unchangeable things, in which it is impossible for God to lie, we who have fled for refuge might have strong encouragement to hold fast to the hope set before us. We have this as a sure and steadfast anchor of the soul, a hope that enters into the inner place behind the curtain, where Jesus has gone as a forerunner on our behalf, having become a high priest for ever after the order of Melchizedek.
> (Heb. 6.13–20)

God sealed the covenant with this oath in order to buttress Abraham's sense of security. For Christians, God's oath acts as an anchor of the soul in the eternal world – an anchor linking us to Jesus, who has already ascended into that world on our behalf to act as our High Priest.

## The aftermath

With God's oath ringing in his head, Abraham descended the mountain and returned to his young men and together they went, appropriately, to Beersheva – the Well of the Oath.

There is no mention of Isaac. As far as the record goes, throughout the searing climax of his ordeal no word was spoken to him and he himself did not speak. What did the silence mean? How was Isaac meant to understand the trauma of what had happened? Where was he now?

Kass remarks:

Isaac, as we know from the story, was not destroyed; what is destroyed, rather, is Abraham's paternal claim to possession of his son. Though Isaac survives the ordeal at least in body, he is set adrift. He will have a long way to go before he can accept what transpired on Mount Moriah . . . The text's silence about Isaac's state of mind and even his whereabouts at the end of the tale is thus wonderfully apt to his existential situation. Isaac only knows that his father was willing to sacrifice him to the Lord but he knows not why: My father took his knife to me – how could he? Why did he? What did the Lord want of him and me?

Yet Isaac knows that his father stopped short, that something summoned him to stop, that his father offered up a ram in his stead and that his life was restored to him even as it was being given up. Even if he did not hear the divine voice he has reason to suspect that he owes his life less to his father more to gracious powers invisible – that his life like any human life is an unmerited gift from beyond . . .

The heart of the story . . . is the conversation between father and son as they went together up the mountain, the conversation that began with Isaac's question: 'where is the lamb' and ended with Abraham's speech that proved prophetic – 'God will see for himself the lamb for the burnt offering, my son'.[13]

One question the text does not answer is whether or not Isaac heard the divine voice telling Abraham to withdraw his knife. If he did hear it, he would surely have linked it with his father's earlier statement that God would provide a lamb. However, Kass concludes:

Even if Isaac did not hear the divine voice that soon after saved his life and even if he subsequently feels estranged from his father and from the God to whom he was offered, he will never forget his father's interpretation of the event. Somewhere in his soul he will always remember that singular conversation of transmission in which Abraham counselled him regarding the deep perplexities of life. *Somewhere in his soul he will always remember that Abraham taught him to place his trust not in his father but in the Lord.*[14]

We need to ask ourselves whether we too have learned that lesson. Does the conviction that we must place our trust in the Lord and no one else dwell in our souls?

And have we transmitted this idea to our children, so they know that God can be trusted to realise their potential, despite their failures – and ours?

# 16

# Applying the Moriah experience

In more ways than one Moriah represented the mountain top of Abraham's journey of faith. Throughout his life he had been presented with graduated lessons in what it meant to trust God. Moriah was the toughest by far.

Trusting God for a son in the face of Sarah's infertility was hard enough, even though it was an exercise of faith in a context that promised a good and welcome outcome in fulfilling Abraham's and Sarah's heart desire.

Not so Moriah.

To a certain extent that experience resembled what Daniel's three friends Shadrach, Meshach and Abednego later faced, when King Nebuchadnezzar commanded them either to bow to his golden idol or be thrown into a fiery furnace. For those courageous men, on one side of the equation was security of job, home, family, success, power and physical life itself. On the other side there stood only one thing: their obedience to God. They deliberately chose God, irrespective of whether he delivered them or not.[1]

The test that God set before Abraham was unique to him. It was connected to the special role God had called upon him to play in the unfolding narrative of redemption. That role was Abraham's, and his alone – which is presumably why in God's mercy others are not called upon to play it in this extreme form.

However, followers of Jesus must also face the same kind of thing in principle. That is, there will be times when God asks us to choose him above other things. It is he who will insist that we confirm the genuineness of our faith by our actions and behaviour, and thereby be justified by our works. That will involve sacrifice.

In order to avoid misunderstanding, it needs to be mentioned in passing that giving up a bad habit, or something morally wrong, is not sacrifice in any sense of the word. It is our moral duty as believers to do so. Sacrifice involves giving up something that is good, wholesome and right in its place, in order to put God first. A woman who hears the call of God to be a missionary in a foreign country may well have to give up the prospects of a secure job in her home country. The job in itself is a good thing, yet she sacrifices it for something better, to which she has been called. The fundamental principle is 'seek first the kingdom [i.e. rule] of God and his righteousness' (Matt. 6.33).

The key consideration here is cost: the cost of obeying God, the cost of following Jesus and putting him first. We see this in Jesus' response to a group of Greeks in Jerusalem who approached one of the disciples, Philip, with the request: 'Sir, we wish to see Jesus.' Jesus told the disciples:

> 'The hour has come for the Son of Man to be glorified. Truly, truly, I say to you, unless a grain of wheat falls into the earth and dies, it remains alone; but if it dies, it bears much fruit. Whoever loves his life loses it, and whoever hates his life in this world will keep it for eternal life. If anyone serves me, he must follow me; and where I am, there will my servant be also. If anyone serves me, the Father will honour him.'
> (John 12.23–26)

Abraham followed the initial call of God because the glory of God appeared to him. Nowadays, we follow Jesus because we see his glory in, for instance, what he did for us on the cross and through his resurrection. It is that dying alone as the seed, being buried and bursting into resurrection life that yielded 'much fruit' in terms of multitudes coming to trust him for salvation.

The cost for the Lord Jesus Christ was incalculable. He provided salvation for us as a gracious – that is, unmerited and unmeritable – free gift. Yet it will cost us to live for him. That cost is to put him first and 'hate' all else. This use of the word 'hate' is an idiomatic, Hebrew way of speaking that is not intended to convey hatred in an absolute sense, but rather preference. For instance, Genesis 29.30 says that Jacob 'loved Rachel more than Leah', whereas the very next verse reads: 'When the LORD saw Leah was hated . . .' Therefore, putting Jesus first and hating all else does not mean that we are, for example, literally to hate our parents – God himself commands us to love and honour them. It means that we are to put Jesus first, above our parents and all else, when we have to make a choice.

That choice may take many forms. Matthew gives the example of a disciple who said to Jesus: "'Lord, let me first go and bury my father.' And Jesus said to him, "Follow me, and leave the dead to bury their own dead"' (Matt. 8.21–22). What the man wanted to do was to stay at home until his father died and not until then set out to follow Jesus. But there is no 'Let me first do this or that' with Jesus. He must take absolute priority.

Paul tells us what following the Lord cost him. Regarding his proud and distinguished pedigree of religious and moral achievement he writes:

> But whatever gain I had, I counted as loss for the sake of Christ. Indeed, I count everything as loss because of the surpassing worth of knowing Christ Jesus my Lord. For his sake I have suffered the loss of all things and count them as rubbish, in order that I may gain Christ and be found in him, not having a righteousness of my own that comes from the law, but that which comes through faith in Christ, the righteousness from God that depends on faith.
> (Phil. 3.7–9)

Paul 'suffered the loss of all things'. We do not know exactly what that meant, but it clearly included his high social standing and acclaim in the religious world, his role as a revered scholar and maybe even his wife and family. It also meant persecution. He was almost beaten to death on more than one occasion, he endured extreme privation, want, loneliness and imprisonment. In the end, his stand for Christ cost him his life, like Stephen and James before him and Peter sometime later.

And in my own lifetime I vividly recall hearing on the radio on 8 January 1956 that five young American missionaries – Jim Elliot, Nate Saint, Ed McCully, Peter Fleming and Roger Youderian – had been speared to death by a group of Huaorani warriors at 'Palm Beach' on the Curaray River in the rain forests of Ecuador. Five seeds had fallen into the ground and died.

They sprang up in the shape of a great wave of Christian missionary activity around the world. The account of it, most memorably that by Jim Elliot's wife Elizabeth entitled *Shadow of the Almighty*, had a profound inspirational effect both on me and on many of my generation. Words from Jim Elliot's journal are etched permanently on many of our minds: 'He is no fool who gives what he cannot keep to gain what he cannot lose.'

That gives me some insight into what was involved on the top of Mount Moriah. For it is easy to talk glibly about 'mountain-top experiences' as if they were all full of joyful exhilaration. Some are and we should be thankful for them, in so far as they are genuine. Yet many are not. Abraham and Isaac's mountain was grim and foreboding. And what shall we say about Calvary?

Have we ever felt as though we were climbing up a narrow, steep and dangerous mountain path, our hearts in turmoil and in the dark about what is going on? Have we ever made the personal and life-changing discovery that 'in the mount of the LORD it shall be provided'?

There is no guarantee of provision *before* that mountain summit is reached. The Lord provides in the hour of need, but not usually before it. Jesus himself prepared his disciples for persecution by saying: 'And when they bring you before the synagogues and the rulers and the authorities, do not be anxious about how you should defend yourself or what you should say, for the Holy Spirit will teach you *in that very hour* what you ought to say' (Luke 12.11–12, emphasis mine). Of course, that is no excuse for laziness and failing to prepare when we can prepare – we are to study to show ourselves approved unto God (see 2 Tim. 2.15). There are, however, occasions when there simply is no time to prepare.

I vividly recall meeting a Siberian believer who had spent some years in the Gulag for his faith in Christ. He was a short man and suddenly he looked up at me and said: 'You couldn't face that sort of thing, could you?'

I was profoundly embarrassed and ashamed, and stammered out: 'N-no.'

He grinned, and said: 'And neither could I! I discovered that the Lord only helped me to deal with such things at the time they happened: never before. I used to faint when I cut myself shaving, but in the camps I had to cope with what no one should ever have to endure – and the Lord provided every time.'

And what shall we say of those many believers throughout the ages who have not returned from such camps, having laid their lives down for the Lord when the knife fell without reprieve? Somewhere in the world, precisely that has almost certainly happened since you started reading this chapter.

There are different kinds of mountains to be climbed and tests to be faced. Another famous test in Scripture is the story of Job. As with Abraham, Job did not know and, as far as the account goes, never got to know what went on behind the scenes.

The story in brief is that God speaks to Satan (the adversary) about Job:

> And the LORD said to Satan, 'Have you considered my servant Job, that there is none like him on the earth, a blameless and upright man, who fears God and turns away from evil?' Then Satan answered the LORD and said, 'Does Job fear God for no reason? Have you not put a hedge around him and his house and all that he has, on every side? You have blessed the work of his hands, and his possessions have increased in the land. But stretch out your hand and touch all that he has, and he will curse you to your face.' And the LORD said to Satan, 'Behold, all that he has is in your hand. Only against him do not stretch out your hand.'
> (Job 1.8–12)

The charge here is that Job's faith in God and reverence for him is essentially puppy love based on all the blessings God has showered upon him in terms of family and possessions. Take those away from Job, Satan suggests, and he will curse God. It can be a sobering question to ask ourselves: and what about me?

It is interesting to compare this with Abraham's situation. There is no mention of Satan there, although Jewish Midrash has many suggestions in that direction.[2]

Also, Abraham believed in God's promise that he would receive such blessings in the future; he did not believe because he already had them.

Only after Isaac was born might it have been said of Abraham that his faith in God was now at least partly based on Isaac as the promised seed. Not quite the same as Job at this stage. But then the stories diverge. Job's story continues with a sequence of disasters devastating him; his children are murdered and his possessions looted.

Nevertheless, Job maintains his trust in God despite his three friends and his wife arguing that he should simply give up and admit he was in the wrong. In the end God declares him to have been righteous all the way through and gives him a new family and great wealth.

Abraham did not in the end lose his son, but Job did. He lost his seven sons and three daughters in a firestorm at their home. His remarkable reaction is often quoted: 'Then Job arose and tore his robe and shaved his head and fell on the ground and worshipped. And he said, "Naked I came from my mother's womb, and naked shall I return. The LORD gave, and the LORD has taken away; blessed be the name of the LORD"' (Job 1.20–21).

Job's loss might well have been harder to come to terms with than the binding of Isaac. Yet every day, around the world, many men and women, whether believers or not, grieve over the untimely loss of their children.

Here we are faced with the problem of suffering and evil, which is probably the hardest problem that anyone faces, whether believer or unbeliever in God. We are all confronted with suffering, much of it caused by evil. It is this issue that drives many people to atheism, even though atheism does not remove the suffering and, indeed, may even make it worse since, by very definition, atheism removes all hope.

There are no simplistic answers here, but the story of Abraham and Isaac on Mount Moriah points the way to the suffering of the Lord Jesus on the cross, which is where many breaking hearts have found an enduring resting place.

For the cross of Christ tells us of a God who has not remained distant or indifferent to human pain and suffering, but has entered into it. By so doing, as Isaiah prophesied centuries before:

Surely he has borne our griefs
and carried our sorrows;
yet we esteemed him stricken,

smitten by God, and afflicted.
But he was wounded for our transgressions;
    he was crushed for our iniquities;
upon him was the chastisement that brought us peace,
    and with his stripes we are healed.
(Isa. 53.4–5)

In dying and being raised from the dead by the almighty power of God, he has done something that enables us to see bright light at the end of the tunnel of grief, by giving us a sure and certain hope. That hope of a personal resurrection is the birthright of every believer in Christ. It doesn't remove grief and sorrow at the loss of a loved one. We sorrow, but not as those who have no hope.

And it is this hope that can infuse the darkness of losing a child. My own sister, some years ago, lost her just-married 22-year-old daughter to a brain tumour. It was devastating, but not only did her daughter hold on to her faith until the end, my sister has also held on to hers. Or, perhaps better, the Lord held on to both of them and has brought her through what was a harrowing experience. According to Scripture, death is still an enemy, but it will one day be overcome as the last enemy (1 Cor. 15.26).

According to Christ himself, Abraham also had this hope: 'Your father Abraham rejoiced that he would see my day. He saw it and was glad' (John 8.56).

And so did Job in his day:

'For I know that my Redeemer lives,
    and at the last he will stand upon the earth.
And after my skin has been thus destroyed,
    yet in my flesh I shall see God,
whom I shall see for myself,
    and my eyes shall behold, and not another.
    My heart faints within me!'
(Job 19.25–27)

In light of that, Job's statement, 'The LORD gave, and the LORD has taken away; blessed be the name of the LORD', is not to be understood as an expression of resigned fatalism. Both Abraham and Job were aware that this is not the only world that exists.

We human beings are only temporary residents on this planet. We shall all have to leave it one day. According to the biblical revelation, God has created far bigger things to come and it is therefore important for us who are believers to realise that the Lord provides until our journey on this earth is done. However, that is not the end of his provision, but the beginning, as we transition from this life and enter the glory of the dwelling in the Father's house that Jesus has already prepared for us (John 14.1–3).

I have written more about the problems of suffering, pain and evil in my books *Gunning for God*[3] and *Where is God in a Coronavirus World?*[4] Also there are numerous interviews and discussions on the subject on my website johnlennox.org.

# Part 5

# GENESIS 22.20—25.11

SUMMARY

A. Abraham learns of (new) relatives (22.20–24)
B. Death of Sarah and purchase of a burial cave (23.1–20)
C. Finding a bride for Isaac from Abraham's kindred. The marriage of Isaac to Rebekah (24.1–67)
D. Abraham's other wives. His death and burial at the age of 175 (25.1–11)

# 17

# Lessons from the life of Sarah

The focus of the narrative now shifts to prepare the way for the grand finale of the Abraham story – the finding of a bride for the promised seed, Isaac. We are told that Abraham is informed about what has been happening back in Mesopotamia. The news, which subsequently proves important, is that Abraham's brother Nahor has eight children, including one Bethuel, who is singled out as the father of Rebekah, for reasons that will soon become obvious.

## The death of Sarah

Sarah died at the age of 127. One wonders whether her death was hastened by shock when she heard what had happened on Mount Moriah.

It had been a long journey together and parting was hard. Abraham mourned. He wept. He missed Sarah greatly. He hastened to find a suitable burying place in Hebron. What happened to her body mattered to him. And what will happen to our bodies should matter to us. For the Bible emphasises the importance of the material dimension to life. God made a physical world and we are repeatedly told that it was good – an attitude that has often been lost to Christians by the unfortunate inroads of philosophies like Platonism, which denigrated the body and held that it defiled and imprisoned the soul.

The glorious message of the resurrection of Christ, the Son of God, and his promise to return and raise bodily from the dead all who trusted him is as far from the Platonic teaching as it could be. The English word 'cemetery' derives from the Greek term *koimeterion* ('a sleeping place'). It bears witness to the Christian teaching that death is like sleep, and resurrection like re-awakening (1 Cor. 15.51).

263

Abraham thought it important to have a permanent burial site not only
for Sarah but also for his family. The account of his purchase of a burying
ground and this, the first description of a burial in Scripture, gives us
a delightful insight into the niceties of Middle-Eastern bargaining at
the time. The transaction took place at the gate of the city, where such
business was done (Gen. 23.10; cf. 23.18; 19.1). Here is the account:

And Abraham rose up from before his dead and said to the Hittites,
'I am a sojourner and foreigner among you; give me property among
you for a burying place, that I may bury my dead out of my sight.'
The Hittites answered Abraham, 'Hear us, my lord; you are a prince
of God among us. Bury your dead in the choicest of our tombs. None
of us will withhold from you his tomb to hinder you from burying
your dead.' Abraham rose and bowed to the Hittites, the people of
the land. And he said to them, 'If you are willing that I should bury
my dead out of my sight, hear me and entreat for me Ephron the
son of Zohar, that he may give me the cave of Machpelah, which he
owns; it is at the end of his field. For the full price let him give it to
me in your presence as property for a burying place.'

Now Ephron was sitting among the Hittites, and Ephron the
Hittite answered Abraham in the hearing of the Hittites, of all who
went in at the gate of his city, 'No, my lord, hear me: I give you the
field, and I give you the cave that is in it. In the sight of the sons of
my people I give it to you. Bury your dead.' Then Abraham bowed
down before the people of the land. And he said to Ephron in the
hearing of the people of the land, 'But if you will, hear me: I give
the price of the field. Accept it from me, that I may bury my dead
there.' Ephron answered Abraham, 'My lord, listen to me: a piece
of land worth four hundred shekels of silver, what is that between
you and me? Bury your dead.' Abraham listened to Ephron, and
Abraham weighed out for Ephron the silver that he had named in
the hearing of the Hittites, four hundred shekels of silver, according
to the weights current among the merchants.

So the field of Ephron in Machpelah, which was to the east of
Mamre, the field with the cave that was in it and all the trees that
were in the field, throughout its whole area, was made over to

Abraham as a possession in the presence of the Hittites, before all
who went in at the gate of his city.
(Gen. 23.3–18)

Abraham commences the discussion by saying that he is a 'sojourner and
foreigner' – legal and technical terms in Hebrew for 'resident alien'. A
Greek equivalent, translated 'exile', is used by Peter to describe Christian
believers: 'Peter, an apostle of Jesus Christ, To those who are elect exiles
of the dispersion in Pontus, Galatia, Cappadocia, Asia, and Bithynia . . .'
(1 Pet. 1.1).

The local Hittites did not accept his modest description of himself,
calling him a prince of God. With apparent generosity they told him that
none of them would deny him their tombs. One would expect that this
would have concluded the matter. However, as Meir Steinberg shrewdly
observes: 'A plurality or community of non-deniers does not yet make a
single giver.'

Steinberg says that the Hittites did not speak their minds:

Whatever the Hittite answer professes, its repetitions and variations
manage among them to evade the heart of Abraham's appeal. 'Give
me a holding for a burial ground with you.' In biblical idiom,
'holding' (*akhuzzah*) unequivocally refers to possession, as distinct
from all other forms of occupying land. The patriarch will not bury
his wife, any more than in the next chapter he will marry his son,
among the people of Canaan . . .[1]

Abraham wanted something that would be his possession in perpetuity.
Yet none of the participants spoke of buying and selling, only of giving.
Steinberg perceives three layers of motive in the negotiation: politeness,
politics and profits.[2]

Abraham was not going to be dependent on their gift any more
than he would accept anything from the king of Sodom. His 'give me',
as Steinberg says, means 'Give me permission to acquire or proceed'.
Abraham had no intention of not paying.

The negotiations now began in earnest as Abraham named a specific
piece of real estate owned by a certain Ephron. The dialogue bears all the

marks of authenticity. Ephron was a practised dealer. The price, neatly slipped obliquely into the conversation, was extortionate for that time – compare the 50 shekels that David paid much later for the site of the Temple (2 Sam. 24.24) or the 17 shekels Jeremiah paid for his cousin's field (Jer. 32.9). Ephron justified his high price by including the field![3]

Abraham paid up front and gave Ephron the silver that sealed the deal. The legal side was important. Abraham wanted to have it all in black and white, so to speak, to avoid any subsequent misunderstanding. That should not surprise us since we are well aware of the amount of trouble that can been caused, even among Christians, through misunderstandings generated by loose promises, vague hints and sloppy negotiations.

In this way, the only piece of land Abraham ever actually owned, the cave of Machpelah, became his burying place. And he paid for it even though the entire land had been promised to him as a gift by God and, notably, even though the Hittites constantly spoke of giving, not selling.

A further interesting detail is to be found in the summary of the legal transaction:

So the field of Ephron in Machpelah, which was to the east of Mamre, the field with the cave that was in it and all the trees that were in the field, throughout its whole area, was made over to Abraham as a possession in the presence of the Hittites, before all who went in at the gate of his city.
(Gen. 23.17–18)

Harrison comments: 'The mention of trees in the narrative reflects the Hittite practice of listing the exact number of trees growing on each piece of property sold.'[4] An uncontrived mark of authenticity.

The fact that the Genesis narrative of the life of Sarah is now complete presents us with an opportunity to look at it as a whole. Sarah is the woman mentioned most often in the Bible, although her name appears only three times in the New Testament:

• 'For this is what the promise said: "About this time next year I will return, and Sarah shall have a son"' (Rom. 9.9).

- 'By faith Sarah herself received power to conceive, even when she was past the age, since she considered him faithful who had promised' (Heb. 11.11).
- '. . . as Sarah obeyed Abraham, calling him lord. And you are her children, if you do good and do not fear anything that is frightening' (1 Pet. 3.6).

It is the third of these passages that raises a number of obvious questions, especially when we see it in its wider context:

> Likewise, wives, be subject to your own husbands, so that even if some do not obey the word, they may be won without a word by the conduct of their wives, when they see your respectful and pure conduct. Do not let your adorning be external – the braiding of hair and the putting on of gold jewellery, or the clothing you wear – but let your adorning be the hidden person of the heart with the imperishable beauty of a gentle and quiet spirit, which in God's sight is very precious. For this is how the holy women who hoped in God used to adorn themselves, by submitting to their own husbands, as Sarah obeyed Abraham, calling him lord. And you are her children, if you do good and do not fear anything that is frightening.
>
> Likewise, husbands, live with your wives in an understanding way, showing honour to the woman as the weaker vessel, since they are heirs with you of the grace of life, so that your prayers may not be hindered.
> (1 Pet. 3.1–7)

In common with Jewish Midrash tradition, which regards Sarah as a prophet and a righteous woman whose actions are worthy of emulation,[5] this passage puts her forward as an example of what it means to be a holy woman and a good wife. Yet the terms used about her – 'respectful and pure conduct', 'gentle and quiet spirit' and submitting to her husband, calling him lord – seem somewhat at odds with the Genesis narrative. There we see a Sarah who is at times not exactly pure, far from respectful, possessing a fiery temper and a woman who bosses Abraham around and gets him to heed her rather than take his views into consideration.

Furthermore, some of the recorded occasions on which she did go along with him lacked moral clarity.

What shall we make of this in light of the fact that biblical teaching on marital relationships, like that just quoted from 1 Peter, often comes under attack as old-fashioned, sexist and even misogynistic? Surely, many say, this is the dominance and subservience, male-centred, power narrative that needs to be overcome after centuries of reigning unchallenged?

Certainly it is old by definition, since the Bible is, after all, a collection of ancient documents. But being old does not imply being old-fashioned. The definition of marriage given in Genesis is exactly the same as the one given by Jesus and Paul many centuries later. Furthermore, if we know anything about the way in which women in the first century were disparaged, we should realise that Jesus and Paul were concerned to elevate that status. Jesus treated women with great respect and defended them. Women were given prominence by the gospel writers as the first witnesses of the resurrection, even though the testimony of women was disregarded by and large in ancient (Jewish) society. Paul felt honoured to have women as his fellow workers, and Peter in the passage just cited calls upon husbands and wives to behave in such a way that the wife's submissiveness is balanced by the husband's self-giving love. Husbands are to honour their wives and treat them, not as inferiors, but as joint heirs of the grace of life, of equal status in the sight of God.

Genesis 1.26 is unquestionably a fundamental text for the foundation of civilised life that gives a unique value and dignity to human beings. It is that God made both men and women in his own image as companions for each other, standing side by side, neither one inferior to the other but complementing each other.

In light of this, what is meant by Peter's injunction that wives should submit to their husbands? Paul says something very similar in the context of his citing of Genesis 2:

Wives, submit to your own husbands, as to the Lord. For the husband is the head of the wife even as Christ is the head of the church, his body, and is himself its Saviour. Now as the church submits to Christ, so also wives should submit in everything to their husbands.

Husbands, love your wives, as Christ loved the church and gave himself up for her, that he might sanctify her, having cleansed her by the washing of water with the word, so that he might present the church to himself in splendour, without spot or wrinkle or any such thing, that she might be holy and without blemish. In the same way husbands should love their wives as their own bodies. He who loves his wife loves himself. For no one ever hated his own flesh, but nourishes and cherishes it, just as Christ does the church, because we are members of his body. 'Therefore a man shall leave his father and mother and hold fast to his wife, and the two shall become one flesh.' This mystery is profound, and I am saying that it refers to Christ and the church. However, let each one of you love his wife as himself, and let the wife see that she respects her husband. (Eph. 5.22–33)

Theologian Alan Richardson wrote:

Indeed, we have in the marriage-metaphor an excellent illustration of the meaning of the doctrine, of the 'one body', 'one flesh', 'one spirit', of the Pauline teaching. For the marriage-relationship is the deepest, richest, and most satisfying personal human relationship of which we have experience; it is an experience of surrender without absorption, of service without compulsion and of love without conditions.[6]

In Paul's first letter to the Corinthians we find another important principle: 'But I want you to understand that the head of every man is Christ, the head of a wife is her husband, and the head of Christ is God' (11.3). The question many ask is: is it degrading, disparaging and insulting to women to say that within the marriage relationship the man is the head of the woman and the wife must submit to her husband?

What is very interesting about the verse just quoted is that not only is the woman said to have a head but so is the man and, even more strikingly, so is Christ himself. We can readily understand Paul saying that the head of the man is Christ in the context of the basic Christian confession that Jesus Christ is Lord. I as a Christian man have agreed to submit to Christ's rule in my life, as he is in every sense superior. However, when it comes to the next stage, that the head of Christ is God, the situation seems very different. For Christ is God and we therefore have to think of this headship in a somewhat different way, which reflects their oneness. For it clearly cannot be insulting to Christ to say that his head is God.

Is this, then, a hierarchy of equals within the godhead as indicated by Jesus' statement that 'the Father is greater than I' (John 14.28)? Reading backwards down Paul's statement we might deduce that likewise the man being head of the woman is a reference to a hierarchy of equals and, therefore, is no insult to women and must not be interpreted as such.

In ordinary life among human beings in our institutions we practise all kinds of hierarchies of equals. In order that a game of football can be played at all, there must be a captain who acts as a leader, directing the play by consent of the other team members of which he (or she) is one. In business there are managers and executives with different roles and responsibilities, but they are all equally human.

Do these biblical passages, then, mean in essence that in the two-person unit that is a married couple, God has chosen that the man is to take the lead but in such a way as to support, love and take responsibility for his wife, enabling her to develop his potential? We should recall that in the ancient world, generally speaking the men were physically stronger than the women and had the responsibility of being the breadwinners, so it would have been natural for the wife to look to her husband to take the lead on where they should live.

Where it says that 'Sarah obeyed Abraham, calling him lord' we can see that one way of understanding this is that she had committed herself to following him and living with him. She certainly had not committed herself to leading a doormat existence allowing him to crush her personality. However, the only time in the Genesis narrative where she uses the term is in Genesis 18.12: 'So Sarah laughed to herself, saying, "After I am worn out, and my lord is old, shall I have pleasure?"' The word translated 'lord' is the Hebrew *adon*, whose modern Hebrew equivalent is a polite form of address ('sir'). We note that it is used in the Genesis narrative by Rebekah in addressing Abraham's servant (Gen. 24.18).

We have the task and the responsibility of applying the principles laid down in Scripture to our own times where, for instance, the woman may be the breadwinner. The key idea is mutual respect and sharing, and each taking their responsibility before the Lord.

Peter was also concerned about the fact that many Christian women had husbands who were not believers and he wanted to encourage them to win their husbands for Christ by their behaviour even more than their words – a situation that still holds today.

This all still leaves us with the question: how can Peter hold Sarah out as a paradigm of godly behaviour to readers, many of whom would have been far more familiar with the Genesis narrative than we are today? Is it that what we have in Genesis is a series of very limited snapshots of Sarah's behaviour over a relatively short time in her long life? We are told almost nothing about her life before or after that time. We noted earlier that Jewish tradition attempted to fill that in with stories about the generosity of the hospitality Abram and Sarai practised during their time in Haran. There is also the Genesis reference to the fact that they entertained angels – an immense privilege for humans in the eyes of Jews – which is picked up in the New Testament as an example of hospitality for Christians to emulate (Heb. 13.2). This alone would give Abraham and Sarah an enviable reputation for hospitality.

For Sarah the arrival of her own child, Isaac, must have released a great deal of the tension, resentment, bitterness, frustration and disappointment that were pent up in her soul. Thereafter, she may well have developed a more equable spirit and her relationship with Abraham may have taken on a new degree of harmony. We clearly should not rush into judgement but rather try to get things into proportion. People change.

We might also note that nowhere in the New Testament are Sarah and Abraham used as illustrations of how not to behave, even though there is plenty of teaching about squabbles and the need to avoid them where reference to them might have been appropriate (see e.g. Gal. 5).

We do not need much experience of life to learn that even in what we would describe as exemplary marriages there can be times of friction

271

and unpleasantness. We are all sinners and we dare not forget it. Marital partners can lose their tempers, they can say and do wrong things that they later regret. Yet if they repent and sort things out before the Lord, the marriage usually gets back on an even keel.

In the case of Sarah we should also recall that on occasion God told Abraham to heed what she was saying, as he was in the wrong and she was right. We husbands are not always right – a very difficult thing for most of us to admit, is it not? It is therefore good when our wives have the courage to flag that up to us – sometimes in no uncertain terms, since no one is as blind as the husband who will not see. Please note – I write as one!

We can imagine that, as in many marriages, times of stress and failure were soon forgotten as life settled down to a much more normal family routine. One could imagine that God then played a far more central role in the family, since they had experienced his faithfulness in delivering the son he had promised.

Furthermore, after Hagar and Ishmael had departed, there may well have been many years of family life during which Isaac grew into manhood; years about which we know nothing. Sarah did not die until Isaac was around 37. Yet she did not live to have the joy of seeing him married.

# 18

# A bride for the promised seed

The sheer length of the account of how Isaac's marriage was arranged is a clear indicator that the narrator thought it important. We recall that, just after the promise Abraham received on Mount Moriah that his offspring would be as the sand of the sea, and just before the account of Sarah's death and burial, a message came from Mesopotamia informing Abraham about his brother Nahor's family. It made special mention of the daughter, Rebekah, of one of them. A hint of things to come.

Abraham then entrusted his most trusted servant with the mission of finding a wife for Isaac. He asked the servant to swear an oath by the Lord, the God of heaven and God of the earth (a name unique to this occasion). He made the servant promise not to look for a wife for Isaac among the local Canaanites but to take the lengthy journey back to Abraham's relatives in Mesopotamia to find someone suitable among them.

The servant knew Abraham well and gave voice to obvious concerns. For instance, what should he do if the woman was not prepared to make the return journey with him? Should he then take Isaac back to the land from which Abraham had come?

Abraham's last recorded words in Genesis follow:

Abraham said to him, 'See to it that you do not take my son back there. The LORD, the God of heaven, who took me from my father's house and from the land of my kindred, and who spoke to me and swore to me, "To your offspring I will give this land," he will send his angel before you, and you shall take a wife for my son from there. But if the woman is not willing to follow you, then you will be free from this oath of mine; only you must not take my son back there.' (Gen. 24.6–8)

Abraham desired a wife for his son who had the same kind of pioneering spirit as he and Sarah had had, a woman who would repeat the journey he had made long before. Abraham insisted, however, that she must embark on the journey of her own free will. If not, the servant was under no obligation to act further. What he must not do under any circumstances was to take Isaac there. Was this a sign that Abraham sensed weakness in Isaac that might lead to losing the whole Seed Project if he were to leave the promised land? If a wife came to Isaac from Mesopotamia, making a sharp break with that culture, there was little likelihood of her, and therefore him, ever returning there.

If Abraham's confidence in Isaac was not strong, his confidence in the Lord was and these, his last words, were very different from his first recorded words that expressed his fear of dying childless. He really now believed that God could repeat for Isaac what he had done for him long ago.

There is an important lesson for younger believers here as they seek a life partner: look for someone who is committed, like you, both to making a clean break with the past and to journeying with the Lord. That is why Paul insisted marriage should be 'in the Lord' (1 Cor. 7.39).

The servant set out with a caravan consisting of ten camels and a great array of gifts. The camels were crucial to the whole enterprise and it is just at this point we meet a common objection: the claim that mention of camels is an anachronism that undermines the historicity of the account. The question 'Do the camels break the Bible's back?' was asked in the context of the claim that camels first appeared in the tenth century BC, long after Abraham. However, Dr Martin Heide of the University of Marburg, an expert in the languages of the ancient Near East, says that there is evidence for Mesopotamian use of domesticated Bactrian camels, including two lexical lists from the Old Babylonian period 'and probably also by [a] Sumerian tablet ... and [a] cylinder seal from the Walters Art Gallery'.

To sum up the early evidence, it is certain that based on archaeological evidence the domesticated two-humped camel appeared in Southern Turkmenistan not later than the middle of the 3rd millennium BCE. From there or from adjacent regions, the domesticated Bactrian camel must have reached Mesopotamia via the Zagros Mountains. In Mesopotamia, the earliest knowledge of the camel points to the middle of the 3rd millennium, where it seems to have been regarded as a very exotic animal. The horse and the Bactrian camel may have been engaged in sea-borne and overland global trading networks spanning much of the ancient world from the third millennium BCE onwards.[1]

Abraham's servant and his camel train headed for the city in Mesopotamia where Nahor, Abraham's brother, lived. He did not make for Nahor's house first of all but went to the local well in the evening, where he knew that the women of the city would come out to draw water for their households. He prayed that the Lord would show *khesed* (steadfast love) towards him and grant his specific request that the woman he would choose to ask to give him water would indicate that she was the right bride for Isaac by offering to water the camels as well. This approach meant that he was not confining the search field to one family, since any of the girls in the city might come to the well.

The test was far from arbitrary. It was not a mere test comparable to Gideon's putting out of a fleece in order to try to calm his nervousness as to whether God would empower him to rid Israel of its enemies (Judg. 6.36–40). It was thoughtfully designed to reveal character and had to do with how a wayfaring stranger would be received (compare the earlier reception of the angels by Abraham – and by Lot!). It was a hospitality test similar to the test in 1 Timothy that widows should only be approved to go on the register for church support if they had 'washed the saints' feet'.

Hospitality, as we have already seen, is one of the prime biblical virtues. It is a vital part of Jewish tradition and especially hospitality to strangers was regarded as a sacred duty. It was repeatedly praised and enjoined by the Lord and his apostles. It was an essential qualification for church leaders.

It often plays a role in marriage. It certainly did for Isaac – and for me! When I arrived as a student in Cambridge two of the leaders in the church I attended were given to hospitality. They regularly filled their homes on Sunday with hungry and appreciative students. The family that invited me the most had four girls. The hospitable attitude of the parents had been passed on to them. To cut a long story short, I married the eldest of them who, from the beginning, made our home a centre of hospitality to many. She has been my wife for more than 54 years. Yes, hospitality makes a huge difference to a marriage and is especially important in training children.

Abraham's servant was a wise and shrewd judge of human character. Before he had finished his prayer, Rebekah arrived (perhaps she saw him pray?). We are told by the narrator – but the servant did not yet know – that she was from the right family. She was also beautiful and a virgin.

How would she react to his request?

The servant duly asked for a drink and she complied, saying: 'Drink, my lord.' But she didn't mention the camels. It must have been a heart-stopping moment for him. Only when he had finished drinking did she offer not only to get water for the camels, but to fetch enough to quench their thirst completely. She was prepared to keep going 'until they [had] finished drinking'. That was a remarkably generous offer, since a thirsty camel can consume 25 gallons before it has had enough! She had to go again and again to the well. For a considerable time she was a whirl of activity, the subject in the text of no fewer than 11 verbs of action and only one of speech (see Gen. 24.16–18). This echoed Abraham's frenzied hospitality to the three 'men' earlier, when he ran to meet them . . . made haste into the tent . . . ran to the tent . . . and made haste to prepare it (see Gen. 18.2–7). This girl was like the man who would become her father-in-law!

She passed the test with flying colours. The servant was in no doubt as to what to do next. The description of what happened as they stood beside the well is a beautiful piece of writing, well worth reproducing in full: 'When the camels had finished drinking, the man took a gold ring weighing a half shekel, and two bracelets for her arms weighing ten gold shekels, and said, "Please tell me whose daughter you are. Is there room in your father's house for us to spend the night?"' (Gen. 24.22–23)

The sight of such gloriously beautiful gold jewellery must have taken her breath away, to say nothing of what she thought when the servant presented it to her. Without giving her name she said to him, 'I am the daughter of Bethuel the son of Milcah, whom she bore to Nahor.'

Answering his second question, she added, 'We have plenty of both straw and fodder, and room to spend the night.' Another indicator of her quality – she stated that there was space, but she did not offer hospitality, as it was not her place to do so.

The man now knew she belonged to Abraham's kin and he

> bowed his head and worshipped the LORD and said, 'Blessed be the LORD, the God of my master Abraham, who has not forsaken his steadfast love and his faithfulness towards my master. As for me, the LORD has led me in the way to the house of my master's kinsmen.' Then the young woman ran and told her mother's household about these things.
>
> (Gen. 24.26–28)

How much she understood of that humble yet telling action of his prayer in her hearing we do not know, but his words must have communicated to her the fact that Nahor was Abraham's kin and that his master Abraham believed in God, although they may well have remembered that fact from the early days when Abraham left.

She then ran to her mother to tell her what had happened, no doubt bursting with excitement as she pondered the meaning of the gold ring and bracelets she was wearing. Why had he given such beautiful and valuable things to her? What was going on?

The next person on the scene was Rebekah's brother Laban. We are told that Laban at once noticed the gold adorning his sister.[2] He listened to what she had to say and greeted Abraham's servant as 'blessed of the LORD' (of course!), inviting him into the house and proffering food.

The servant, however, regarded his mission as more important than food and refused to eat until he had told his story. One can imagine him, in the great tradition of Hebrew storytelling, regaling the household at length with a gripping account of their relatives Abraham and Sarah, their wealth, their exploits, their son and heir. It was all a build-up to his description of Isaac's pressing need for a wife and the mission of the servant ending in his encounter with Rebekah. No doubt she listened to this incredible narrative with a mounting thrill of understanding and anticipation. The servant finished his speech by telling the assembled company about his prayer for guidance at the well and its detailed fulfilment under the complex interweaving of God's providential direction and the choices both of the servant and of Rebekah.

It was this final argument – divine providence – that appeared to weigh most with the listeners. Laban and Bethuel claimed, rather over-piously one might think, to have recognised the hand of the Lord in it all, though we might well ask how much, if anything, they knew about the Lord. More gifts were showered on Rebekah and her mother and brother – and they were duly noted by the onlookers. The family's request for a delay in the manner of the culture was firmly rejected by the servant. His mission must take precedence.

They called Rebekah and put to her the crucial question: 'Will you go with this man?'

'I will go,' she said.

Test passed. Mission accomplished!

What had convinced her? First, the gifts she had been given showed that her prospective in-laws were both wealthy and generous. Second, there was the fact that they had shared kinship. Third, there was the story of Abraham and Isaac's life and the sheer romance of the servant's mission culminating in his prayer for guidance and its fulfilment. One would imagine that the credibility of Abraham's servant played an important role: his kindness, his love for his master and his transparent faith in God. Perhaps she also understood that the servant had tested her in the way he did in order to learn something of her character before he told her more of the story behind his visit. It all added up convincingly in her mind and pointed in one, and only one, exciting direction.

Many years earlier the God of glory had appeared to Abram and it had set him on the journey to Canaan. History was now repeating itself as Rebekah was shown Isaac's glory and it set her on the very same journey.

Eventually, the caravan train reached the Negev. The Genesis narrator takes up the story:

Now Isaac had returned from Beer-lahai-roi and was dwelling in the Negeb. And Isaac went out to meditate in the field towards evening. And he lifted up his eyes and saw, and behold, there were camels

coming. And Rebekah lifted up her eyes, and when she saw Isaac, she dismounted from the camel and said to the servant, 'Who is that man, walking in the field to meet us?' The servant said, 'It is my master.' So she took her veil and covered herself. And the servant told Isaac all the things that he had done. Then Isaac brought her into the tent of Sarah his mother and took Rebekah, and she became his wife, and he loved her. So Isaac was comforted after his mother's death.
(Gen. 24.62–67)

This entire remarkable account gives us insight into the complex workings of God's guidance within the personal trajectories of our lives, and yet there is no hint in it of a micro-managing determinism that removes the freedom of choice of the individuals involved, down to Rebekah's evidence-based response to the question 'Will you go with this man?'[3]

How can we apply this story, as many of its aspects are clearly unique?

We saw earlier the way in which the story of father and son on the mountain of sacrifice projects onto the greater story of Father and Son on Calvary. Now we have learned how the father Abraham sends his servant back to the Gentiles to win a bride for his son. The servant reveals to the potential bride the wealth and glory of the son, so that she begins to fall in love with him, a man she has never seen. Her trust is awakened and she embarks on the long journey to Canaan, eventually to meet and marry the man of whom she has heard so much.

It would be difficult to read this without thinking of a very similar kind of narrative at a much higher level – the story of God the Father in heaven sending his Spirit to witness to his Son by revealing his glory and attracting people of all nations to take their faith journey to him. Jesus equipped his disciples for this task:

'Nevertheless, I tell you the truth: it is to your advantage that I go away, for if I do not go away, the Helper will not come to you. But if I go, I will send him to you. And when he comes, he will convict the world concerning sin and righteousness and judgement: concerning sin, because they do not believe in me; concerning righteousness, because I go to the Father, and you will see me no longer; concerning judgement, because the ruler of this world is judged.

'I still have many things to say to you, but you cannot bear them now. When the Spirit of truth comes, he will guide you into all the truth, for he will not speak on his own authority, but whatever he hears he will speak, and he will declare to you the things that are to come. *He will glorify me, for he will take what is mine and declare it to you. All that the Father has is mine; therefore I said that he will take what is mine and declare it to you.'*
(John 16.7–15, emphasis mine)

To think of the servant's quest for a bride for Isaac in this way does not mean regarding the story as an allegory but rather as a prototype. Nor am I trying to *deduce* teaching about the Holy Spirit from Genesis. Such teaching is explicit in the New Testament. It is the fact that we are called to go into all the world and tell men and women of a journey into life that they can undertake. How will we persuade them? God has sent his Holy Spirit to help us show them the wealth and glory of our Lord and Saviour Jesus Christ so that they might be attracted to put their trust in him, and themselves become Abraham's children by faith.

On our part we need to get to know the riches of God's word because we cannot share what we do not know. God has promised his Spirit to help us, but that does not exempt us from making every effort to soak our minds and hearts in Scripture in order, as Paul said to his protégé Timothy, to show ourselves approved unto God, workers that have no need to be ashamed (2 Tim. 2.15).

Some of my most precious memories are of sitting in a room telling a group of people the story of the Father God who sent his Son into the world to find sheep that were lost and show them the way to the fold. What a privilege to be able to put to people the most important question of all: 'Will you go with this man?'

I have watched, as doubtless many of you have watched, while eyes fill with wonder and even tears as the Spirit of God reveals the glory of Christ and opens hearts and minds to receive him as Saviour, and decide to take the greatest step of all: 'I will go with this man.'

Their new life journey starts at that point, a journey of following the Lord, living for him and dying without ever having seen him. As Peter put it: 'Though you have not seen him, you love him. Though you do not now see him, you believe in him and rejoice with joy that is inexpressible and filled with glory, obtaining the outcome of your faith, the salvation of your souls' (1 Pet. 1.8–9). We do so in the knowledge that one day, as he promised, he will return to take us to himself.

> For the Lord himself will descend from heaven with a cry of command, with the voice of an archangel, and with the sound of the trumpet of God. And the dead in Christ will rise first. Then we who are alive, who are left, will be caught up together with them in the clouds to meet the Lord in the air, and so we will always be with the Lord. Therefore encourage one another with these words.
> (1 Thess. 4.16–18)

Thus shall we ever be with the Lord.

## Cities and their foundations

Not only that but, according to the book of Revelation, we, as part of the Church that Christ calls his bride, will participate in an indescribably glorious wedding, the marriage supper of the Lamb, with which the eternal ages to come shall begin (Rev. 19.6–9). We shall at last have reached the city with foundations for which Abraham looked and of which he has long since been a citizen.

That city, variously called the New Jerusalem and the Bride of the Lamb, is contrasted in the book of Revelation with Babylon the Great, a city on earth that is a prostitute.

The great cycle of the Abraham narrative commenced with the building of Babel/Babylon, which became a byword in the ancient world for religion that is polyamorous in its trust in many gods and therefore is unfaithful to the one true God. In other words it behaves as a prostitute, seducing the faithful where possible. Abraham is called to leave it and trust God, and live a life that is a protest against such idolatrous unfaithfulness.

His narrative comes to its end with a repetition of his call, this time to a young woman, to leave the region Abraham had left and travel to become the faithful bride of a man she had never seen and thereby to join Abraham in carrying his vision in living for the city with foundations whose builder and maker is God.

This beautiful account gives us some important principles for seeking guidance in our everyday lives. At the simplest level we see that Abraham trusted God for a wife for his son and one presumes Isaac was content to go along with that, although there is no record of them discussing it. And one of the things Christian families (should) do as they watch their children (and grandchildren) growing up is to pray for them that the Lord will in due course give them a suitable partner for life. Looking back over our own lives as Christians, recognising that we are all different, it is nevertheless instructive to trace at a very different, more normal, level how various aspects of the biblical narrative played a role. One example in my case is how I found my wife, which I spoke of briefly earlier.

First, there was the decision to leave my home and country of birth to study in Cambridge. Unlike Abraham my home background was Christian and credible. My parents lived what they believed, yet did not impose their views on me so that I was allowed to come to my own convictions. Among them was the importance of leaving home in order to be free to discover and develop what God had for me.

My headmaster suggested I try for Cambridge. We took advice from a Christian friend who had studied there and we prayed about it. I sat the examinations and was accepted. Before I set out, the friend made a laconic remark to me in the quasi-biblical language he sometimes used when having fun: 'There is a man in Cambridge with four daughters . . .' When I got there the family of this man turned out to be very hospitable and I was invited to their home. In this way I met my future wife in the context of very generous hospitality that her family showed to students who were away from home. She shared the gospel vision.

We eventually married in Cambridge and immediately left to live and work in another country – Wales. It was necessary and important for my wife to leave home also. It has not been difficult to trace the hand of God behind all our many journeys since.

In addition, we have always sensed that our journeys do not have their goal in this world. Like Abraham we believe that there is another world, and like him we are headed towards that city where he has been (in earthly terms) for centuries.

# 19

# The last days of Abraham – and beyond

We are told that Abraham, at this late stage in his long life, took another wife, Keturah, and had six sons by her, half-brothers to Isaac. The mind boggles at his vigour at this time of life! Their families eventually became nomadic tribes east of Jordan and in the Arabian peninsula. However, the narrator informs us that Abraham kept these other children separate from Isaac, giving them gifts and sending them away during his lifetime. To Isaac he gave everything.

At length, Abraham died at the ripe old age of 175. Isaac and Ishmael came together to bury him alongside Sarah in the cave of Machpelah in Hebron. It would be fascinating to know what Abraham talked about in that final conversation with his sons – that is, if they did have a discussion.

The narrative of Abraham's earthly life ends with the words: 'After the death of Abraham, God blessed Isaac his son. And Isaac settled at Beer-lahai-roi' (Gen. 25.11). This is the place that recalls the importance of the presence behind the narrative of El Roi, the God who sees – in the sense of observation and provision. It is also the place where God spoke to Hagar when she had been thrown out by Sarah. Hagar had given the place its name and it had stuck. Presumably Isaac knew this and was nevertheless content to live there with the memory. One wonders what the name meant to him.

The transition to the next major section of Genesis that deals with Isaac and his sons contains a paragraph informing us that Ishmael flourished and produced 12 sons who became princes of their respective tribes. He died at the age of 137 years. God had fulfilled his promise to Hagar about him. Yet the tension between the two parts of the family was set to continue. For instance, Isaac's son Esau, to spite his father, eventually married one of Ishmael's daughters (Gen. 28.9).

When Jesus the promised Seed of Abraham came, he said that the Old Testament itself implied that the story of Abraham was not terminated by his physical death – just the earthly part of it. For as far as God is concerned, Abraham is still alive: 'And as for the resurrection of the dead, have you not read what was said to you by God: "I am the God of Abraham, and the God of Isaac, and the God of Jacob"? He is not God of the dead, but of the living' (Matt. 22.31–32).

This text comes from Exodus 3.6, which refers to events that occurred centuries after Abraham's death. It does not say, as might have been expected, that God *was* the God of Abraham, but that he (still) *is* the God of Abraham. In other words, Abraham is still alive.

The fact that Abraham is not only still alive but alive in God's heavenly kingdom is something Jesus himself emphasised on a number of other occasions. For instance, recall Jesus' reaction to the faith of the Roman centurion who asked him to heal his servant simply by speaking a word rather than coming to his house:

> When Jesus heard this, he marvelled and said to those who followed him, 'Truly, I tell you, with no one in Israel have I found such faith. I tell you, many will come from east and west and recline at table with Abraham, Isaac, and Jacob in the kingdom of heaven, while the sons of the kingdom will be thrown into the outer darkness. In that place there will be weeping and gnashing of teeth.'
> (Matt. 8.10–12)

God promised Abraham that he would bring blessing to the nations of the world and this is an example of it – many Gentiles like this centurion would come to faith in Jesus, become children of Abraham and ultimately join him in the world to come in his kingdom.

The tragedy, as Jesus warned, is that many physical descendants of Abraham, sons of the kingdom in that sense, will not be in that kingdom because they never repented of their evil deeds nor trusted God.

In the parallel passage in Luke it says:

> 'In that place there will be weeping and gnashing of teeth, when you see Abraham and Isaac and Jacob and all the prophets in the

kingdom of God but you yourselves cast out. And people will come from east and west, and from north and south, and recline at table in the kingdom of God. And behold, some are last who will be first, and some are first who will be last.'
(Luke 13.28–30)

That same motif – that those rejected by the Lord will see Abraham – is also found in the story Jesus related about a rich man and Lazarus, the beggar who sat at his gate. Lazarus died and was carried by the angels to Abraham's side. Friendless in life God compensated him in death by bringing him together with Abraham the friend of God. The rich man also died, was buried and found himself in torment in Hades, from where he saw Abraham 'far off and Lazarus at his side'. There then follows a remarkable discussion between him and Abraham – two men communicating *after* death.

And he [the rich man] called out, 'Father Abraham, have mercy on me, and send Lazarus to dip the end of his finger in water and cool my tongue, for I am in anguish in this flame.' But Abraham said, 'Child, remember that you in your lifetime received your good things, and Lazarus in like manner bad things; but now he is comforted here, and you are in anguish. And besides all this, between us and you a great chasm has been fixed, in order that those who would pass from here to you may not do so, and none may cross from there to us.' And he said, 'Then I beg you, father, to send him to my father's house – for I have five brothers – so that he may warn them, lest they also come into this place of torment.' But Abraham said, 'They have Moses and the Prophets; let them hear them.' And he said, 'No, father Abraham, but if someone goes to them from the dead, they will repent.' He said to him, 'If they do not hear Moses and the Prophets, neither will they be convinced if someone should rise from the dead.'
(Luke 16.24–31)

Scholars have pointed out that this story is not likely to be a parable.[1] It is, in all probability, a rare factual insight into the nature of the world beyond the grave. What is very striking about it is that it doesn't mention God. Abraham conducts the discussion. The context is judgement and it immediately calls to mind that Abraham had discussed with God the matter of judgement on Sodom. Now he is being allowed to speak – presumably because in his life on earth he had passed the tests that qualified him to do so.

This is consistent with the teaching of Jesus to his disciples that the reward for faithful stewardship in this life would be real administrative responsibility in the world to come – for instance, in the parable of the minas in Luke 19.11–27. Also, Paul rebuked some church members in Corinth for going to law before unbelievers by pointing out to them that believers will in a future day be given responsibility to judge the world and to judge angels:

> When one of you has a grievance against another, does he dare go to law before the unrighteous instead of the saints? Or do you not know that the saints will judge the world? And if the world is to be judged by you, are you incompetent to try trivial cases? Do you not know that we are to judge angels? How much more, then, matters pertaining to this life!
> (1 Cor. 6.1–3)

The story of Abraham, the rich man and Lazarus gives us another glimpse into the eternal world beyond this one. During his lifetime on earth Abraham had been wealthy yet generous spirited in hospitality. He had learned to trust God and not his material wealth. The rich man, by contrast, had trusted his wealth, been mean spirited and ungenerous and had ignored both Lazarus and God.

That was the first reason the rich man's request to have Lazarus come and cool his tongue was refused by Abraham. Second, as Abraham pointed out, it was in any case impossible for anyone to pass in either direction between where the rich man was and where Abraham and Lazarus were. On earth the rich man could easily have helped alleviate Lazarus's hunger and disease, but he erected a barrier of greed and selfishness between them. He could have lifted that barrier but didn't, with the result that an eternally impassable barrier separated the rich man from Lazarus, Abraham and heaven.

One of the most solemn features of the account is that it gives no indication the rich man wanted to get out of where he was. Instead he asked for Lazarus to come and relieve him. The rich man then requested that Lazarus should be sent back into the world to warn his five brothers and bring them to repentance. Abraham denied that request also, on the basis that the brothers already had access to Moses and the Prophets. If they did not heed them, they wouldn't believe even if someone were to rise from the dead.

Abraham's final message from the as yet unseen heavenly world warns of the deadly seriousness of failing to heed what Scripture has to say – so serious that it was the reason the rich man found himself eternally separated from God.

This is a crucially important issue that many people fail to grasp. David Gooding explains it as follows:

> Abraham persisted in his refusal to send Lazarus to warn his brothers, and it is instructive to notice why. It was not that Abraham, or God either, was determined to give people no more than the minimum of evidence. If seeing and hearing an apparition would have brought the brothers to repentance, every room they sat in, every street they walked down, would have been alive with apparitions. But apparitions would not have helped them.
>
> They did not need to be convinced that the afterlife is real, or that after death there comes the judgment, or that there is a hell. They needed to be convinced that their neglect of God's law was serious enough to land them personally in hell. And that was a moral issue, and ultimately a question of God's moral character. The highest possible evidence in the matter therefore was the plain statement of his Word directed to the brothers' moral conscience and judgment. And so it is with us. If our moral judgment is so irresponsible that it can make light of the Bible's warnings of our guilt before God (see John 3:18; Rom 1:18, 20; 2:1–3:20), no amount of seeing of apparitions would convince us that we personally were in danger of perdition unless we repented.[2]

The point is that apparitions might frighten us, but fear is not the same as moral conviction, and it is moral conviction that is essential to bring us to repentance.

These are strong words and, just in case we are tempted to ignore them as too extreme, we need to remind ourselves that the warnings came from no less than the Lord Jesus himself, the one whose love for his fellow human beings was unique in its commitment. It is precisely this love that makes the warning so serious – just as the love of parents for their children will add weight to a warning not to go skating on thin ice on a deep lake.

It is, therefore, appropriate to conclude the story of Abraham listening to him plead with us from heaven to take the word of God seriously and to bring it to bear on a world that desperately needs it

What will our reaction be? Are we going to prove to be true and genuine children of Abraham by standing firm in our faith in Christ, spending time and energy getting to know God's living word and taking it to the world?

Are we also going to put our energy into learning to explain that message to the next generation of believers to empower them to resist the raging storms of secularism, relativism and outright atheism? Is the eternal city, for which Abraham looked, a living, vibrant prospect for us? Are we building its foundational principles of faith in the unseen God into our lives and thereby allowing him to shape our identity, as he did for Abraham, rather than trying – and failing – to do so in our own strength?

Abraham is one of the cloud of many witnesses who would encourage us, whatever our situation, to lift up our eyes and, looking to Jesus the Author and Finisher of our faith (Heb. 12.2), to run the race eagerly, saying: 'Amen. Come, Lord Jesus!' (Rev. 22.20).

In the meantime God would call to us as to Abraham at the beginning: *Lech lecha!* Get going!

# Appendix 1
# A brief history of Israel

Here, as promised, we return to the question of the fulfilment of the promise of land to Abraham's offspring in light of the tortuous history of claim and counter-claim; of challenge, protest, violence, war and successive attempts by international authorities to solve the problems. In short the question is: why did all of this happen in the way it did? What are the main issues involved?

First, Abraham's story is a story of faith in God. He trusted God for his inheritance of children and land. This did not carry the implication that his descendants could enjoy the inheritance without themselves having the same kind of personal faith in God as Abraham did. And this is where the major problem lies with subsequent history. For, as Stephen pointed out in his overview of the history of Israel in Acts 7, many of those who were leaders in Israel rebelled against God and against the series of saviours God raised up to rescue them from their enemies and their sins – the patriarchs themselves rejected Joseph and sold him into Egyptian slavery. Yet the man they rejected saved them. Perhaps that is part of the explanation for the slavery the nation later suffered in Egypt?

After that period God appointed Moses to lead them out of slavery and yet the fathers and leaders of the nation rejected Moses' authority for a considerable period. And, when he eventually led them across the desert, at various junctures they again rebelled against Moses and God, and turned in their hearts back to Egypt. Eventually, when Moses was absent at Sinai, receiving the law, they got Aaron to make golden idols for them to worship. God stepped in, disciplined them severely and warned them through Moses that such behaviour would always bring severe judgement on the nation.

Here is one of the typically strong warnings Moses delivered to Israel before the nation crossed the border and entered the promised land:

'Do not make yourselves unclean by any of these things, for by all these the nations I am driving out before you have become unclean, and the land became unclean, so that I punished its iniquity, and the land vomited out its inhabitants. But you shall keep my statutes and my rules and do none of these abominations, either the native or the stranger who sojourns among you (for the people of the land, who were before you, did all of these abominations, so that the land became unclean), lest the land vomit you out when you make it unclean, as it vomited out the nation that was before you. For everyone who does any of these abominations, the persons who do them shall be cut off from among their people. So keep my charge never to practise any of these abominable customs that were practised before you, and never to make yourselves unclean by them: I am the LORD your God.'
(Lev. 18.24–30)

It is important to note the strong moral emphasis here. When the nation entered the land eventually, under the leadership of Joshua, they dispossessed certain tribes that were already there. Moses tells them that this dispossession would not be arbitrary but it would form God's judgement on their 'abominable customs'.

In consequence, if Israel got seduced into practising such things the land would 'vomit them out' also. God is no respecter of persons and so, even though he had promised the land as an inheritance to the descendants of Abraham, they would not enjoy it if they failed to keep his moral and spiritual standards.

The period of the Judges followed, some of whom led the nation in godly ways, others did not and we see a degeneration towards the end of that period when the priesthood failed through immorality and Samuel the prophet became the leader. His dynasty did not last either and the people craved a king 'like the other nations'. Saul was chosen as king and he failed in his commitment to God. Samuel was told to anoint David secretly as king even before the death of Saul, although David waited for God's timing and did not do anything to hasten Saul's demise.

King David took control of Jerusalem around 1000 BC and for a time the nation enjoyed prosperity. It may have seemed that Abraham's vision was being fulfilled at last. Solomon built a temple to the Lord in Jerusalem and, again for a time, reigned gloriously.

It was not long before things began to go wrong and the nation split in two, with Israel in the north and Judah in the south. God sent prophets to warn them as Moses did of the dangers of idolatry and failing to keep God's law. For instance, Isaiah warned Israel of impending captivity by Assyria, and Jeremiah warned Judah of impending captivity by Babylon.

Here is what Jeremiah told the people of Judah:

'You have neither listened nor inclined your ears to hear, although the LORD persistently sent to you all his servants the prophets, saying, "Turn now, every one of you, from his evil way and evil deeds, and dwell upon the land that the LORD has given to you and your fathers from of old and for ever. Do not go after other gods to serve and worship them, or provoke me to anger with the work of your hands. Then I will do you no harm." Yet you have not listened to me, declares the LORD, that you might provoke me to anger with the work of your hands to your own harm.

'Therefore thus says the LORD of hosts: Because you have not obeyed my words, behold, I will send for all the tribes of the north, declares the LORD, and for Nebuchadnezzar the king of Babylon, my servant, and I will bring them against this land and its inhabitants . . . This whole land shall become a ruin and a waste, and these nations shall serve the king of Babylon seventy years. Then after seventy years are completed, I will punish the king of Babylon and that nation, the land of the Chaldeans, for their iniquity . . .'"
(Jer. 25.4–12)

Just as Abraham was informed that his nation would be slaves in Egypt for a stated period of 400 years, so now Jeremiah tells Judah that, because of their flirtation with idolatry, they will be taken into Babylonian captivity for a period of 70 years. The punishment fitted the crime, since Babylon was the most idolatrous empire of that time.

The predicted fall of the Temple and Jerusalem to the Babylonians occurred in 586 BC and the subsequent exile lasted around 70 years. One of the Jewish captives, Daniel, rose to a senior position in the administration of the empire – first the Babylonian and then the Medo-Persian. Towards the end of the 70 years he read Jeremiah's prediction:

> This is what the LORD says: 'When seventy years are completed for Babylon, I will come to you and fulfil my good promise to bring you back to this place. For I know the plans I have for you,' declares the LORD, 'plans to prosper you and not to harm you, plans to give you hope and a future. Then you will call on me and come and pray to me, and I will listen to you. You will seek me and find me when you seek me with all your heart.'
> (Jer. 29.10–13, NIV)

He was so concerned for the future of his people that, when he read the above prophecy of Jeremiah, he did pray to God about what would happen to Jerusalem and the people of Israel in the future. God sent the angel Gabriel to give Daniel a sombre message about the future:

> 'Seventy weeks are decreed about your people and your holy city, to finish the transgression, to put an end to sin, and to atone for iniquity, to bring in everlasting righteousness, to seal both vision and prophet, and to anoint a most holy place. Know therefore and understand that from the going out of the word to restore and build Jerusalem to the coming of an anointed one, a prince, there shall be seven weeks. Then for sixty-two weeks it shall be built again with squares and moat, but in a troubled time. And after the sixty-two weeks, an anointed one shall be cut off and shall have nothing. And the people of the prince who is to come shall destroy the city and the sanctuary. Its end shall come with a flood, and to the end there shall be war. Desolations are decreed.'
> (Dan. 9.24–26)

Daniel was told in this much discussed prophecy that, even though the 70 years of exile were nearly at an end, it would take 70 times 7 (that is, 490) years to sort things out and realise the goals of God's original promise. Important events along the way are predicted. First, the decree to rebuild

Jerusalem. In my book on Daniel[1] I argue that this decree was obtained by the prophet Nehemiah from the Persian king Artaxerxes in 444 BC.

Second, after 62 times 7 (that is, 483 BC) the anointed one would be cut off. The indicated time is around AD 30 and the Anointed One is of course the Christ: 'Christ' is Greek for 'anointed'.

Third, there is the prediction of the fall of Jerusalem in AD 70 by the Romans.

In 538 BC King Cyrus of Persia, who had conquered the Babylonian Empire, permitted some Jewish exiles in Babylonia to return to their land and rebuild the Temple. The work was completed in the reign of Darius I in 515 BC. The rebuilding of the city took place later, under Nehemiah's leadership, as indicated above.

The Greeks eventually conquered the whole region, and their Hellenistic rulers allowed the Temple to function. The Greek historian Polybius, of the second century BC, described the Jews of the time as a nation dwelling around the famous Temple in Jerusalem.[2] Its sanctity was savagely violated by Antiochus Ephiphanes II in 169 BC, who sacrificed a pig on the altar. Its services were restored three years later when Judas Maccabeus retook the Temple Mount and cleansed it, an event celebrated in the annual Jewish festival of Hannukah.

Greek rule gave way to Roman occupation, and a puppet Roman king, Herod the Great, undertook a massive reconstruction, refurbishment and extension of the Temple Mount. Starting around 20 BC he took 46 years to rebuild and remodel it from ground up. This was the Temple of the time of Jesus the Messiah, who 'came to his own, and his own people did not receive him' (John 1.11).

It was bad enough to have rejected leaders and saviours like Joseph, Moses and many of the prophets. It was in an altogether different category to reject and crucify Jesus the Messiah, the Son of God. This 'cutting off of the Anointed One' by the leaders of his own Jewish people could not but have massive implications for the inheritance.

Jesus had warned those leaders on many occasions that they were playing with fire. Here is a parable where he likens them to tenants of a vineyard:

And he began to tell the people this parable: 'A man planted a vineyard and let it out to tenants and went into another country for a long while. When the time came, he sent a servant to the tenants, so that they would give him some of the fruit of the vineyard. But the tenants beat him and sent him away empty-handed. And he sent another servant. But they also beat and treated him shamefully, and sent him away empty-handed. And he sent yet a third. This one also they wounded and cast out. Then the owner of the vineyard said, "What shall I do? I will send my beloved son; perhaps they will respect him." But when the tenants saw him, they said to themselves, "This is the heir. Let us kill him, so that the inheritance may be ours." And they threw him out of the vineyard and killed him. What then will the owner of the vineyard do to them? He will come and destroy those tenants and give the vineyard to others.' When they heard this, they said, 'Surely not!' But he looked directly at them and said, 'What then is this that is written:

"The stone that the builders rejected
    has become the cornerstone"?

Everyone who falls on that stone will be broken to pieces, and when it falls on anyone, it will crush him.'
    The scribes and the chief priests sought to lay hands on him at that very hour, for they perceived that he had told this parable against them, but they feared the people.
(Luke 20.9–19)

The leaders of the nation wanted the inheritance for themselves. However, you cannot have the inheritance by rejecting its owner, the Messiah – so they lost it and everything else.
    In his Olivet discourse Jesus explicitly predicted how that would soon happen. He foretold Jerusalem's downfall and the destruction of Herod's Temple by the Romans in AD 70. He warned of desolations and exile for the nation leading far into the future up to his coming:

'For there will be great distress upon the earth and wrath against this people. They will fall by the edge of the sword and be led captive among all nations, and Jerusalem will be trampled underfoot by the

Gentiles, until the times of the Gentiles are fulfilled . . . And then they will see the Son of Man coming in a cloud with power and great glory.' (Luke 21.23–24, 27)

In other words, the answer to the longings of all those who believed the promises of God to Abraham would not be fulfilled until Christ's return to restore all things – including the kingdom to Israel.

In the meantime the task of those who believed was to proclaim the message to the world. They would have to preach it in the midst of all kinds of trouble and difficulty. For not long after this the deacon Stephen became the first Christian to be martyred for his faith and the Church was scattered and suffered increasing persecution from the Roman (and Jewish) authorities.

There now follows a very brief sketch of the subsequent history of the land up to the present. As Jesus had predicted, the Temple at Jerusalem was destroyed in AD 70 by the Roman legions led by Titus. Since then the region has been conquered and reconquered. During the Bar Kokhba rebellion of AD 132–35, Jerusalem was liberated and a Jewish government established in it. The rebellion was quashed and the Roman emperor Hadrian built a temple to Jupiter on the Temple Mount and turned Jerusalem into a Roman city. Not much happened until the reign of Julian the Apostate, who attempted to rebuild the Temple in AD 363, but was foiled by an earthquake. During this time Jews continued to make pilgrimage to the site, but Christians showed no interest.

The Muslim conquest occurred in the seventh century and lasted until the fall of Jerusalem to the Crusaders in AD 1099. Muslim tradition says that Mohammed was supernaturally carried at night to Jerusalem on his horse al-Buraq, together with the angel Gabriel. There he met Abraham, Moses, Jesus and other prophets, after which he ascended to heaven from the Rock on the Temple Mount. During that period the Muslims built various structures on the Temple site. In particular, at the end of the seventh century and beginning of the eighth, the Dome of the Rock and the Al-Aqsa Mosque were built.

Next came the period of the Crusaders, who used the Al-Aqsa Mosque as their administrative centre, renaming it Templum Salomonis. The Dome of the Rock was renamed Templum Domini.

Jerusalem was reconquered by the Muslims in 1187. Then came the Mameluke (or Mamluk) period from 1260 to 1516. The Mamelukes were armies of slaves established during the Abbasid era that later won political control of several Muslim states. Under the Ayyubid sultanate, Mameluke generals ruled Egypt and Syria from 1250 to 1517.

This period was followed by the Turkish Ottoman Empire, whose rule lasted until the end of the First World War, when the British Mandate was set up. This Mandate for Palestine was a League of Nations mandate for British administration of the territories of what was then called Palestine and Transjordan. Its objective was to provide for the former territories of the Ottoman Empire 'administrative advice and assistance by a Mandatory until such time as they are able to stand alone'. The Balfour Declaration was made in 1917, in which the British undertook to set up a Jewish homeland for the then minority Jewish population of Palestine.

British administrative control of Palestine lasted for three decades, during which there was increasing tension between the Jewish and Arab communities, which led to an Arab revolt in 1936–39 and a Jewish insurgency from 1944 to 1948.

In between the two there was the most horrific attempt to wipe the Jews from the face of the earth, the Nazi holocaust – a blot on the face of humanity.

The UN attempted to solve the problem of the division of land between the various factions by creating a Partition Plan for Palestine in 1947. The idea was to set up separate Jewish and Arab states in an economic union and put Jerusalem into UN trusteeship. The Mandate ended on 15 May 1948, upon which the Jewish community immediately issued a Declaration of Independence for Israel.

Intensification of war ensued, with the Arab nations of Lebanon, Syria, Iraq and Egypt sending troops. The UN plan failed and in 1949 Mandatory Palestine was divided between Israel, Jordan (the annexation of the West Bank) and Egypt (the Egyptian All-Palestine Protectorate in the Gaza Strip).

The History website says:

The Israelis, though less well equipped, managed to fight off the Arabs and then seize key territory, such as Galilee, the Palestinian coast, and a strip of territory connecting the coastal region to the western section of Jerusalem. In 1949, U.N.-brokered cease-fires left the State of Israel in permanent control of this conquered territory. The departure of hundreds of thousands of Palestinian Arabs from Israel during the war left the country with a substantial Jewish majority.

During the third Arab-Israeli conflict – the Six-Day War of 1967 – Israel again greatly increased its borders, capturing from Jordan, Egypt, and Syria the Old City of Jerusalem, the Sinai Peninsula, the Gaza Strip, the West Bank and the Golan Heights. In 1979, Israel and Egypt signed a historic peace agreement in which Israel returned the Sinai in exchange for Egyptian recognition and peace. Israel and the Palestine Liberation Organization (PLO) signed a major peace accord in 1993, which envisioned the gradual implementation of Palestinian self-government in the West Bank and Gaza Strip. The Israeli-Palestinian peace process moved slowly, however . . .[3]

There is still conflict and violence today.

Is that it, then? Is that all we can ever expect? Should we not be ashamed to associate ourselves with it or embarrassed to associate the name of God with it? Yes, indeed – if that was the whole story. But it isn't. It never was. For we are forgetting that the messiness of the story was to be expected – indeed was clearly predicted, not once, but many times over.

God told Abraham, Moses and Joshua to expect trouble and conflict. The prophets told Israel and Judah to expect it and, most important of all, Jesus told Israel to expect it. Thereafter, the apostles told Christian believers to expect it. And the reason? The same in all cases: moral failure and rebellion against God and his word.

Therefore, we find two lines of prediction weaving in and out of the biblical narrative – one full of gloom at the prospect of Israel's constant misbehaviour and rebellion against God and its devastating consequences for the nation's prosperity, and the other full of hope for the eventual realisation of God's promise to Abraham of an inheritance for his offspring.

In addition, we should also keep in mind that, for the last 20 centuries, there have been around the world, and in the land of Israel, Jewish believers in Christ, Arab believers in Christ and believers from many other nations – sometimes all meeting in the same church which, although small scale maybe, might indicate that a change of hearts and minds can make a difference. It is hard to believe that the problems will ever end without massive change on an unprecedented scale.

And that, according to Paul, is exactly what will happen – and Paul was no starry-eyed optimist who had no knowledge of the sad history outlined above. On the contrary, he knew it better than most others and the scriptures related to it. That is evident in Romans 9–11, where he tackles a related issue that gave him great concern as a Jew: how could it be that the very nation that had produced Messiah, descended from Abraham and David, had turned against him? Did that not contradict God's promise to Abraham?[4] Paul's answer is: no, the word of God had not come to nothing because, in the first place, there were at least some Jews, ethnic Jews like himself, who believed in Jesus as the Messiah. In addition there were many Gentiles. In fact, the Jewish rejection of Jesus had led to the gospel flowing out to the Gentiles. However, that situation will change dramatically one day when the Jews are at last reconciled to their true King and Messiah. Paul wrote:

> Lest you be wise in your own sight, I want you to understand this mystery, brothers: a partial hardening has come upon Israel, until the fullness of the Gentiles has come in. And in this way all Israel will be saved, as it is written,

> 'The Deliverer will come from Zion,
>    he will banish ungodliness from Jacob';
> 'and this will be my covenant with them
>    when I take away their sins.'

> As regards the gospel, they are enemies of God for your sake. But as regards election, they are beloved for the sake of their forefathers. For the gifts and the calling of God are irrevocable.
> (Rom. 11.25–29)

It must be stressed once more: the inheritance cannot be enjoyed by those who reject its king. Such people cannot be genuine offspring of Abraham, as Jesus sternly told them: 'They answered him, "Abraham is our father." Jesus said to them, "If you were Abraham's children, you would be doing the works Abraham did, but now you seek to kill me, a man who has told you the truth that I heard from God. This is not what Abraham did' (John 8.39–40). The promise to Abraham can only be realised fully when the nation repents of this attitude.

In spite of all that has happened, Paul believes that this repentance will take place one day. He has an unshakeable hope that, just as Jesus had appeared to him as the Messiah and Son of God, so he will appear to the nation as a whole and, this time, they will not reject him but will repent and receive him as King. Their conversion, compared with anything that has happened before, will be like 'life from the dead' (Rom. 11.15).

The key thing here is that 'the gifts and the calling of God are irrevocable'. That will be seen when 'the Deliverer' comes 'to Zion' in fulfilment of his promise to return – made publicly to his judges in the court of the high priest and privately to his disciples in the upper room and confirmed by his ascension and the subsequent repeated teaching that Jesus would come again to set up his kingdom. The biblical teaching on the kingdom in its varied aspects is quite complicated and we shall confine ourselves to the basics here.[5]

First, the idea that Messiah would come to reign is not peripheral but central to the biblical storyline. And it is familiar to all of us who enjoy Handel's magnificent oratorio on Isaiah 9:

For to us a child is born,
    to us a son is given;
and the government shall be upon his shoulder,
    and his name shall be called
Wonderful Counsellor, Mighty God,
    Everlasting Father, Prince of Peace.
Of the increase of his government and of peace
    there will be no end,
on the throne of David and over his kingdom,

to establish it and to uphold it
with justice and with righteousness
    from this time forth and for evermore.
The zeal of the LORD of hosts will do this.
(Isa. 9.6–7)

This promise was repeated to Mary by the angel Gabriel:

And the angel said to her, 'Do not be afraid, Mary, for you have
found favour with God. And behold, you will conceive in your
womb and bear a son, and you shall call his name Jesus. He will be
great and will be called the Son of the Most High. And the Lord
God will give to him the throne of his father David, and he will
reign over the house of Jacob for ever, and of his kingdom there
will be no end.'
(Luke 1.30–33)

As predicted by Zechariah the prophet, it was as King that Jesus entered
Jerusalem shortly before he was crucified:

This took place to fulfil what was spoken by the prophet, saying,

'Say to the daughter of Zion,
"Behold, your king is coming to you,
humble, and mounted on a donkey,
and on a colt, the foal of a beast of burden."'
(Matt. 21.4–5, citing Zech. 9.9)

The crowds understood what was happening – at least initially:
'And the crowds that went before him and that followed him were
shouting, "Hosanna to the Son of David! Blessed is he who comes in
the name of the Lord! Hosanna in the highest!"' (Matt. 21.9).

    Yet just before this event Jesus had warned his disciples that the
situation was not quite as they imagined. He told them a parable to
correct his disciples' erroneous impression that this would mean he
would soon take over the kingdom:

As they heard these things, he proceeded to tell a parable, because he was near to Jerusalem, and because they supposed that the kingdom of God was to appear immediately. He said therefore, 'A nobleman went into a far country to receive for himself a kingdom and then return. Calling ten of his servants, he gave them ten minas, and said to them, "Engage in business until I come." But his citizens hated him and sent a delegation after him, saying, "We do not want this man to reign over us."'
(Luke 19.11–14)

That was exactly the attitude of the leaders of the nation, who soon rejected him as he and Isaiah had foretold (Isa. 53). Jesus was put on trial for the 'offence' of claiming to be the Christ-King, and the chief priest condemned him because of these messianic claims:

And the high priest said to him, 'I adjure you by the living God, tell us if you are the Christ, the Son of God.' Jesus said to him, 'You have said so. But I tell you, from now on you will see the Son of Man seated at the right hand of Power and coming on the clouds of heaven.' Then the high priest tore his robes and said, 'He has uttered blasphemy. What further witnesses do we need? You have now heard his blasphemy. What is your judgement?' They answered, 'He deserves death.'
(Matt. 26.63–66)

They did not miss his reference to the vision the prophet Daniel saw of a man coming on the clouds of heaven to take over the government. For that claim they sent him to the Romans to get him crucified. The inscription on his cross read 'The King of the Jews' and Pilate the governor refused to change it.

None of them had any idea that the death of Jesus would be God's solution to the sin, disobedience, bitterness and war of centuries – that it would ultimately lead to the fulfilment of the promise to Abraham.

Jesus' disciples did not understand it at first. When they saw that he did not resist arrest, they all forsook him and fled in bitter disappointment. Yet when he rose from the dead three days later, their hope was greatly revived that he would now take over control of the country, get rid of the

Roman occupation and restore the kingdom to Israel. And so, as Luke records, they very naturally wanted to know, and asked him: 'Lord, will you at this time restore the kingdom to Israel?' (Acts 1.6).

Their question was precise. It was not: 'Lord, do you intend to restore the kingdom to Israel?' They would not have asked that question for the simple reason that they all expected such a restoration – it was their key hope as Jewish believers holding on to the promises that were made to Abraham and renewed through the prophets.

They had not understood the parable mentioned above that Jesus told them before he entered Jerusalem as King on Palm Sunday – a parable in which he referred to himself as a nobleman who, while away obtaining the authority to rule, was rejected by his servants who did not wish him to reign over them. The disciples had failed to grasp that Jesus would, like that nobleman, have to go away and then return.

So they pressed the matter of whether he was going to reign right away. Their question therefore had to do, not with the *fact* of restoration (because they had no doubt about that), but with the *timing* of restoration. Not 'Are you going to do it?' but 'Are you going to do it *now*?' Jesus replied accordingly: 'It is not for you to know times or seasons that the Father has fixed by his own authority. But you will receive power when the Holy Spirit has come upon you, and you will be my witnesses in Jerusalem and in all Judea and Samaria, and to the end of the earth' (Acts 1.7–8).

There are three main thrusts to Jesus' reply: first, the disciples were not to concern themselves regarding the timing of the restoration; second, that timing had already been fixed by the Father, so the restoration would happen at a time of his choosing; third, their task now was to concentrate on being his witnesses in the power of the Holy Spirit who would soon come to them at Pentecost.

The next event Luke records is the ascension of Jesus. His leaving earth to return to heaven was an unmistakable indication that he was not going to restore the kingdom to Israel with himself as King at that time!

In his day of Pentecost sermon Peter pointed out that the ascension had been prophesied long before by King David:

'This Jesus God raised up, and of that we all are witnesses. Being therefore exalted at the right hand of God, and having received from the Father the promise of the Holy Spirit, he has poured out this that you yourselves are seeing and hearing. For David did not ascend into the heavens, but he himself says,

"The Lord said to my Lord,
Sit at my right hand, until I make your enemies your
    footstool."

Let all the house of Israel therefore know for certain that God has made him both Lord and Christ, this Jesus whom you crucified.' (Acts 2.32–36)

The manner in which the ascension of Jesus took place had a positive message to convey that was relayed to the disciples by two men in white robes who suddenly appeared beside them: 'Men of Galilee, why do you stand looking into heaven? This Jesus, who was taken up from you into heaven, will come in the same way as you saw him go into heaven' (Acts 1.9–11).

The ascension was staged in such a way as to demonstrate to the disciples that, just as Jesus had left them visibly and physically, he would return equally physically and visibly. It was to this future return of Christ that Peter pointed in his second major sermon in Acts. Addressing those who had called for Jesus' execution, he said:

'And now, brothers, I know that you acted in ignorance, as did also your rulers. But what God foretold by the mouth of all the prophets, that his Christ would suffer, he thus fulfilled. Repent therefore, and turn again, that your sins may be blotted out, that times of refreshing may come from the presence of the Lord, and that he may send the Christ appointed for you, Jesus, *whom heaven must receive until the time for restoring all the things* about which God spoke by the mouth of his holy prophets long ago.'
(Acts 3.17–21, emphasis mine)

Like the nobleman in the parable, Jesus would go away and return. That return would trigger the restoration of all things, which Peter understood to be what the prophets had foretold. It would also involve the restoration of the kingdom to Israel, as Jesus himself promised in his final words to his disciples in Acts 1, as indicated above.

In fact, Jesus had himself earlier told his first disciples that they would one day have a very special role in this restoration: 'You are those who have stayed with me in my trials, and I assign to you, as my Father assigned to me, a kingdom, that you may eat and drink at my table in my kingdom and sit on thrones judging the twelve tribes of Israel' (Luke 22.28–30).

If we ask when this will happen, Matthew supplies more detail given a wider context to the same incident:

> Then Peter said in reply, 'See, we have left everything and followed you. What then will we have?' Jesus said to them, 'Truly, I say to you, in the new world, when the Son of Man will sit on his glorious throne, you who have followed me will also sit on twelve thrones, judging the twelve tribes of Israel. And everyone who has left houses or brothers or sisters or father or mother or children or lands, for my name's sake, will receive a hundredfold and will inherit eternal life. But many who are first will be last, and the last first.'
> (Matt. 19.27–30)

The word translated 'new world' is the Greek for 'regeneration' and it is clearly referring to the time when Jesus the Messiah will come and sit on his throne to reign.

That, of course, raises the question of what precise territorial boundaries that future kingdom will have in light of the fact that the geographical extent of Israel has varied considerably throughout history. However, we may not need to address this question, because of an interesting extension to the scope of the original promise to Abraham. Discussing that promise, Paul in Romans 4 says the following:

> For the promise to Abraham and his offspring *that he would be heir of the world* did not come through the law but through the righteousness of faith. For if it is the adherents of the law who are to be the heirs, faith is null and the promise is void. For the law brings

wrath, but where there is no law there is no transgression. That is why it depends on faith, in order that the promise may rest on grace and be guaranteed to all his offspring – not only to the adherent of the law but also to the one who shares the faith of Abraham, who is the father of us all.

(Rom. 4.13–16, emphasis mine)

When God originally made the promise to Abraham it concerned the land of Canaan that was around him. But here we see that Paul refers to the whole world, and not just part of it, as being the inheritance of all those people who share the faith of Abraham.

This is an altogether different scale of things and the obvious response to it is: if such a mess has been made of sorting out an inheritance limited to the geography of Palestine, how could we possibly believe that the whole world will one day be involved? Once again, we must emphasise that the difference is made by the prospect of repentance and return to God and his Messiah on the part of the nation. The principle that repentance and renewed faith in God can bring renewed prosperity has been seen in microcosm at the national level in the past under the leadership of Joseph, Moses, Joshua, and some of the prophets and kings, like David and Josiah. It has also been seen at the individual level in the case of millions of people from every nation whose lives have been radically changed for the good through faith in Christ – even though they may have suffered in their life's journey, their hope transcended death.

Abraham was told that in him and in his seed all the nations of the world would be blessed. This is an indicator of something large-scale, so in spite of appearances Paul's conviction that the inheritance will extend to the entire world is not entirely unexpected.

Paul's teaching elsewhere is consistent with this view. Writing to the church at Corinth about their incapacity to sort out their church disputes internally, he says:

When one of you has a grievance against another, does he dare go to law before the unrighteous instead of the saints? Or do you not know that the saints will judge the world? And if the world is to be

judged by you, are you incompetent to try trivial cases? Do you not know that we are to judge angels? How much more, then, matters pertaining to this life!
(1 Cor. 6.1–3)

Here we are told that the saints – that is, believers – will one day judge the world and will judge angels. This is no hyperbolic slip of the pen. There is a world to come, reigned over by Christ, in the administration of which his original apostles will have special roles regarding Israel, but even wider than that, believers of all kinds will also be involved. The word translated 'judge' here has the wider connotation of 'administer' or 'lead' and is not confined to making legal decisions. For instance, the judges in the Old Testament were leaders in the general sense.

Again, these ideas of believers being involved in his kingdom in the future originate with Jesus himself. His parables often referred to administrative positions given as rewards for faithful service. For instance, the parable of the nobleman and the ten minas that we have just discussed mentions this. Recall what Jesus said:

'A nobleman went into a far country to receive for himself a kingdom and then return. Calling ten of his servants, he gave them ten minas, and said to them, "Engage in business until I come." But his citizens hated him and sent a delegation after him, saying, "We do not want this man to reign over us." When he returned, having received the kingdom, he ordered these servants to whom he had given the money to be called to him, that he might know what they had gained by doing business. The first came before him, saying, "Lord, your mina has made ten minas more." And he said to him, "Well done, good servant! Because you have been faithful in a very little, you shall have authority over ten cities." And the second came, saying, "Lord, your mina has made five minas." And he said to him, "And you are to be over five cities."'
(Luke 19.12–19)

It is interesting that the rewards are administrative positions over various numbers of cities, depending on how well the servants had traded. This city imagery fits in very well with the fact that Abraham and the heroes of faith were looking for the 'city that has foundations whose designer and builder is God'.

Finally, we should take into account the book of Revelation, which builds on the uniform testimony of earlier Scripture that Jesus will come as Messiah and Son of God to reign on this earth. After the vivid description of the Son of Man coming on a white horse as King of kings and Lord of lords to reign, John the apostle writes about the setting up of that reign:

> Then I saw thrones, and seated on them were those to whom the authority to judge was committed. Also I saw the souls of those who had been beheaded for the testimony of Jesus and for the word of God, and those who had not worshipped the beast or its image and had not received its mark on their foreheads or their hands. They came to life and reigned with Christ for a thousand years. The rest of the dead did not come to life until the thousand years were ended. This is the first resurrection. Blessed and holy is the one who shares in the first resurrection! Over such the second death has no power, but they will be priests of God and of Christ, and they will reign with him for a thousand years.
> (Rev. 20.4–6)

This is the only place in Scripture where a period of a thousand years (the millennium) is mentioned, for which (to my mind unconvincing) reason some think that it is not meant as a real reign on earth, even though a real reign on this earth is at the heart of biblical expectation.

We should note that Revelation here is not talking about the new heavens and the new earth. That is yet to come. It is talking about planet Earth as we know it.

And this makes sense. How could it be that the world could reject and murder its Creator and Redeemer – the Word become human – and expect to have heard the last of him? It must know his reign before its course is done. Paul explains this to the Corinthian church:

> But in fact Christ has been raised from the dead, the firstfruits of those who have fallen asleep. For as by a man came death, by a man

has come also the resurrection of the dead. For as in Adam all die, so also in Christ shall all be made alive. But each in his own order: Christ the firstfruits, then at his coming those who belong to Christ. Then comes the end, when he delivers the kingdom to God the Father after destroying every rule and every authority and power. For he must reign until he has put all his enemies under his feet. The last enemy to be destroyed is death.
(1 Cor. 15.20–26)

The book of Revelation confirms that the last enemy to be overcome will be death – after the reign of Christ on this earth.

Here, in conclusion, is the wisdom of God:

Yet among the mature we do impart wisdom, although it is not a wisdom of this age or of the rulers of this age, who are doomed to pass away. But we impart a secret and hidden wisdom of God, which God decreed before the ages for our glory. None of the rulers of this age understood this, for if they had, they would not have crucified the Lord of glory. But, as it is written,

'What no eye has seen, nor ear heard,
    nor the heart of man imagined,
what God has prepared for those who love him' –

these things God has revealed to us through the Spirit. For the Spirit searches everything, even the depths of God.
(1 Cor. 2.6–10)

There are then much greater things to come. If we can grasp this wisdom of God that has been revealed we shall have fewer difficulties in believing that God's promise to Abraham will reach undreamed-of fulfilment – and we who trust Christ will have a part in it.

# Appendix 2
# How do we know that God speaks?

Central to the Abraham narrative is the claim that God spoke to him. The same is true of the entire Christian story. It is summed up in first words of the book of Hebrews: 'Long ago, at many times and in many ways, God spoke to our fathers by the prophets, but in these last days he has spoken to us by his Son, whom he appointed the heir of all things, through whom also he created the world' (1.1–2).

One of those who was convinced that God spoke through his Son was the apostle Peter, who set out to follow Jesus on a journey that, like Abram's, was to have implications for the entire world. He, together with two other apostles James and John, was marked for life by another experience of the voice of God on a mountain top, in Galilee at the transfiguration of Jesus. The importance of this event is underscored by the fact that it is recorded four times in the New Testament: Matthew 17, Mark 9, Luke 9 and 2 Peter 1. Peter later wrote to explain the significance of what happened:

> For we did not follow cleverly devised myths when we made known to you the power and coming of our Lord Jesus Christ, but we were eyewitnesses of his majesty. For when he received honour and glory from God the Father, and the voice was borne to him by the Majestic Glory, 'This is my beloved Son, with whom I am well pleased', we ourselves heard this very voice borne from heaven, for we were with him on the holy mountain.
> (2 Pet. 1.16–18)

Peter stressed what he saw – the majestic glory of Christ – and what he heard: the voice from heaven. This is what Abraham and Paul also experienced at the start of their respective journeys. And Jesus assured all of his followers that he was the Shepherd of the sheep and his sheep would hear his voice and recognise it (John 10).

We reasonably ask how that actually happens today. First, there is no reason to reject all reports from people, especially those from a Muslim background, who claim to have become Christians by hearing the voice of God either audibly or in dreams. Here is one example among many related by Darren Carlson:

A friend of mine tells of a Persian migrant who arrived at a refugee centre at 6 a.m., visibly upset. He told his story to a Persian pastor: During the night he saw someone dressed in white raise his hand and say, 'Stand up and follow me.' The Persian man said, 'Who are you?' The man in white replied, 'I am the Alpha and the Omega. I'm the way to heaven. No one can go to the Father, except through me.'

He began to ask the Persian pastor: 'Who is he? What am I going to do? Why did he ask me to follow him? How shall I go? Tell me.'

In response, the pastor held out his Bible and asked, 'Have you seen this before?'

'No,' he replied.

'Do you know what it is?'

'No.'

The pastor then opened to the Book of Revelation: 'I am Alpha and Omega, the beginning and the end.' The man started crying and said, 'How can I accept him? How can I follow him?' So the pastor led him in prayer and peace came over him. The pastor then gave the man a Bible and told him to hide it, since the Muslims in the camps could cause him trouble.

But the man replied, 'The Jesus that I met today, he's more powerful than the Muslims in the camp.' He left and an hour later returned with ten more Persians and told the pastor, 'These people want a Bible.' No one had to teach him an evangelistic strategy.[1]

I do not expect the Lord to speak to me that way, although of course he could do if he so desired. On the other hand, I believe that God has indeed spoken to me in several different ways. This is what Scripture teaches. Apart from an audible voice, there is what is often called general revelation, which occurs in two ways. First, through creation, in the sense of the observable universe outside us: 'The heavens declare the glory of God,' says Psalm 19.1. Paul explains this in Romans 1.19–20:

> For what can be known about God is plain to them, because God has shown it to them. For his invisible attributes, namely, his eternal power and divine nature, have been clearly perceived, ever since the creation of the world, in the things that have been made. So they are without excuse.

This means creation is a powerful witness. So much so that, according to Paul, it leaves people without excuse as to God's existence and power. This fact justifies looking for pointers to God in nature and science and has been a primary motivation in some of my life's work.

Creation is a witness outside us, so to speak. There is a second witness inside us, conscience, through which God communicates moral concepts to us. Paul explains this in Romans 2:

> For when Gentiles, who do not have the law, by nature do what the law requires, they are a law to themselves, even though they do not have the law. They show that the work of the law is written on their hearts, while their conscience also bears witness, and their conflicting thoughts accuse or even excuse them on that day when, according to my gospel, God judges the secrets of men by Christ Jesus.
> (Rom. 2.14–16)

We human beings are created in God's image as moral beings. Our conscience is connected to God's law, although we need to be aware that it can become dulled or even seared and give us a false reading, as it were, so we need constantly to refresh it with our reading of the Scriptures.

Perhaps the most important way in which God speaks is by special revelation in his word, the Bible. In John 16.12–15 Jesus made the following promise to his disciples:

> 'I still have many things to say to you, but you cannot bear them now. When the Spirit of truth comes, he will guide you into all the

truth, for he will not speak on his own authority, but whatever he hears he will speak, and he will declare to you the things that are to come. He will glorify me, for he will take what is mine and declare it to you. All that the Father has is mine; therefore I said that he will take what is mine and declare it to you.'

Here, the Lord Jesus gives divine supernatural authority to the writings of the apostles, an authority that the Old Testament Scriptures already possessed. That is made evident in the second part of the passage we considered above (2 Pet. 1.19–20), where Peter outlines how we in our day can experience the glory and hear the voice of God through his word.

For many of us, the first time we hear God speaking is when we listen to someone preach from a passage of Scripture that suddenly and forcefully gets to our conscience and heart, convicting us of our sinfulness and need for a Saviour and leading us to trust Christ for salvation. We hear a voice, the human voice of the speaker, and yet we detect behind it the authentic voice of God.

Or, we may suddenly be filled with a sense of wonder as we see the way in which Scripture fits beautifully and convincingly together, mediating a deep conviction of truth embedded in an awareness of God's immediate presence. The effect can be life-changing – and that is exactly what happened to me.

The apostles Peter, James and John were privileged to hear the direct and audible voice of God, who spoke to them as Jesus was transfigured before them on the mountain. For them it was conclusive evidence that Jesus was the Son of God. Yet, even as Peter relates the incident, he has not forgotten the vast majority of us who were not present. For he goes on to write:

And we have something more sure, the prophetic word, to which you will do well to pay attention as to a lamp shining in a dark place, until the day dawns and the morning star rises in your hearts, knowing this first of all, that no prophecy of Scripture comes from someone's own interpretation. For no prophecy was ever produced by the will of man, but men spoke from God as they were carried along by the Holy Spirit.
(2 Pet. 1.19–21)

Here Peter tells us that we – that is, his fellow believers of all generations – have something 'more sure' than his experience on the mountain; namely, the prophetic word of Scripture.

His statement could be understood in different ways. First, the transfiguration on the mountain inevitably had a strong subjective dimension in terms of psychological impact and, as we said above, we all know what scepticism certain psychologists and psychiatrists, especially those of the Freudian school, can show towards people claiming to 'see' and 'hear' things. This does not mean that his experience was not authentic, but it could make it difficult to convince others of the fact. Peter may well, therefore, mean here that Scripture, ranging as it does over many authors and centuries, is another source of seeing the glory and hearing the voice that is not so easily explained away.

The reason for this, as Peter explains, is that Scripture does not come from clever human analysis of situations; it is not a human production at all. It has a source external to the biblical authors: God's Holy Spirit moving in their hearts and minds. Therefore, because of its thoroughly supernatural nature, Scripture can act as a powerful light 'in a dark place, until the day dawns and the morning star rises in your hearts'.

Peter reminds us that Jesus will return in glory as the Day Star and, using a magnificent metaphor, tells us that in the meantime paying attention to Scripture can make this hope so real for us that we sense the rising of the 'star' in our hearts in a genuine experience of the voice of God. Peter is not only saying that Scripture *can* do this, but that this is its *prime intention* and because of this it gives us insight into how we should approach the word of God.

As I write these words my mind goes back some years to the death of a close friend from Cambridge days, Nigel Lee. He was diagnosed with an inoperable tumour and, knowing that it was terminal, he asked me to speak at his funeral. I asked him what he would like me to say. Without hesitation he replied: 'Tell them to do what we did all those years ago in our student Bible study group in Cambridge – to soak our minds prayerfully in Scripture until the face of God appears.' He added: 'And then they will have something to say.'

I had learned this from my mentor, the late Professor David Gooding, and it had proved to be the key to living experience of God. How shall one

315

describe such experiences? That is not easy, since they are subjective by definition. Yet they are, I believe, direct and valid perceptions of reality. They are in a way like perception of the beauty of music, flowers, birds, mountains or stars and sunsets – our perception is direct and immediate without any intermediate chain of reasoning required to support it. We have no hesitation in thinking such perceptions are real. All I can do is humbly testify that they are real. God does fulfil his promise to speak through the word, but he may wait to see how serious we are about hearing his voice.

How easily we content ourselves with looking at Scripture simply to prepare material for others – talks, meditations, sermons and so on – all important in their place, but if we do that without waiting on God to speak through the word, we have missed the whole purpose of Scripture. As a result, the talks we produce often have neither spiritual authority nor impact. However, if we are prepared to spend time prayerfully in the word of God, there come times when we may be overwhelmed by the sense of truth that we are seeing.

It is elementary logic that if we have not heard God's voice in this way, if we have not sensed his glory in the face of Jesus Christ in the word, we will have little to say to the world that will count. Therefore, as we study together the call and life of Abraham, our prayer should be that the Lord will speak to us, reveal his glory and deepen our grip on what he has in store for us.

A question remains in my mind that I sometimes ask myself. Would I wish to hear the voice in the same direct audible way as did Abraham, Moses, Gideon, Samuel, Daniel and the apostles, among others?

To them, the voice of God spoke things that were of massive import for the whole history of the world. They were words of calling and commission to bear an enormous weight of responsibility as they engaged in huge tasks that required immense courage, resourcefulness and, in some cases, great pain and suffering. Think, for instance, of the responsibility placed on the young Samuel to bring a message of devastating judgement on the high priest Eli and his house. Think of the weight of knowledge given to Abraham about the lengthy future suffering of his offspring. However, it is true that when God calls someone to a task at any level he equips the person called for it – as the lives of Abraham and Samuel exemplify.

I have often pondered the fact that whether God speaks directly or not is clearly a complex matter. This is seen, for instance, in that at least one major biblical figure, Joseph, seems to be an exception. Yes, he had dreams from God that played an important role in his life, but dreams are much more open to interpretation than God's audible voice. As I have pointed out in my book on the life of Joseph, it would seem that an important element in equipping him for his pivotal role was the fact that he had to live with the silence of God.[2]

In addition, in the case of those to whom God speaks directly, there is the matter of when he does so. For instance, Job suffers his massive losses and the pressures from his wife and friends to admit guilt, before God speaks and exonerates him.

In light of all this, I feel deeply honoured to have a very real, personal and indeed precious sense of calling, mainly mediated by God's current normal way of communicating through his word – where I have to wrestle before God to understand it and where I may often have no clear sense of his guidance. We less prominent members of the Christian body are also privileged to serve in the train of the mighty saints of God – indeed, God himself regards us as necessary (1 Cor. 12).

Nevertheless, I have no doubt that God can and still does speak directly to people – often in dreams, as numerous reports from people of, for example, a Muslim background testify, and the quality of their conversion establishes.

It is one thing when God himself takes the initiative to speak to someone. It is an entirely different thing when people on their own initiative strive to hear the divine voice in an audible form. Experience shows that they may not really understand what they are wishing for themselves. It would appear to be much wiser to leave the matter entirely to God.

What we need to beware of is the all-too-common danger of seeking to hear an audible voice from God (or to have some spectacular 'supernatural' gift or equivalent) that we think will give us assurance of really being true believers rather than getting our confidence from God's word.

The words of Jesus are apposite. When the disciples were in danger of falling into that trap and placing their confidence even in the genuine gifts God had given them, he warned them not to rejoice in that but to rejoice that their names were written in heaven (Luke 10.20).

In the end, whether audibly or not, God will speak to his children and authenticate his word in their hearts and minds. It carries his unique authority. We will hear the 'still small voice' if, and only if, we are prepared to spend time in Scripture listening for it. Then our convictions will be rooted in the word of God, where they should always be.

For me, that rooting of convictions began at home when I learned to love Scripture and had a desire to follow it. It continued when I arrived at university determined to nail my Christian colours to the mast from the beginning. It continued as I began to teach the Bible to individuals, then gradually to larger and larger groups. The voice of God in Scripture was enough to drive this work and enable me to mature as a Christian.

Yet, having said all that, there have been occasions when I have sensed God speaking in a much more direct way in the context of leading me to a radically new sphere of activity. I will mention two in particular.

The first occurred in 1975 when I was in Germany on a research year. I met a Hungarian believer in Berlin who, out of the blue, took out his diary and asked me to give him a date when I would come to Hungary. Very embarrassed and not wishing to offend I said: 'July next year,' and specified a date. I confess that I thought I could worm my way out of it later. And yet I could not get it out of my mind and, leaving my wife and family behind in Cardiff, I drove to Budapest, and what I experienced there changed the direction of my Christian work profoundly. It became very clear in the end that, through the voice of a humble Hungarian believer, I had heard God's voice calling me to do Bible teaching in Eastern Europe.

Fourteen years later, I was equally clearly directed to the former Soviet Union – a story for another time.

For all these reasons I am convinced that God speaks. He is, after all, the living God, and speech is one evidence of intelligent life.

# Notes

## Introduction

1  J. Sacks, *The Great Partnership: God, science and the search for meaning* (London: Hodder & Stoughton), p. 8.

2  Christopher Watkin, *Biblical Critical Theory* (Grand Rapids: Zondervan, 2022), p. 227.

3  Alfred Edersheim, *The Life and Times of Jesus the Messiah* (London: Longmans, Green and Co., 1883), p. 272.

4  I have found that when speaking with my Jewish friends it is better to use the original Hebrew names rather than their Westernised equivalents.

5  Colin Hemer, *The Book of Acts in the Setting of Hellenistic History* (Tubingen: J. C. B. Mohr, 1989).

6  Peter J. Williams, *Can We Trust the Gospels?* (Grand Rapids: Crossway, 2018).

7  Alan Millard, private communication, reproduced with permission.

8  Alan Millard, *Treasures from Bible Times* (Tring: Lion, 1985), p. 59.

9  Kenneth Kitchen, *On the Reliability of the Old Testament* (Grand Rapids: Eerdmans, 2003), pp. 364–8.

10  Kitchen, *On the Reliability*, p. 366.

11  R. K. Harrison, *Introduction to the Old Testament* (Grand Rapids: Eerdmans, 1969), p. 112.

12  A. R. Millard and D. J. Wiseman (eds), *Essays on the Patriarchal Narratives* (Leicester: IVP, 1980).

13  Robert Alter, *The Art of Biblical Narrative* (New York: Basic Books, 1981), p. 51.

14  Leon Kass, *Founding God's Nation: Reading Exodus* (New Haven: Yale University Press, 2021), p. 66.

15  Leon Kass, *The Beginning of Wisdom – Reading Genesis* (Chicago: University of Chicago Press, 2006), pp.18–19.

## 1 The city that reached for the sky

1 Robert Alter, *Genesis Translation and Commentary* (New York: Norton, 1996).

2 K. A. Kitchen, *On the Reliability of the Old Testament* (Grand Rapids: Eerdmans, 2003), p. 427.

3 The ancient inhabitants had no agreed name for their land and simply vaguely called it 'the Land', or 'Sumer', 'Akkad', 'Babylon', although these were sub-regions.

4 *The Antiquities of the Jews*, 1.109–1.119.

5 For a fascinating perspective on the history of city culture, see the Sunday Times Book of the Year, *The Dawn of Everything: A new history of humanity* (London: Allen Lane, 2021), by the late anthropologist (and political activist) David Graeber and archaeologist David Wengrow. This book challenges much of the generally received understanding of the early history of humanity – particularly the ideas that we are wiser than our ancient ancestors and that social history advanced in a linear way from the primitive to the more sophisticated.

6 See: www.britannica.com/place/Babylon-ancient-city-Mesopotamia-Asia (accessed 3 May 2023).

7 Sumer, the southernmost part of Mesopotamia.

8 L. Wittgenstein, *Tractatus Logico-Philosophicus*, Proposition 5.6 (1922).

9 Aristotle, *The Politics*, tr. T. A. Sinclair, revised and re-presented by Trevor J. Saunders (London: Penguin Books, 1992), 1253a7.

10 C. Lord (ed. and tr.), *Aristotle's Politics*, 1st edn (Chicago: University of Chicago Press, 1984), pp. 35, 36–7.

11 *Diaspora* is Greek for 'scattering of seed' (see Acts 8.1).

12 Leon Kass, *The Beginning of Wisdom – Reading Genesis* (Chicago: University of Chicago Press, 2006), p. 231.

13 *The Times*, Credo, 31 August 2013.

14 Jacques Ellul, *The Meaning of the City* (Grand Rapids: Eerdmans, 1970), p. 16.

15 For an application of these ideas at the personal level, see chapter 2 of David A. Smith, *Hidden Agendas* (Fearn: Christian Focus Publications, 2022).

16 Philip Nobel, *Lust for Height*, American Enterprise Institute, 23

February 2007, available at: www.aei.org/articles/lust-for-height/ (accessed 3 May 2023).

17 From Assyrian *ziqquratu*, meaning 'height' or 'pinnacle'.

18 Latin for 'man god' or 'god man'.

19 For more on this important issue, see my *2084: Artificial Intelligence and the future of humanity* (Grand Rapids: Zondervan, 2020).

20 Gordon Wenham, *Genesis* (Grand Rapids: Zondervan, 2015), p. 235.

21 1 Samuel 25 tells of a foolish man called Nabal.

22 Wenham, *Genesis*, p. 209.

23 A common biblical metaphor for powerful nations or leaders.

24 For more detail on this see the author's *2084*.

25 Old English for 'six miles'.

26 The earliest commentary on the Tower of Babel is found in the book of Jubilees X.18–27 (c. 200 BC), where we read: 'And they built it: forty and three years were they building it; its breadth was 203 bricks, and the height (of a brick) was the third of one; its height amounted to 5433 cubits and 2 palms, and (the extent of one wall was) thirteen stades (and of the other thirty stades).' That would make it about 1.6 miles high – higher than the Burj Khalifa – but less than 'sax myle'!

27 See my book *2084*.

28 Comment, 13 May 2021. Interview with Anne Snyder, available at: www.cardus.ca/comment/article/forging-a-people-sustaining-a-nation/?mc_cid=2f66d06550&mc_eid=19b161f5a7 (accessed 3 May 2023).

29 'Why the past ten years of American life have been uniquely stupid', *The Atlantic*, 11 April 2022.

30 Martin Gurri, *The Revolt of the Public* (San Francisco: Stripe Press, 2018).

31 See D. A. Carson, *The Intolerance of Tolerance* (Grand Rapids: Eerdmans, 2013).

32 Dorothy L. Sayers, *Christian Letters to a Post-Christian World* (Grand Rapids: Eerdmans, 1969), p. 152.

33 *Christianity Today*, 21 April 2022.

34 'Does Free Exercise of Religion Deserve Constitutional Mention?', 54, *American Journal of Jurisprudence*, 41 (2009).

35 Entry under Nimrod, at: www.jewishencyclopedia.com/articles/11548-nimrod (accessed 17 March 2023).

36 Yuval Noah Harari, *Homo Deus* (London: Vintage, 2017), p. 49.

37 Harari, *Homo Deus*, p. 24.

38 For an introduction to artificial intelligence and a critique of Harari, see my book *2084*.

39 *That Hideous Strength*, The Cosmic Trilogy (London: Bodley Head, 1989), p. 618.

40 'LEWISIANA: George Orwell on C. S. Lewis, That Hideous Strength', *lewisiana.nl*.

41 (Oxford: Lion Hudson, 2015).

## 2 From Shem to Abram

1 K. A. Kitchen, *On the Reliability of the Old Testament* (Grand Rapids: Eerdmans, 2003), pp. 358–9.

2 Some have questioned whether this is really too early for Abraham and have argued that he lived at the earlier time of those Sumerian city-states.

3 Kitchen, *On the Reliability*, p. 320.

4 G. Roux, *Ancient Iraq* (London: Penguin Books, 1992).

5 Roux, *Ancient Iraq*, pp. 86ff.

6 Not as large as the much later construction at Babylon in the reign of Nebuchadnezzar (sometimes written as Nebuchadrezzar). It had a square base 91 metres per side and reputedly had seven storeys, making it around 90 metres high.

7 Roux, *Ancient Iraq*, p. 137.

8 See Roux, *Ancient Iraq*, p.19. See also K. R. Nemet-Nejat, *Daily Life in Ancient Mesopotamia* (Peabody: Hendrickson Publishers, 2002).

9 *Cuneus* is Latin for 'wedge'.

10 See O. Neugebauer, *The Exact Sciences in Antiquity* (Providence Rhode Island: Brown University Press, 1957). An interesting account of mathematics, medicine and astronomy is to be found in H. W. F. Saggs, *op. cit.*, chapter 14.

11 This is shown by the fact that it contains medieval names for countries in Europe.

12 There is also an eighteenth-century literary forgery by Jacob with the same name.

13 Book of Jasher, chapter 9.

14 Roux, *Ancient Iraq*, p. 85.

15 Jubilees Midrash and in Qur'an.

16 Leon Kass, *The Beginning of Wisdom – Reading Genesis* (Chicago: University of Chicago Press, 2006), p. 39.

17 For more detail, see the author's *Seven Days that Divide the World*, 10th anniversary rev. edn (Grand Rapids: Zondervan, 2021).

## Part 2 Introduction

1 Although Egypt is not explicitly mentioned in C, it is nevertheless implied to be identified later in Exodus.

## 3 The call of Abram

1 Despite appearances the city Haran (Kharran) and the person Haran do not bear the same name – Hebrew has two different letters (*heh* and *het*) that are often rendered by the English 'h', although the second would be better represented as ch or kh.

2 R. Alter, *The Art of Biblical Narrative* (New York: Basic Books, 1981), p. 182.

3 See: www.mentalhealth.org.uk/a-to-z/h/hearing-voices (accessed 20 March 2023).

4 I have argued the case for this supernaturalist view in a number of books, including: *Gunning for God, Cosmic Chemistry* and *Can Science Explain Everything?*

5 See my *Can Science Explain Everything?*

6 This in my view is too restrictive a definition since it equates science with applied naturalism and so prevents following evidence if that evidence arguably points beyond the natural. I have discussed this important issue in my book *Cosmic Chemistry* (Oxford: Lion Hudson, 2021).

7 Contrary to what some think, the natural sciences and rationality are not co-extensive. History, literature, philosophy and many other disciplines are rational, but are not science.

8 *Lech* is the imperative of the verb 'to go'. *Lecha* is usually understood to be made up of the preposition *Le* that means 'to', 'toward', 'for', together with a suffix *cha* that makes it masculine second person singular 'you': hence 'to you, for you'. The interesting thing is that

although the words are identical without vowel pointing, they are pronounced slightly differently and are grammatically unrelated. It would seem to have an aura of poetry about it, with an implication of deeper meaning.

9 Available at: https://rabbisacks.org/covenant-conversation-5768-lech-lecha-the-heroism-of-ordinary-life/ (accessed 6 May 2023).

10 Available at: https://rabbisacks.org/covenant-conversation-5768-lech-lecha-the-heroism-of-ordinary-life/ (accessed 21 March 2023).

11 A delightful Jewish children's song about it can be heard at: www.chabad.org/kids/article_cdo/aid/528140/jewish/Lech-Lecha-II.htm (accessed 8 May 2023).

## 4 From Haran to Canaan

1 Presumably meaning they were bought as slaves.

2 Available at: www.jmtour.com/media/Bible-Age-of-Humans-Genetic-Entropy-WUBC.pdf (accessed 8 May 2023).

3 The oldest person in the world at the time of writing is said to be 118. Life expectancy has roughly doubled in the past 100 years.

4 Leon Kass, *The Beginning of Wisdom – Reading Genesis* (Chicago: University of Chicago Press, 2006), p. 263.

5 Christopher Booker, *The Seven Basic Plots* (London: Continuum, 2006).

6 J. Sacks, *The Great Partnership* (London: Hodder & Stoughton, 2011), p. 8.

7 *Tractatus Logico-Philosophicus* 6.4.

8 *Antiquities* i. 7, § 8.

9 *Delphi Collected Works of Eusebius* (Delphi Classics, 2019), ch. 17.3.

10 For detailed examples in the book of Acts, see David Gooding, *True to the Faith* (Belfast: Myrtlefield House, 2013).

11 Near Nablus in the West Bank.

12 See: www.cardus.ca/comment/article/forging-a-people-sustaining-a-nation/?mc_cid=2f66d06550&mc_eid=19b161f5a7 (accessed 21 March 2023).

13 Bethel means 'house of God'.

14 Altars were made of different materials; e.g. Moses was instructed to make an altar of earth in Exodus 20.24 and another of wood and so on in Exodus 27.1.

## 5 From Canaan to Egypt

1 See my *Determined to Believe?* (Oxford: Lion Hudson, 2017).
2 Available at: www.chabad.org/therebbe/article_cdo/aid/110320/jewish/Torah-Studies-Lech-Lecha.htm (accessed 21 March 2023).
3 See: www.cardus.ca/comment/article/forging-a-people-sustaining-a-nation/?mc_cid=2f66d06550&mc_eid=19b161f5a7 (accessed 21 March 2023).
4 See the comments on longevity in Chapter 4.
5 Cited by Christ in Matt. 19.5 and by Paul in Eph. 5.31.
6 L. Kass, *The Beginning of Wisdom* (Chicago: University of Chicago Press, 2006), p. 275.
7 Kass, *The Beginning*, p. 266.
8 Andrew Sims, *Is Faith Delusion?* (London/New York: Continuum, 2009).
9 M. Parris, *The Times*, 27 December 2008.
10 See Karen Rhea Nemet-Nejat, *Daily Life in Ancient Mesopotamia* (Peabody: Hendrickson, 2002), pp. 131–41.
11 See the Jewish Women's Archive available at: https://jwa.org/encyclopedia/article/sarah-midrash-and-aggadah (accessed 22 March 2023).
12 *Antiquities* i. 7, § 8.
13 See Robert Alter, *Genesis Translation and Commentary* (New York: W. W. Norton & Co., 1996), p. 52.

## 6 Abram and Lot

1 See my book *Joseph: A Story of Love, Hate, Slavery, Power, and Forgiveness* (Grand Rapids: Crossway, 2019).
2 This is the only place where Abram is described as a Hebrew.
3 R. Alter, *Genesis Translation and Commentary* (New York: W. W. Norton & Co., 1998), p. 51, n. 5.
4 P. Copan, *Is God a Moral Monster?* (Grand Rapids: Baker Books, 2011). See also chapter 6 of my book *Gunning for God* (Oxford: Lion Hudson, 2011).

## 7 Abram and Melchizedek

1 According to the principle enunciated in Hebrews 7.7: 'It is beyond dispute that the inferior is blessed by the superior.'

2 Available at: www.christianity.com/bible/nlt/genesis/14-21 (accessed 6 May 2023). Calvin held the same view.

3 Available at: https://biblehub.com/commentaries/genesis/14-23.htm (accessed 6 May 2023).

4 R. Alter, *Genesis Translation and Commentary* (New York: W. W. Norton & Co., 1996). p. 61, ns. 19 and 20.

5 See: www.britannica.com/contributor/Theodorus-P-van-Baaren/134 (accessed 23 March 2023).

6 See: www.quora.com/What-is-the-oldest-monotheistic-religion (accessed 23 March 2023).

7 The Hebrew word translated 'said' is a technical term designating an oracle, or solemn prophetic statement of God.

8 David Gooding, *An Unshakeable Kingdom* (Belfast: Myrtlefield House, 2013).

9 See my *Determined to Believe* (Oxford: Lion Hudson, 2017).

10 D. Gooding, *According to Luke* (Belfast: Myrtlefield House, 2013), p. 357.

11 I refer readers interested in having more detail on these issues to my book *A Good Return* (Fearn: Christian Focus Publications, 2023).

## 8 Justification by faith

1 See the entries on Justification and Righteousness in *Vine's Complete Expository Dictionary of Old and New Testament Words* (Nashville: Thomas Nelson, 1996).

2 Betrand Russell, *Human Society in Ethics and Politics* (London: Allen and Unwin, 1954).

3 Richard Dawkins, *The Selfish Gene* (Oxford: Oxford University Press, 1976), p. 330.

4 *Vine's Complete Expository Dictionary of Old and New Testament Words.*

5 *The Guardian*, 19 October 2006.

6 Aristotle, *Metaphysics*, Book 1 (London: Penguin Classics, 1998), 980a.

7 C. E. B. Cranfield, *The International Critical Commentary*, *The Epistle to the Romans* Vol. I (Edinburgh: T & T Clark Ltd, 1975), p. 95.

## 9 God's covenant with Abram

1 For a very instructive treatment of covenants, see the excellent book detailing how the New Testament uses the Old by David Gooding,

*The Riches of Divine Wisdom* (Belfast: Myrtlefield House, 2013), ch. 10.

2 It refers to the covenant made between God and Israel at Sinai – more about that later.

3 The word for 'wealth' is that used earlier for 'goods' – that particular topic is still in the background.

4 For more detailed analysis see my *Gunning for God* (Oxford: Lion Hudson, 2011), pp. 124ff.

5 E. Wiesel, *Night* (New York: Hill and Wang, 1960), p. 32.

## 10 The new covenant

1 Louis Berkhof, *Systematic Theology* (Grand Rapids: Eerdmans, 1949), pp. 262–3. He also says that *berit* is 'derived from the Assyrian word *beritu*, meaning "to bind." This would at once point to the covenant as a bond. The question of the derivation is of no great importance for the construction of the doctrine. The word *berith* may denote a mutual voluntary agreement (dipleuric = two sided, gk pleura = side), but also a disposition or arrangement imposed by one party on another (monopleuric). Its exact meaning does not depend on the etymology of the word, nor on the historical development of the concept, but simply on the parties concerned. In the measure in which one of the parties is subordinate and has less to say, the covenant acquires the character of a disposition or arrangement imposed by one party on the other. *Berith* then becomes synonymous with *choq* (appointed statute or ordinance), Ex. 34:10; Isa. 59:21; Jer. 31:36; 33:20; 34:13. Hence we also find that *karath berith* (to cut a covenant) is construed not only with the prepositions *'am* and *ben* (with), but also with *lamedh* (to), Jos. 9:6; Isa. 55:3; 61:8; Jer. 32:40.

The Greek word διαθηκη (*diatheke*), usually translated "covenant" in English versions of the Bible, is a legal term denoting a formal and legally binding declaration of benefits to be given by one party to another, with or without conditions attached. In secular contexts it was most often used of a "last will and testament." In the Greek version of the Old Testament διαθηκη was used as the ordinary rendering for the Hebrew word ברית. ברית (*berith*) is also translated "covenant" in English versions, but, like διαθηκη, it also refers to legal dispositions or pledges which may or may not have the character of an "agreement." Sometimes a ברית is more in the nature of a one-sided promise or grant.'

2 'Remember' is a technical legal term here and refers to the process in a trial of reading the record of what the person in the dock is accused of.

## 11 A surrogate son

1 R. Clarke, *Forty Women: Unseen women from Eden to Easter* (London: IVP, 2021), ch. 2.

2 Peter Saunders, in *Nucleus*, CMF Publications, Spring 2003.

3 See: www.cmf.org.uk.

4 E. Margesson and S. McGowan, *Just the Two of Us?* (Leicester: IVP, 2010).

5 R. K. Harrison, *Introduction to the Old Testament* (Grand Rapids: Eerdmans, 1969), p. 109. See also Karen Rhea Nemet-Nejat, *Daily Life in Ancient Mesopotamia* (Peabody: Hendrickson, 2002), p. 140.

6 A female member of a religious order, sometimes called a 'sister of a god'.

7 J. B. Pritchard, *Ancient Near Eastern Texts in Relation to the Old Testament (ANET)*, (Princeton: Princeton University Press, 1969), p. 543.

8 Pritchard, *Ancient Near Eastern* Texts, p. 172; CoS 2. 345.

9 See e.g. G. Wenham, *Genesis*, Word Biblical Commentary, Vol. 2 (Grand Rapids: Zondervan, 2015), p. 8.

10 Clarke, *Forty Women*, p. 5.

11 Ishmael means 'God hears'.

12 Clarke, *Forty Women*, pp. 8, 9.

13 Compare this with the experience of Leah, Jacob's wife, in Genesis 29.32ff.

14 Our Daily Bread Publishing have produced a book called *God Sees Her: 365 devotions for women by women* (2020).

15 See article by Richard Alleyne, Science Correspondent, *Daily Telegraph*, 7 September 2009.

16 For an excellent account of the implications of being made in the image of God, written by a Christian professor of neonatal medicine and bioethics, see John Wyatt, *Matters of Life and Death* (Leicester: IVP, 2009), pp. 51–63.

17 C. S. Lewis, *The Abolition of Man* (London: Fount, 1943), pp. 34, 42.

18 CMF file 47 (2012) – Surrogacy. See: www.cmf.org.uk/resources/publications/content/?context=article&id=25772 (accessed 29 March 2023).

19 See, for example, the webpage in previous note.

## 12 The covenant of circumcision

1 Christopher Watkin, *Biblical Critical Theory* (Grand Rapids: Zondervan, 2022), p. 229.

2 The imagery of building is once more of interest.

3 See Dr Peter Saunders, at: www.cmf.org.uk/resources/publications/content/?context=article&id=25716 (accessed 29 March 2023).

4 Many use infant baptism to fulfil this role, although care is needed here that neither the parents nor the child, when older, mistakenly think that the ceremony itself conveys regeneration.

5 The Hebrew word here for laughed is *tsachaq*, from which 'Isaac' is derived.

6 See: https://blogs.webmd.com/womens-health/20200622/am-i-too-old-to-have-a-baby (accessed 30 March 2023).

7 Reminding Abraham of the meaning of 'Ishmael' ('God hears'). This is a play on words in Hebrew, where two words convey what takes six in English translation.

## 13 The judgement of Sodom

1 J. Sacks, *The Great Partnership* (London: Hodder & Stoughton, 2011), p. 299.

2 Contrast the use of 'know' to describe God's appraisal of Sodom referred to in verse 21.

3 C. S. Lewis, *The Four Loves* (London: William Collins, 1960).

4 Ancient Canaanite cities had a large room or chamber at the gate, in which business and administration were conducted.

5 See my YouTube debate with Dawkins, 'Has Science Buried God?' at: www.youtube.com/watch?v=OVEuQg_Mglw (accessed 31 March 2023).

6 *Vine's Complete Expository Dictionary of Old and New Testament Word* (Nashville: Thomas Nelson, 1996), p. 139; *The Brown–Driver–Briggs*

*Hebrew and English Lexicon* (Peabody: Hendrickson Publishers, 2020)., p. 613b. Compare Genesis 15.5.

7 Another parallel with Noah, who got drunk after the Flood (see Gen. 9.20–27).

8 We might compare the case of Tamar who, in her desperation to have children, seduced Judah, her father-in-law (see Gen. 38).

9 The name can be read as *me'av* ('from the father'), thus referring to his incestuous origin. Ammon probably derives from *ammi* ('my people') – which may indicate that the women were proud of what they had done.

10 The name Molech (sometimes written Moloch) derives from combining the consonants of the Hebrew *melech* ('king') with the vowels of *boshet* ('shame').

11 L. Kass, *The Beginning of Wisdom – Reading Genesis* (Chicago: University of Chicago Press, 2006), p. 329.

## 14 Sarah and Hagar

1 His name means 'my father is king'.

2 Derek Kidner, *Genesis* (Leicester: IVP, 1967), pp. 138–9.

3 The conception had an evident supernatural dimension. Its description is reminiscent of the account of the conception of John the Baptist in the Gospel of Luke chapter 1.

4 R. K. Harrison, *Introduction to the Old Testament* (Grand Rapids: Eerdmans, 1969), p. 109.

5 Fergus Millar, *Rome, the Greek World and the East, Vol. 3. The Greek World, the Jews and the East* (Chapel Hill: University of North Carolina Press, 2006), pp. 351–77.

6 I have investigated in detail that matter of God's sovereignty and human responsibility in my book *Determined to Believe?* (Oxford: Lion Hudson, 2017).

7 D. Gooding, *The Riches of Divine Wisdom* (Belfast: Myrtlefield House, 2013), p. 228.

8 T. Holland, *Dominion: The making of the Western mind* (London: Little, Brown, 2019).

9 Jürgen Habermas, *Time of Transitions* (New York: Polity, 2006), pp. 150–51.

10  Gooding, *The Riches*, p. 235.

11  Gooding, *The Riches*, pp. 236–8.

12  Gooding, *The Riches*, pp. 238–9.

13  It could also be translated as 'Well of Seven'.

14  See John Rhinehart's book, *Gospel Patrons* (Minneapolis: Reclaimed Publishing, 2013).

15  All genuine gifts of God are by definition supernatural, the more important ones being, according to the New Testament, teaching, evangelism and pastoring.

## 15  God tests Abraham

1  In a letter to his friend Robert Klopstock, June 1921.

2  See Daniel Conway (ed.), *Kierkegaard's Fear and Trembling: A critical guide* (Cambridge: Cambridge University Press, 2015).

3  See his contribution to that book.

4  Muslims believe that God told Abraham to sacrifice Ishmael (Ismail) – although the Qur'an does not name the son. There is, however, considerable difference of opinion on the matter among Muslim scholars.

5  Aryeh Amihay, *Theory and Practice in Essene Law* (Oxford: Oxford University Press, 2017), p. 74.

6  See David S. Stern, 'The Bind of Responsibility, Kierkegaard, Derrida and the Akedah of Isaac', *Philosophy Today*, 47 (1), 2003, 34–43.

7  An identical situation was faced by Zacharias and Elizabeth in Luke 1 regarding John the Baptist.

8  Calvin, *Institutes* I, 565.

9  Available at: https://outorah.org/p/21996 (accessed 6 April 2023).

10  2 Chronicles 3.1 says that Solomon built the Temple on Mount Moriah.

11  D. Gooding, *The Riches of Divine Wisdom* (Belfast: Myrtlefield House, 2013), p. 337.

12  C. S. Lewis, *The Screwtape Letters* (London: Fontana Books, 1955), Letter XXIX, p. 149.

13  L. Kass, *The Beginning of Wisdom – Reading Genesis* (Chicago: University of Chicago Press, 2006), p. 359.

14  Kass, *Beginning of Wisdom*, p. 361, my emphasis.

## 16 Applying the Moriah experience

1 See my book *Against the Flow* (Oxford: Lion Hudson, 2015).
2 See Albert van der Heide, *'Now I know': Five Centuries of Aquedah Exegesis* (Cham: Springer, 2017), p. 10.
3 John C. Lennox, *Gunning for God* (Oxford: Lion Hudson, 2011), ch. 5.
4 John C. Lennox, *Where is God in a Coronavirus World?* (London: The Good Book Company, 2020).

## 17 Lessons from the life of Sarah

1 In Meir Steinberg's essay, 'Double Cave, Double Talk: The indirections of biblical dialogue, in Jason P. Rosenblatt and Joseph C. Sitterson, Jr (eds), *Not in Heaven: Coherence and complexity in biblical narrative* (Bloomington: Indiana University Press, 1991), pp. 32, 31.
2 Rosenblatt and Sitterson, *Not in Heaven*, p. 34.
3 See Robert Alter, *Genesis Translation and Commentary* (New York: Norton, 1996), p. 111.
4 R. K. Harrison, *Introduction to the Old Testament* (Grand Rapids: Eerdmans, 1969), p. 112.
5 See the Jewish Women's Archive at: https://jwa.org/encyclopedia/article/sarah-midrash-and-aggadah (accessed 10 April 2023).
6 Alan Richardson, *An Introduction to the Theology of the New Testament* (London: SCM Press, 1958), p. 258.

## 18 A bridge for the promised seed

1 Martin Heide, 'The Domestication of the Camel: Biological, Archaeological and Inscriptional Evidence from Mesopotamia, Egypt, Israel and Arabia, and Literary Evidence from the Hebrew Bible', *Ugarit-Forschungen* (Munster: Ugarit-Verlag, 2011), pp. 358–9.
2 Which, incidentally, gives us insight into the rather greedy character that he later displayed in his involvement in the betrothal of Jacob, Rebekah's son.
3 For more on God's providence, freewill and determinism, see my book *Determined to Believe?* (Oxford: Lion Hudson, 2017).

## 19 The last days of Abraham – and beyond

1 For instance, parables do not give the names of people. See also David Gooding, *According to Luke* (Belfast: Myrtlefield House, 2013), p. 291, footnote 3.

2 Gooding, *According to Luke*, p. 291.

## Appendix 1 A brief history of Israel

1 J. Lennox, *Against the Flow* (Oxford: Lion Hudson, 2015), p. 297.

2 Josephus, *Jewish Antiquities*, 12.136.

3 Available at: www.history.com/this-day-in-history/state-of-israel-proclaimed (accessed 18 April 2023).

4 For more detail on this, see my *Determined to Believe?* (Oxford: Lion Hudson, 2017), ch. 16.

5 The interested reader is referred to the appendix on the kingdom in my book *Against the Flow*.

## Appendix 2 How do we know that God speaks?

1 See www.thegospelcoalition.org/article/muslims-dream-jesus/ (accessed 3 May 2023).

2 John C. Lennox, *Joseph* (Grand Rapids: Crossway, 2019).

# Bibliography

Alter, Robert, *The Art of Biblical Narrative*, New York: Basic Books, 1981.
——, *Genesis Translation and Commentary*, New York: Norton, 1996.
Amihay, Aryeh, *Theory and Practice in Essene Law*, Oxford: Oxford University Press, 2017.
Aristotle, *The Metaphysics*, Book 1, London: Penguin Classics, 1998.
Berkhof, Louis, *Systematic Theology*, Grand Rapids: Eerdmans, 1949.
Booker, Christopher, *The Seven Basic Plots*, London: Continuum, 2006.
Carson, D. A., *The Intolerance of Tolerance*, Grand Rapids: Eerdmans, 2013.
Clarke, Ros, *Forty Women: Unseen Women from Eden to Easter*, London: InterVarsity Press, 2021.
Conway, Daniel (ed.), *Kierkegaard's Fear and Trembling: A Critical Guide*, Cambridge: Cambridge University Press, 2015.
Copan, Paul, *Is God a Moral Monster?*, Grand Rapids: Baker Books, 2011.
Cranfield, C. E. B., *The International Critical Commentary, The Epistle to the Romans Vol. I*, Edinburgh: T & T Clark Ltd, 1975.
Ellul, Jacques, *The Meaning of the City*, Grand Rapids: Eerdmans, 1970.
Eusebius, *Collected Works*, Delphi Ancient Classics, Book 94, 2019.
Gooding, David, *True to the Faith*, Belfast: Myrtlefield House, 2013.
——, *According to Luke*, Belfast: Myrtlefield House, 2013.
——, *The Riches of Divine Wisdom*, Belfast: Myrtlefield House, 2013.
Graeber, David and David Wengrow, *The Dawn of Everything: A New History of Humanity*, London: Allen Lane, 2021.
Gurri, Martin, *The Revolt of the Public and the Crisis of Authority in the New Millennium*, San Francisco: Stripe Press, 2018.
Habermas, Jürgen, *Time of Transitions*, New York: Polity, 2006.
Harrison, R. K., *Introduction to the Old Testament*, Grand Rapids: Eerdmans, 1969.
Holland, Tom, *Dominion: The Making of the Western Mind*, London: Little, Brown, 2019.

Josephus, Flavius, *Antiquities of the Jews*, Loeb Classics, 1965.

Kass, Leon, *The Beginning of Wisdom – Reading Genesis*, Chicago: University of Chicago Press, 2006.

——, *Founding God's Nation: Reading Exodus*, New Haven: Yale University Press, 2021.

Kidner, Derek, *Genesis*, Leicester: InterVarsity Press, 1967.

Kitchen, Ken, *On the Reliability of the Old Testament*, Grand Rapids: Eerdmans, 2003.

Lennox, John C., *Gunning for God*, Oxford: Lion Hudson, 2011.

——, *Against the Flow – Lessons from Daniel in an Age of Relativism*, Oxford: Lion Hudson, 2015.

——, *Determined To Believe?*, Oxford: Lion Hudson, Monarch Books, 2017.

——, *Joseph: A Story of Love, Hate, Slavery, Power, and Forgiveness*, Grand Rapids: Crossway, 2019.

——, *Where is God in a Coronavirus World?* London: The Good Book Company, 2020.

——, *Seven Days that Divide the World*, 10th anniversary rev. edn, Grand Rapids: Zondervan, 2021.

——, *Cosmic Chemistry*, Oxford: Lion Hudson, 2021.

——, *Artificial Intelligence and the Future of Humanity*, Grand Rapids: Zondervan, 2020.

Lewis, C. S., *That Hideous Strength*, The Cosmic Trilogy, London: Bodley Head, 1989.

——, *The Abolition of Man*, London: Fount, 1943.

——, *The Four Loves*, London: William Collins, 1960.

Lord, C. (ed. and tr.), *Aristotle – The Politics*, Chicago: University of Chicago Press, 1984.

Millar, Fergus, Hannah H. Cotton and Guy MacLean Rogers, *Rome, the Greek World and the East* Vol. 3. *The Greek World, the Jews and the East*, Chapel Hill: University of North Carolina Press, 2008.

Millard, Alan, *Treasures from Bible Times*, Tring: Lion, 1985.

Millard, A. R. and D. J. Wiseman (eds), *Essays on the Patriarchal Narratives*, Leicester: IVP, 1980.

Neugebauer, O., *The Exact Sciences in Antiquity*, Providence Rhode Island: Brown University Press, 1957.

Pritchard, James B., *Ancient Near Eastern Texts in Relation to the Old Testament (ANET)*, Princeton: Princeton University Press, 1969.

Nemet-Nejat, Karen Rhea, *Daily Life in Ancient Mesopotamia*, Peabody: Hendrickson Publishers, 2002.

Rhinehart, John, *Gospel Patrons*, Minneapolis: Reclaimed Publishing, 2013.

Richardson, Alan, *An Introduction to the Theology of the N.T.*, London: SCM Press, 1958.

Rosenblatt, Jason P. and Joseph C. Sitterson JOR (eds), *Not in Heaven, Coherence and Complexity in Biblical Narrative*, Bloomington: Indiana University Press, 1991.

Roux, George, *Ancient Iraq*, London: Penguin Books, 1992.

Sacks, Jonathan, *The Great Partnership*, London: Hodder & Stoughton, 2011.

Sayers, Dorothy, *Christian Letters to a Post-Christian World*, Grand Rapids: Eerdmans, 1969.

Sims, Andrew, *Is Faith Delusion?* London/New York: Continuum, 2009.

Smith, David A., *Hidden Agendas*, Fearn: Christian Focus, 2022.

Van der Heide, Albert, *'Now I know': Five Centuries of Aquedah Exegesis*, Cham: Springer, 2017.

*Vine's Complete Expository Dictionary of Old and New Testament Words*, Nashville: Thomas Nelson, 1996.

Watkin, Christopher, *Biblical Critical Theory*, Grand Rapids: Zondervan, 2022.

Wenham, Gordon, *Genesis*, Vols I and II, Word Biblical Commentary, Grand Rapids: Zondervan, 2015.

Wiesel, Elie, *Night*, New York: Hill and Wang, 1960.

Wittgenstein, Ludwig, *Tractatus Logico-Philosophicus Proposition* (1922).

Wyatt, John, *Matters of Life and Death*, Leicester: IVP, 2009.

# Index of Scripture references

# Index of Scripture references

25.1–11 *261*
25.11 *284*
25.12 *xxv*
25.12—35.29 *xxv*
25.19 *xxv*
26.18–22 *228*
28.9 *284*
29.30 *254*
30.3 *166*
36.1 *xxv*
36.1—50.26 *xxv*
37.2 *xxv*
45.8 *97*

**Exodus**
8.1 *250*
12.26–27 *172*
19.5 *134*
20.1–6 *33*
20.2 *21*
24.3, 6–8 *220*
24.7–8 *135*

**Leviticus**
17.1 *142*
18.5 *219*
18.21 *200*
18.24–30 *292*
20.1–5 *234*

**Numbers**
25 *200*

**Deuteronomy**
8.2 *233*
9.4 *89*
10.16 *174*
12.31 *89*
18.10 *89*
25.1 *120*
30.6 *174*

**Joshua**
10.12–13 *31*
24.2 *31*
24.2–3 *30*

**Judges**
6.36–40 *275*
7 *88*

**2 Samuel**
1.17–18 *31*
12.10–15 *199*
18.18 *93*
24.24 *266*

**2 Chronicles**
3.1 *234*
20.7 *187*

**Job**
1.8–12 *257*
1.20–21 *258*
19.25–27 *259*

**Psalms**
19.1 *313*
37.34 *156*
83.6 *224*
90.10 *51*
110 *98, 102*
110.1, 4 *95, 96, 97*
118.6 *73*
139.2 *160*

**Proverbs**
22.6 *172*

**Isaiah**
3.9 *191*
9.6–7 *301–2*
14.13–14 *14*
15.5 *200*

19.24–25 *78*
30.1–3 *77*
40.31 *156*
41.8 *187*
44.9–20 *33–4*
51.1–2 *226*
53 *303*
53.4–5 *258–9*
54.1 *225*

**Jeremiah**
9.25 *174*
25.4–12 *293*
29.10–13 *294*
31.31–34 *136, 146, 222*
32.9 *266*
34.18–20 *129*

**Daniel**
9.24–26 *294*

**Habakkuk**
2.4 *114*

**Zechariah**
9.9 *302*

MIDRASH

**Genesis Rabbah**
50.4 *194*
50.6 *195*

NEW TESTAMENT

**Matthew**
1 *xxiii*
1.1–2 *xv*
2.13–23 *78*

3.5–10 *xvii*
3.17 *46*
6.19–21 *229*
6.24, 25 *230*
6.31–33 *109*
6.33 *254*
7.21–23 *232*
8.10–12 *285*
8.21–22 *255*
10.34–39 *48*
16.24–28 *49*
17 *311*
17.5 *46*
19.27–30 *139, 306*
19.28 *145*
21.4–5 *302*
21.9 *302*
22.31–32 *285*
22.41–46 *96*
24.37 *xxvi*
26.63–66 *303*

**Mark**
9 *311*
10.45 *244*
12.32–33 *237*
14.31 *105*
16.16 *176*

**Luke**
1.18 *180*
1.30–33 *302*
1.54–55 *249*
1.68–75 *249*
3 *xxiii*
7.29 *121*
8.1–3 *229*
9 *311*
9.61–62 *196*
10.17–20 *231*
10.20 *318*
12.11–12 *256*

338

# Index of subjects

hospitality of 275–6
other gods 30
Nanna/Sin 29, 80
Nathan 199
Nebuchadnezzar
conquest of Jerusalem 25
Shadrach, Meshach and Abednego 253
Nehemiah 295
New Testament
Abraham's influence and xiii
on cataclysms xxvi
dialogue with Jesus 44–9
Nietzsche, Friedrich 47
Nimrod xxxviii
Abraham and 22–3, 42
Babel and 4, 6, 11, 13
rule of 16
Nineveh
library of 31
Nimrod and 6
Nippur, library of 31
Noah xxv
Abraham and 30–1
covenant with God 130
God saves xxxviii
judgement of times 186–7
Nimrod and 4
sons of 4
Nobel, Philip 13

*On the Reliability of the Old Testament*
(Kitchen) xxii–xxiii
Orwell, George 25
Ottoman Empire 298

Palestine and Palestinians 298–9
Palestinian Liberation Organization
(PLO) 299
parenthood, responsibility and 171–3
Parris, Matthew 70–1
Paul the apostle
on behaviour of believers 198

on children of Abraham xx, 306–8
on circumcision 175–6, 177–80
on communion 149
compared to Abraham 57–8
on controversies 20
creation as witness 313
on flesh or Spirit 213–15
God's righteousness 142
on governments 59
on Hagar and Ishmael 162–3
on Hagar and Sarah 215–23
Isaac and Ishmael 212–13
on Jerusalem as mother 223–7
on justification xvii–xviii
on the law 219–20
on loyalty 76
on marriage 268–70
on the new covenant 137–9
persecution for faith 230–1
on righteousness 122
sacrifices to follow Jesus 255
on sexual transgressions 83
on sin and salvation 123–5
the Sinai covenant 218–19
on trouble in Israel 300
understanding our actions 163–4
on wealth 110
Peladi, Zsolt and Geza xviii
Peleg 5
Perizzites 80
Peter the apostle
on ascension 304–7
denies Jesus 105–8
on exiles/Christians 265
fears 209
on immoral teachers 195–6
on Lot 197–8
on the Messiah 97
on return of Jesus 315
sacrifice for Jesus 255
on Scripture 314–15
voice of God 311, 314

# Index of subjects